Craftsman
of the
Cumberlan

Craftsman of the Cumberlands

Tradition & Creativity

MICHAEL OWEN JONES

THE UNIVERSITY PRESS OF KENTUCKY

Publications of the American Folklore Society, New Series,
Patrick Mullen, General Editor.

This book is an extensive revision of
The Hand Made Object and Its Maker
(University of California Press, 1975).

Editorial and Sales Offices: Lexington, Kentucky 40506-0336

The illustration "Types and subtypes of slat-back chair" on page 235
is from *Patterns in the Material Folk Culture of the Eastern United States*
by Henry Glassie. © 1968 by the Trustees of the University of
Pennsylvania Press. Reprinted by permission.

Library of Congress Cataloging-in-Publication Data

Jones, Michael Owen.
   Craftsman of the Cumberlands : tradition and creativity / Michael
Owen Jones.
      p.   cm. -- (Publications of the American Folklore Society)
   Bibliography: p.
   Includes index.
   ISBN 0-8131-1672-4 (alk. paper) -- ISBN 0-8131-0183-2
(pbk. : alk. paper)
     1. Chairs--Kentucky--History--20th century.   2. Furniture-
-Kentucky--History--20th century.   3. Chair-makers--Kentucky-
-Psychology.   I. Title.   II. Series: Publications of the American
Folklore Society. New series (Unnumbered)
NK2715.J57   1989
749'.32'097691--dc19
                89-5542
                CIP

To the Memory of . . .

My parents, Woodrow Owen Jones (1915-1973) and Anne Elizabeth (nee Blackford) Jones (1915-1976), the former a farmer as well as a tool designer, and the latter a public school teacher; their influence was strong and lasting.

Richard M. Dorson (1916-1981), historian and folklorist, who inspired many of us in his charge, whether or not we followed the path of folklore studies quite as he did.

Chester Cornett (1913-1981), chairmaker, who taught me about craftsmanship, and whose life and work forced me to reflect on the human condition.

Other Books by Michael Owen Jones

Inside Organizations: Understanding the Human Dimension (co-editor, 1988)

Exploring Folk Art: Twenty Years of Thought on Craft, Work and Aesthetics (1987)

The World of the Kalevala (editor, 1987)

Foodways and Eating Habits: Directions for Research (co-editor, 1981)

People Studying People: The Human Element in Fieldwork (co-author, 1980)

The Hand Made Object and Its Maker (1975)

Why Faith Healing? (1972)

Contents

Preface

This book is about craftsmen living in southeastern Kentucky in the 1960s. Known simply as "chairmakers," many of them made baskets, musical instruments, and other furniture, such as tables and cabinets, as well as chairs.

Who were these craftsmen? How did they design and construct chairs? How did families, friends, and customers respond to the craftsmen and their works? How did the attitudes and expectations of others affect the craftsmen and the things they made?

I focus on one woodworker, Chester Cornett. Born in 1913, he learned chairmaking from his grandfathers and his uncle. Of the fifteen or more furniture makers I met or learned of, he seemed the most knowledgeable and dedicated. Many admired his chairs for their comfort, durability, and appearance. He often experimented with materials, techniques of construction, and designs; for example, he created dining chairs with seven or eight legs and two-in-one rocking chairs with eight legs and four rockers.

Although a master at his craft, Chester Cornett led a troubled life. Through his chairmaking and other expressive forms, he attempted to cope with marital discord, poverty, and illness. Some of his chairs fulfilled a craving for old-timiness, security, and a sense of self-esteem.

The discoveries about chairmakers in southeastern Kentucky raise larger questions. What compels people to give aesthetic value to some aspects of their daily lives, even the making of utilitarian objects? How does style develop? Why are traditions perpetuated? This study also concerns methods, including concepts and ways of researching folk art. It grows out of my doctoral dissertation at Indiana University (1970), several articles on folk art and aesthetics, and especially a book entitled *The Hand Made Object and Its Maker* (University of California Press, 1975).

The book I published in 1975 differed from other studies at the time in the amount of information on the craftsmen's lives. The few biographies of folk artists before it dealt with painters or sculptors, not with those who produced utilitarian objects like chairs. Most research on folk craft focused on the techniques of construction and the historical and geographical distribution of forms. My book was of interest to those who felt there was more to the study of folk art than a preoccupation with painting and sculpture or an attempt to set the makers of objects within a cultural context as simply transmitters of tradition; they realized the pervasiveness of the aesthetic impulse and the importance of the individual.

I have rewritten that book rather than simply reprinting it. The introduction and conclusion of the present version are entirely new. In other chapters, while retaining some of the earlier themes and information, I have reorganized and expanded both description and analysis. I have substituted some illustrations and added others. My intent is to provide greater detail about chairs, chairmaking, and chairmakers in southeastern Kentucky and to place this descriptive matter within the broader context of folklore research.

People often ask folklorists how their field differs from anthropology or other related disciplines. They inquire about what folklorists do, and how and why they proceed in this fashion. They want to know what folklorists can contribute that is uniquely theirs. As I reflect on my research among chairmakers in southeastern Kentucky in the late 1960s, I realize that what I perceived to be significant, what I questioned and sought answers to, and what I reported grew out of my orientation as a folklorist rather than as a specialist in some other field. After all, I had chosen to study traditions, and to do so in certain ways.

What intrigued me was the continuities and consistencies in people's symbolic expressions through time and space. I examined these expressions with regard to the immediate circumstances in which they were generated. I focused on the activity of making chairs, including the tools, materials, and traditional techniques of construction. I compiled information about the experiences of chairmakers that shaped their perceptions, motivated them, and informed their craftsmanship, as well as gave meaning to what they made. I also explored the relationship between craftsmen and their customers, particularly the economics of chairmaking and the taste and aesthetics of consumers. Attention to these matters in this combination seemed to me, as a folklorist, to best answer the question of why specific objects existed and exhibited particular features.

Much of what I learned about chairmaking had not been reported before, especially the ways in which the craft fulfilled a need to express and an urge to create. My research challenged some long-standing assumptions about tradition and the individual; it offered new perspectives on some old issues concerning creativity and aesthetics. It seems fitting, therefore, to conceptualize this inquiry into the activities of chairmakers of the Cumberlands as a case study in the methods of folklore research.

My thesis is that the chairs owe their traits and features to the tools, materials, and techniques used in construction; to designs learned from other chairmakers; to preferences and expectations of customers as stated by them or inferred by the craftsmen; and to each maker's unique discoveries and inventions on the one hand, and his self-concept, values, and aspirations on the other.

This study illustrates that many objects people make are both means of achieving some practical goal and ends in themselves, to be admired for their form. Technological and creative processes, therefore, are intertwined; evaluations of products admit considerations of both fitness for use and appearance.

Moreover, tradition is not an enemy of creativity, innovation, or change. Modeling in behavior does not exclude perfecting skills and mastering techniques to produce excellent forms; neither does it exclude transforming designs rather than simply imitating and repeating them.

Finally, it appears that even the simplest chair made by hand may communicate much. Produced by one person in interaction with others, using traditional techniques and inspired by designs that have been repeated through time and space, a hand-made chair exhibits continuities and consistencies, as well as elements of originality and uniqueness, specific to the circum-stances of manufacture. A crucial question is, what can be in-ferred about human behavior through a study of these objects?

In conclusion, this book has three purposes. One is to report on chairs, chairmaking, and chairmakers in southeastern Ken-tucky for the intrinsic interest this subject might hold. A second is to reassess the meanings and application of certain terms. The third is to demonstrate the use of methods of folklore research. I hope the volume achieves these objectives, but more, that it contributes to the understanding of particular individuals, spe-cific societies or subgroups, and perhaps the species of homo sapiens as a whole—which, I believe, is the ultimate purpose of folklore studies.

I am indebted to many individuals, not only for assistance in writing and publishing this volume, but also for their help, advice, and support in earlier research embodied in this book. I want to thank Professor Warren R. Roberts for introducing me to the study of folk art and technology and encouraging the orig-inal research project in 1965-67. To Professor David E. Smith I owe my gratitude for a number of kindnesses connected with my original investigations, from stimulating research to assisting me in obtaining the necessary funds. Professors Richard M. Dor-son, John C. Messenger, and Roy Sieber provided constructive criticism and helpful insights. I benefited in the early years from discussions with many other people, including Henry Glassie, Carlos C. Drake, Willard B. Moore, Robert B. Klymasz, and David Bidney.

I would like to express my appreciation as well to the many students in my classes who not only tolerated my attempts to express some of the ideas in this volume, but also helped me articulate them. To mention only a few of the graduate students over the years with whom I have had important exchanges of ideas about folk art, there are Anne Armstrong, Barbara Allen, Carole and Michael Bell, Jackson Braider, Jennie Chinn, Don Christensen, Norine Dresser, Robin Evanchuk, Kay Hardman

Enell, Deirdre Evans-Pritchard, Sara Selene Faulds, Magda Ferl, Russell Frank, Rachel Fretz, Bruce S. Giuliano, Barry Glass, Susan Gordon, Verni Greenfield, Clodagh Harvey, Judith Haut, Michael Heisley, Joanne Farb Hernandez, Teresa Keeler, Roberta Krell, Robert Leibman, Erica Meltzer, Susan O'Brien, Colin Quigley, Judith Samuel, Sue Samuelson, Anthony Shay, Sharon Sherman, David Shuldiner, Chris Simon, Amy Skillman, Steven Stern, Patricia Atkinson Wells, Diane Vidal, Daniel Wojcik, and Patricia Mastick Young.

In regard to the preparation of the present book I want to thank Simon J. Bronner, Leslie Prosterman, Eugene Metcalf, and others who urged me to return to the subject after a dozen years, rewriting my earlier book as I had often said I wanted to do. Individuals who assisted in various ways, particularly through encouragement and the exchange of ideas over the years, include Kenneth L. Ames, Michael J. Bell, John A. Burrison, Kristin G. Congdon, Keith and Kathi Cunningham, C. Kurt Dewhurst, William R. Ferris, Gladys-Marie Fry, Robert A. Georges, Joyce Ice, Barbara Kirshenblatt-Gimblett, Yvonne Lockwood, Marsha MacDowell, Stephen Ohrn, Elliott Oring, Gerald L. Pocius, Richard Poulson, Thomas J. Schlereth, Robert Trent, John Michael Vlach, William A. Wilson, Don Yoder, and Charles Zug, III. I am indebted also to Judith Haut for editorial suggestions and to John D. Alexander, Jr., for technical assistance.

Finally, I wish to thank the many people in southeastern Kentucky of two decades ago who answered my questions and permitted me to photograph the chairs in their possession, particularly the several craftsmen who revealed to me details of their lives and art. Some of these people are identified in this book by their actual names; others are not.

On 5 September 1981, Chester Cornett died in the Veterans Administration Hospital in Cincinnati, Ohio. The subject of my research twenty years ago and of the present book, he had been ill for two years and had made no chairs during this time. Fortunately, however, the last chair he built was documented in detail by Herbie Smith and his wife, Elizabeth Barret, in a ninety-minute film called *Hand Carved*.

ONE

The Chairmaking Business

The afternoon was hot, the humidity high, the air still. It was one of those dog days of August. My wife Jane and I headed northeast from Hazard on Highway 80, traveling slowly because the road was narrow and winding and because we were looking for a craftsman we had read about two months before in the *Louisville Courier-Journal*. How we would find him we did not know. The brief article mentioned only a workshop near Dwarf, "deep in the mountains of Perry County."

The steep, wooded hills on our right did not invite human habitation. To the left, however, between the road and the river, an occasional wide spot held a home or country store amid the box elder and weeping willow trees. Suddenly the greenery was broken. In isolation stood a decrepit building that once had been a coal company office and weigh station but now seemed to be used as a house. Covered with gray and black shingles, the two-story building blended with the coal dust of the yard.

A sign mounted high on the south side of the structure proclaimed in bright orange letters that this was the home of

hand Mad Furniture
maker of the Cornett chaires
we make iney thin
ar hit Cant be mad

A similar sign adorned the building's north side, we discovered as we continued past the house and down the highway, not stopping until we were a mile away.

I was about to begin my second year as a graduate student in folklore and American studies at Indiana University. Because I was interested in American folk art, the article about this chairmaker in the Louisville paper, dated 20 June 1965, had attracted my attention. At the urging of Warren Roberts, one of my mentors, my wife and I had driven from Bloomington, Indiana, to southeastern Kentucky in mid-August 1965 to meet Chester Cornett. Although familiar with European masterpieces of painting and sculpture through training in the history of art, I knew nothing about woodworking and had had no previous interest in chairs.

I was writing my master's thesis on the traditions of a Kansas farmer who was my parents' neighbor in a rural area near Wichita where I was born and reared. The traditional forms included custom, belief, and play, but not art. I had long been intrigued by the aesthetic impulse, however, having had aspirations at one time to be an easel painter and then a photographer. Thomas Hart Benton, the regionalist noted for his murals and lithographs depicting traditional life in the Ozarks, and W. Eugene Smith, a photographer from Wichita whose visual essays on a country doctor, a midwife, a Spanish village, and Welsh miners treated ordinary people with depth and feeling, inspired me. Although I took studio courses in art at the University of Kansas, I majored in American history, international relations, and art history. It was not until my senior year that I enrolled in a course in folklore studies. Early in the class, I realized that this field was what I had been seeking for so long. I applied for admission to the graduate program in folklore at Indiana University; at the time, UCLA offered only the master's degree in folklore studies, and I knew little about the program at the University of Pennsylvania (the University of Texas and Memorial University of Newfoundland had not yet established folklore programs).

By the summer of 1965, I had taken a dozen courses in folklore. I was writing my master's thesis. I had done fieldwork in southern Indiana on various topics. I was anticipating the preparation of a doctoral dissertation, one that would focus on contemporary folklore and be based on field research rather than the use of library or archive materials. But about what? I hoped this craftsman in southeastern Kentucky would warrant study. Emphasizing that his chairs were made without glue or nails and that these large and elaborate works were created with a few simple tools, the newspaper article led me to believe there was sufficient complexity to chairmaking, and enough skill and artistry in this man's efforts, to engage a student of folk art in search of a suitable subject.

We did not stop the first two times our car crept past Chester Cornett's house. In the yard stood a barefoot man in dingy blue overalls, his long hair and beard masking his features. He was flanked by two teenage boys brandishing planks; their jerky movements indicated something might be wrong with them. Contributing to the foreboding quality of the scene was the coal dust, which smothered the grass and clung to the siding, deepening the shadows cast by the building as the sun set. The only bright spot was the craftsman's hand-lettered sign, with the promise it implied.

The next day we forced ourselves to drive to the chairmaker's home from our motel in town. This time we stopped. I shuddered to think of my embarrassment later if I were to return to Bloomington empty-handed because I had been afraid to talk to the craftsman. What would I tell Professor Roberts, an experienced fieldworker, who had urged me to meet Chester Cornett and who had equipped me with tape recorder and cameras? And besides, the morning sunshine had dispelled some of our misgivings of the night before.

Introducing ourselves to Chester Cornett, we mentioned the newspaper article we had read about him, tried to explain our interest in studying things that people make, and asked if we could photograph him at work. "Didn't you fellas drive by here last night?" he asked. We were trying to find his house, I said lamely, and once we located it, it seemed too late to stop. Rushing on, I again expressed an interest in his work, saying I wanted to learn more about chairmaking. The situation was awkward, not only because I was unsure of myself and uncertain of what I wanted to know, but also because the chairmaker seemed equally ill at ease. He did, however, begin to tell us about shaping chair "posts" (legs) with a drawing knife, the task he had been engaged in when we drove up.

We spent a week with Chester, asking him about his chair-

1 The chairmaker Chester Cornett, his wife, Ruth, and three youngest children, with settin' chairs at their home near Dwarf, Kentucky (July 1967).

making and taking pictures of his tools, work procedures, and the objects he made. We also devoted several days to tracking down some of his earlier chairs, among which were a couple of two-in-one rockers he had described to us, but which we could not envision.

As the days passed, Chester became more amicable and animated; he was a master craftsman whose expertise was beginning to awe his audience. Both he and I gained confidence, but he never lost his nervousness entirely. Interviewing was often difficult. When Chester talked, he tended to dip his face down and mumble into his beard or turn his head aside to avoid direct eye contact.

In addition, his and his wife's dialect was more pronounced than other people's. Chester and Ruth dropped the final "g" from many words, such as "anythin'." Sometimes Chester did not say the "w" in a word, as in "al'ays." Both Chester and Ruth often, though not always, said "hit" instead of "it"—usually at the beginning of a sentence or at the start of a phrase after a pause, and sometimes perhaps for emphasis. Fascinated, I found myself attempting to capture the rhythms of their speech, some of which I present here.

This first visit was exciting and trying for my wife and me, as no doubt it was for the Cornett family. Obviously, Chester was skilled, imaginative, and sophisticated in his work. But he also seemed to have difficulty relating to other people, and the tension between him and his wife, Ruth, was palpable. "My wife don't think much of this here chairmakin'," he told us soon after we met him.

The family's poverty was acute, as it had been for years despite Chester's efforts to attract wealthier clients. Moreover, the older male children were mentally retarded and physically crippled. In his early twenties, the eldest sat or lay in bed day and night, sometimes making buzzing sounds. About nineteen, the second son paced the yard, flailing his arms and muttering to himself. The fifteen-year-old was only slightly more coordinated and coherent. The twelve-year-old girl and three-year-old boy were normal enough; indeed, Billy was precocious, as the other boys had been at his age. Perhaps the same fate awaited Billy that had befallen his brothers; Chester wondered aloud about this one day as he watched the youth imitate him at work.

During our visit I learned how furniture could be constructed without the use of glue or nails and with only a few tools, including handmade ones. I even tried to mortise a back, shave a post, and carve a peg.

The key to how Chester and other craftsmen of the Cumberlands made furniture lay in knowing the characteristics of the wood they worked, especially what happens to it as it dries. Unlike furniture made in a factory, the homemade chairs depend on a mastery of working green or "wet" wood.

The sawn lumber used in factory-made furniture is cut against the natural grain of the wood and hence must be worked dry or seasoned. Pieces cannot be bent readily for fear they will break, and the only way to hold components together is with glue and nails or screws. Wet woodworking takes advantage of the pliability of wood split along its grain and of the shrinkage that occurs as the components season after the chair has been built. The result is not only a chair that stays together forever, but also types of chairs in which the back posts and the slats are bent for greater comfort. Among these forms are the so-called mule-eared settin' chairs so pervasive in the South (fig. 1).

Aptly named, a settin' chair renders the act of sitting an enjoyable experience unknown to those of us accustomed to factory-made side chairs. The back posts, flattened on the front and bent slightly outward at the top, are reminiscent of the long, pointed ears of a mule (for the parts of a chair, see figs. 2, 3, and 4). This kind of chair is comparatively small, usually measuring only about 40 inches high in back; the seat is perhaps a third (or less) of that distance from the floor. Made of hickory, birch, or sassafras, or occasionally of ash or oak, the chair is lightweight but sturdy. The seat, woven of splints from the inner bark of a hickory sapling, gives under one's weight, and conforms to the contour of one's posterior.

Slats in the back of the chair are curved to accommodate the rounding of the human form. Back posts may be bent backward and outward, just as one's back widens. If the rear posts are angled backward somewhat, then the center of gravity shifts to

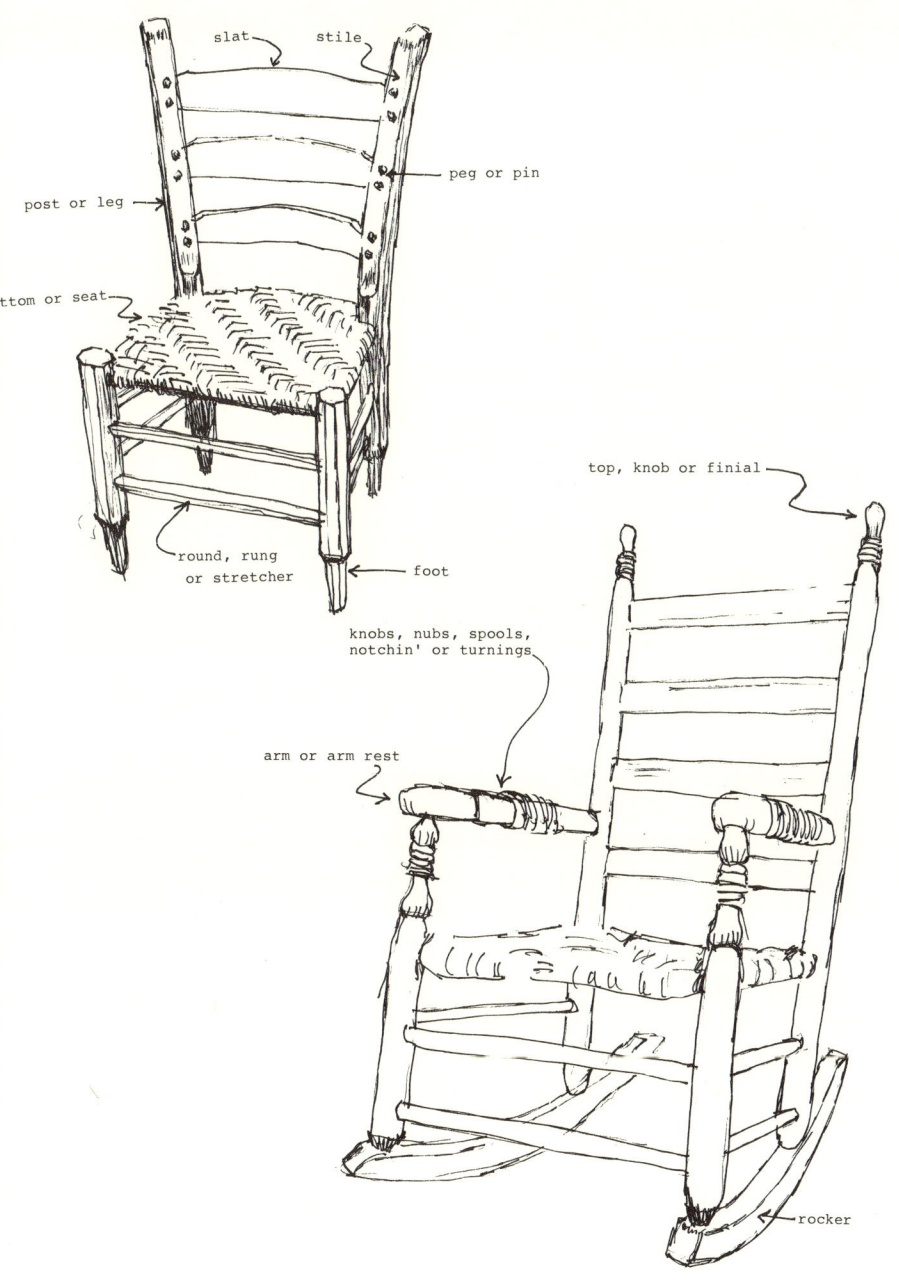

2 Parts of a settin' chair.   **3** Parts of a rocking chair.

the back of the seat, which encourages one to sit straight instead of slumping forward. The slightest effort is sufficient to tip the chair backward, permitting one to remain comfortably at this angle for long periods of time, to lean against the wall or to rock back and forth.

Not surprisingly, this simple but pleasing and efficient form is the kind of chair made often by many craftsmen of the Cumberlands, although they also produced dining chairs, rocking chairs, and stools. Probably the first rocking chair ever made was a side chair mounted on rockers; certainly the technology as well as the basic design of the settin' chair is relied upon today in the South to construct rocking chairs by hand.

Make a Chair from a Tree: An Introduction to Working Green Wood by John D. Alexander, Jr. (1978) contains the most thorough analysis of how wet woodworking avails itself of the natural properties of wood, along with detailed instruction for building a chair. An attorney in Baltimore who is an aficionado of fine furniture, Alexander devoted years to examining antiques, perusing studies of craft work, including some of mine, and talking with wood scientists in order to solve the mystery of traditional craftsmanship. "The key was the wood," he finally realized. "I turned some wet wood and I was fascinated, it was so easy and so beautiful. Suddenly I knew it was the way to make chairs, not with that hard, dry stuff you buy at the lumberyard" (p. 7).

Alexander also discovered that if a very dry round (rung or stretcher) is inserted into a mortise or hole in a post that is green or only partially seasoned, the dry round as it absorbs moisture from the post will swell, forming a lasting joint (figs. 4 and 5). It helps if the end of the round is shaped as a tenon—a projecting member left by cutting away the wood around it—and the sides of the tenon are flattened (to avoid splitting the post). In addition, the round and post must have been riven out of a log along its grain rather than sawed, which cuts into the grain.

Wood shrinks differently along its rays or grain from the way it shrinks in tangent to the radial axis. Tangential shrinkage (approximately 10 percent) is about twice as great as radial. This is why a drying log always cracks along lines radiating from the center outward. Building a chair without glue or nails demands

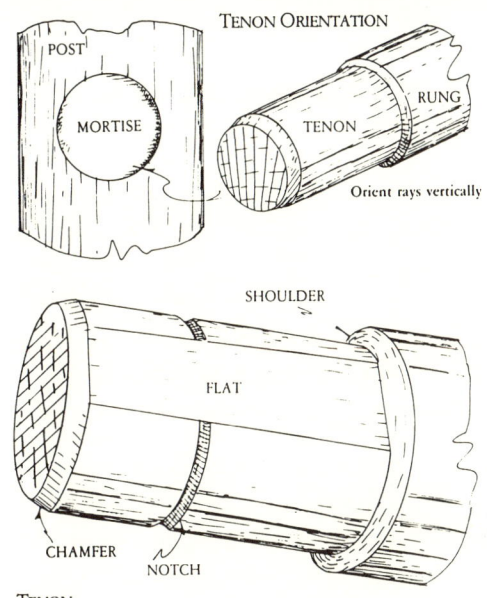

TENON ORIENTATION

POST

MORTISE

RUNG

TENON

Orient rays vertically

SHOULDER

FLAT

CHAMFER

NOTCH

TENON

4 and **5** A dry round is inserted into a mortise or hole in a green post; as it absorbs moisture from the green wood, the round swells, while the mortise tightens around it as the post dries. Drawings from Alexander, *Make a Chair from a Tree*, pp. 75, 93. Copyright 1978 by John D. Alexander, Jr. Used with permission.

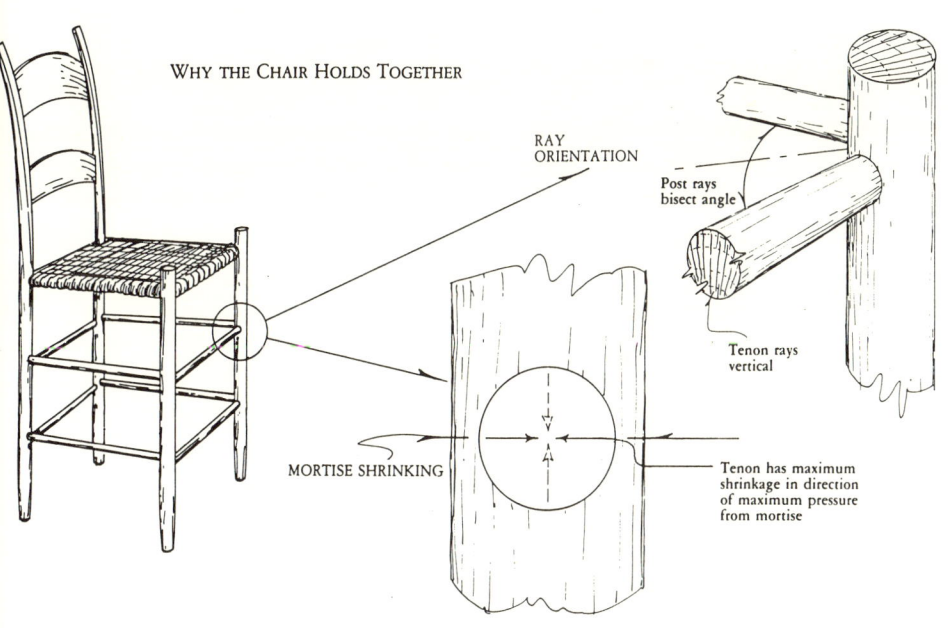

WHY THE CHAIR HOLDS TOGETHER

RAY ORIENTATION

Post rays bisect angle

Tenon rays vertical

MORTISE SHRINKING

Tenon has maximum shrinkage in direction of maximum pressure from mortise

avoiding maximum shrinking and swelling of the wood, while using the same properties to prevent the chair from cracking or splintering and holding the joint fast. This technique has long been known by traditional craftsmen.

TOOLS

Many people who encounter handmade chairs, especially those constructed with patience and attention to detail, wonder about the tools, as those who admire a fine photograph may ask "what kind of camera was used and what film?" The simpler the equipment, the greater the astonishment at the results. So, too, with chairmaking.

Chairmaking tools number about a dozen, several of which the craftsmen make themselves. (Some of these tools are shown in use in the figures accompanying the next section on construction techniques.) A saw and an ax, of course, are needed to fell trees from which to obtain the wood for the parts of a chair and to strip bark for the seats. Splitting a bolt from the fallen log requires the use of two handmade implements: a maul (or club made of hickory or other hardwood), and a glut (or large wedge of dogwood or similar material that will not crack when hit) (fig. 6). Also vital are a hatchet to rough out the posts and slats; a chisel and hammer or hatchet to mortise the backs for the slats; a brace and bit or drill to make holes for the rounds and pegs; a knife and some sort of measuring device. Chester used his hands and thumbs as a ruler—two hands extended with one thumb overlapping the other equaled one foot, one hand with thumb extended was six inches, and the width of one thumb equaled an inch (fig. 7).

Dressing a post or round or shaping a slat is done with a drawing knife on a homemade drawing or shaving horse. Shaving horses differ in size, material, and construction, but all exploit a single principle: the greater the pressure exerted to shape a piece, the more securely the piece is held in place.

The drawing horse is simply a beam, plank, or runner on short legs (fig. 8). Near the center on top of this beam is the head, a large, heavy block of wood that drops down onto the piece being worked. The head is attached at an angle to a lever arm bolted to the beam and extending below it so the craftsman, seated on the horse, can press the lever with his foot as he pulls the drawing knife toward him, its blade biting into the piece of wood to be shaved.

Chester's drawing horse was 80 inches long, 4 inches wide, and 32 inches high. The beam or runner was locust, the legs hickory, the head sassafras. Of one piece, the head and lever portions were from a limb that had a crook in it. The longer and more slender leg of this inverted V extended down through a hole in the runner and was held in place with a peg serving as a pivot. The shorter end, which gripped the piece of wood to be shaved, was covered with a section of tire tacked in place with cobbler's nails. Chester's maternal grandfather, Cal, had used horseshoe nails driven through the head and runner, rather than a piece of rubber to hold the slat or post being shaped. The nails actually bit into the wood being worked. Once the piece was finished, the scarred end was cut off, a procedure that seemed wasteful to Chester.

Chairmakers also make their own presses that produce the desired curvature in posts, slats, and rockers. Chester's post press, constructed about 1950 of hickory and mulberry, was 45½ inches wide, 33 inches high, and 6 inches deep. One of the slat presses, made of swamp willow and hickory, was 32 inches long, 22 inches wide, and 2 inches thick; the other (fig. 9) was 58 inches long, 25½ inches wide, and 2¾ inches deep. The former would bend a set of three slats for a settin' or dining chair, while the latter produced up to seven matching slats for a rocking chair. The rocker press of beech and hickory was 39 inches wide, 35 inches high, and 8½ inches thick. Slat presses are not as deep as post and rocker presses. A slat is only ⅜ to ½ inch thick, compared with a post or rocker 2½ or more inches thick.

I discovered later that some chairmakers do not bend rockers; they seek naturally curving pieces or they saw the rockers in a curved form from a larger board, as Chester sometimes did, too. Moreover, other chairmakers' slat and post presses tended to be more makeshift than Chester's were. Whatever the size, material, and design, all presses function similarly. They exert pres-

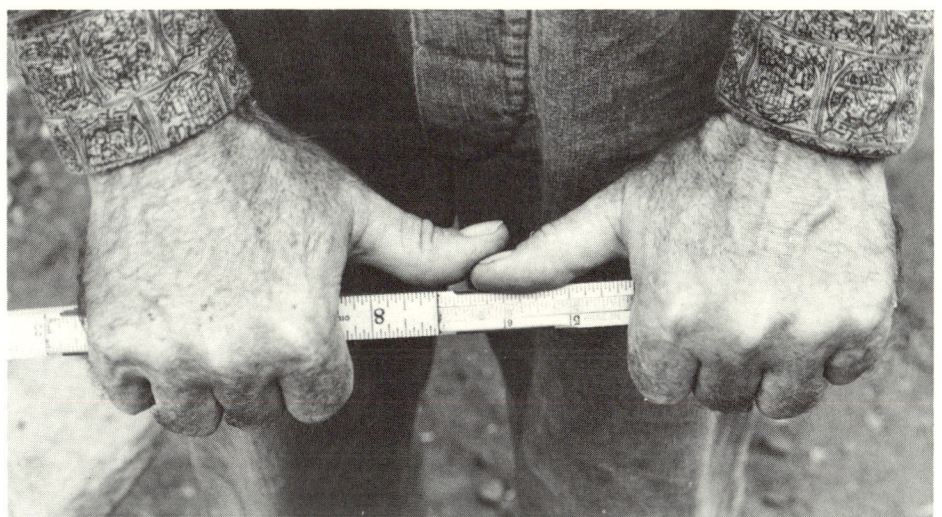

6 *Opposite,* Chester splits a bolt with a hickory maul and the edge of an ax;
once the split was started, he used a dogwood glut.   7 Chester used his
hands as a ruler; two hands with thumbs overlapped equaled 12 inches; the
width of one thumb was an inch.   8 Chester at the drawing horse measures
with a thumb where he will begin to shave a stile on the post.

9 Chester's slat press had room enough to bend at least seven slats.

sure in the same direction at the ends of a piece of wood, but in the opposite direction in the middle. When a piece of wet wood is bent under constant pressure, it acquires curvature, which it retains after drying. Because the piece of wood was riven out of a plank along the grain, it does not crack or break under pressure—the occasional exception being walnut, which few craftsmen other than Chester were willing to use for chairs.

Another handmade tool is the work bench or vise bench. Chester's bench was half a split log about six feet long. Toward the middle were three hickory stobs or pegs. By inserting two wedges, Chester could hold chair posts or other pieces in place while he worked on them without their moving around. Made about 1957, his vise bench was of oak with locust legs. The stobs were 3 inches high by 1¼ inches square and were set into the log about 6 inches deep; the two front pegs were about 6 inches apart and about 7 inches from the third stob. The two wedges were triangular in shape, about 8 inches long, 2¼ inches thick, and 1½ inches in width, tapering to ¾ inch.

At the time I met him in August 1965, Chester was not using a turning lathe. All other chairmakers I later met or heard about depended on a lathe to turn the rounds and posts of a chair. The lathe was usually an electric one, either bought new or used or else built from salvaged materials. The first chairs Chester made as a youth had square posts. He whittled the rounds with a knife. Later he turned posts and rounds on a handmade, foot-powered lathe similar to one he had operated for his grandfather as a teenager in the 1920s.

It is nearly impossible to shape a square piece of wood, even if it is green, on a foot-powered lathe because it cannot be spun consistently fast enough to overcome the impact of a chisel blade suddenly being thrust against it. Hence, the post or round is usually roughly hewed with an ax or drawing knife from a square to an eight-sided piece before it is placed in the lathe.

About 1950 Chester ceased to use the foot-powered lathe. He could not find a blacksmith to repair certain parts, and lacking a helper to operate the lathe, he found it awkward and tiring to pump the pedal and chisel a whirling post simultaneously. I wonder, however, whether Chester had come to consider the lathe an intrusion that distanced him from the materials he seemed to take great pleasure in handling. Unlike other chair-makers, then, Chester did not turn posts and rounds. He hewed them with an ax or hatchet, then carefully shaped them eight-sided with a drawing knife, and finally used a pocketknife to cut "notchin'" reminiscent of chisel work done on a lathe.

TECHNIQUES

Not every chairmaker procures all his materials or executes by himself all the many possible steps in making a chair. Because Chester was the first chairmaker I observed at work and because he did so much of the work himself, I use him as a model in the following description, with occasional reference to other crafts-men I met later. Even Chester did not always use the full range of steps described here.

Sometimes Chester cut the timber in the hills, preferring to do so in the fall and on the "olden moon" when the wood is relatively dry and less subject to cracking during seasoning. Lacking an automobile or even work animals, he had to "pack in" the logs or log sections ("bolts") on his back, or tie strips of hickory bark around the logs and drag them. But the trees that provided the bark woven into chair seats or bottoms could be stripped (skinned) in the woods (see figs. 10-13). Chester had a system of grading hickory, the source of bark, from 1 to 5, depending on length, number of knots, and straightness of the tree. A number 1 pole had no knots, was perfectly straight, and grew about 30 feet from the butt to the section where it began to branch. The day I went into the hills with him to get bark we found a number 4 pole that had 15 feet of usable length, was slightly crooked, and contained numerous knots on the lower part of the log.

While his grandfather Cal almost invariably used maple for the posts of a chair, yellow locust for the rounds, and the inner bark of a shagbark hickory pole for the seats, Chester tended to rely in the early years on locust for rounds and maple, white oak, or ash for the posts, owing to the relative strength of these woods. He first used sassafras about 1950. "It's good bendin', an' you can shape it better'n any kind of wood I ever worked," he said. In addition, the tree grows in gnarled and twisted shapes already naturally bent for slats, rockers, or posts. About 1960 Chester began using walnut for chairs, making four dining chairs at the request of a customer. Walnut, he said, is "pretty, but it'll burst up on you, an' hit's hard to bend—hit'll break 'fore it'll bend—unless it has a lot of white wood" (the thick wood between the bark and the inner part of a black walnut tree). He found a bit of white an attractive contrast on walnut chairs, but some customers did not, Chester said. The two other chair-makers I interviewed who made black walnut chairs (Aaron and Hascal) did not bend the posts.

Once he had a bolt cut in the hills or culled from a sawmill, Chester split it into quarters to make the posts of a chair (fig. 6). He drove an ax into the bolt to start a cut and then split the log using a hickory maul and dogwood glut, a method that pre-served the natural strength of the wood by cleaving along the grain.

Next Chester roughly shaped the planks into posts about 4 inches square by hacking many slight cuts into the plank and gently slicing them off so that the hatchet blade did not gouge into the wood. Then he cut off each corner of the square, thus forming an octagon-shaped piece. He cut off the ends to make the posts the same length and eliminate splintering. He pre-pared the dowels for rounds and pegs from smaller pieces of wood. For some of his cheaper chairs, he shaped the pieces entirely with a hatchet rather than finishing them with a drawing knife.

He shaped slats in much the same way (fig. 14). Once he had roughly hewn a block to about 4 inches in thickness, he split it into slats ½ or ¾ inch thick. Two or more slats could be riven from a single board, like shake shingles, using the edge of a hatchet as a froe or cleaving tool. Later he trimmed the slats at the drawing horse, "cooked" them in hot water to make them pliable (fig. 15), put them in a press to dry, and finally dressed them with a drawing knife at the shaving horse once again.

After he hewed out pieces for the posts, Chester measured them with his hands and thumbs to mark off the holes for slats and rounds. Next he shaved them roughly with a drawing knife. The post in figure 8 is white oak, destined for the back leg of a settin' chair. The face of the post, or stile, is cut out more deeply for the sake of comfort and appearance. To do this, Chester oriented the post so the face was toward him and then took small cutting bites to start the curve just above the seat. Turning the knife at a 30-degree angle, he began the cut at the extreme left end of the knife, drawing it forward to the right end. The movement was long and smooth.

To make the slats and posts pliable enough to put into the presses in which they seasoned into curved shapes, Chester cooked the slats for twenty minutes and the posts for an hour (or a week, if the posts were completely unseasoned). The board in the tub holds the pieces under the boiling water (fig. 15), preventing their floating to the top. The next step was to insert the slats and posts into a press. Sometimes Chester pressed more posts than needed for a chair in progress because he had orders for others and because a post might split.

To increase the curvature of slats, Chester put small blocks of wood behind them. For the slats on his rocking chairs with eight posts and four rockers (the two-in-one rockers), he bent the slats a full 180 degrees; the blocks were therefore very large. The slat press in figure 9, containing three slats for a settin' chair in progress, was made to accommodate as many as seven slats for a regular rocker.

Seasoning time depended on the type of wood, when it was cut, and the part of the chair for which a piece was to be used. The fastest drying wood is sassafras; it can be seasoned by the fire. Willow dries nearly as quickly. The wood requiring the most time to season is oak. Wood cut when the sap is up takes longer to cure. Chester stored hickory pieces for rounds under a vegetable stand, sassafras by the stove in the living room or the oven in the kitchen, and other pieces in a cardboard box left on the stovepipe above the potbellied stove. He leaned presses with slats and posts against a tub in the yard with the fire burning for at least two days. Slats loosened in the presses as they dried; Chester also sometimes shook a press, determining from the rattle whether the slats were loose enough to remove. He air-dried the rounds and the dowels for pegs at least six months and then cooked them in the oven for thirty to forty minutes before final assembly. A settin' chair may take three or four months to season fully; the bark seat requires at least a week, during which time it should be sat on to put "swag" into it.

After cooking, breaking, pressing, and seasoning the posts by a fire, Chester shaved them once again to remove soiling and scarring. If he removed too much of the seasoned wood, he would have to drive the posts into the press again.

In figure 16, Chester mortises the back posts for the slats—held in place by two wedges and three stobs projecting from the face of the handmade workbench. Each mortise required about twenty-five separate strokes with a hammer (or hatchet) and chisel.

The next step was to check the angle at which to drill holes for the rounds or stretchers (fig. 17) and then to determine the proper length of the slats (fig. 18). Chester trimmed off the excess length, beveling the end of the slat with his pocketknife to assure a proper fit in the mortise. On a few chairs he cut a hole all the way through the post for the slat so it would stick out.

Chester marked the rounds for the notchin', that is, the decorative detail equivalent to turnings on posts and rounds fashioned on a lathe (fig. 19). He called the procedure "layin' off the rounds" (or "postees"). With his pocketknife he incised the wood about ⅛ inch deep at each mark and then cut notches. To complete the round, he carved a tenon on each end. Because they are less dry (having been seasoned a shorter time), the legs shrink around the stretchers or rounds, the tenon equalizing the pressure of the leg on the stretcher, which prevents its cracking.

The chair was then ready for assembly (fig. 20). Using a hickory maul to avoid scarring the wood, Chester drove the pieces of the back together. He tapped each joint with the head of a hatchet, listening closely for the sound indicating that the pieces were secure.

Chester drilled holes in the posts at each end of a slat into which he later drove walnut pegs. "I have to use twelve pegs an' hit takes a right smart time," he said (fig. 21).

At this time Chester was using walnut pegs on light-colored

chairs such as hickory, sassafras, and white oak. He put the lighter-colored hickory pegs in chairs made of red oak or walnut. Both the large number of pegs and the contrasting colors served decorative purposes. Only a thin peg or pin at each end of the top slat in back was needed to protect the chair against abuse; the differential rate of seasoning of pieces prevented the chair's coming apart under normal use.

After Chester pegged the back of the chair, he assembled the front posts and stretchers or rounds, and then attached the sides. The chair was ready for "barkin'" or "bottomin'," that is, weaving a seat (fig. 22). At any time, Chester might find it necessary to peel bark, a difficult and unpleasant task. On finding an appropriate tree, he had to fell it, remove the rough outer bark with a drawing knife, being careful not to cut into the inner bark, and strip off the inner bark with a pocketknife before any of it dried. "The worst thing I had to learn was jerkin' bark," he said. He preferred to use the bark straight from the tree because it was easier to weave and lighter in color; often, however, he had to store bark and then soak it in a tub of hot water for twenty minutes or so (which darkens it) to restore its pliability.

When weaving the seat, Chester used the thicker butt end of the strip of bark as the needle and the thinner tip for joining to another splint. In contrast to many chairmakers, he used bark of different widths and wove a variety of patterns, depending in part on the amount he hoped to charge for a chair. The widest strip was 2½ inches, the narrowest was ⅜ inch; he varied the pattern of overlapping splints from two-weave to five-weave, for the widest and narrowest strips. He said that the thicker and wider the bark, the longer it would last, and the easier and quicker it was to weave. He preferred narrow bark. The seat on one of the larger rocking chairs required about 160 feet of wide bark and 400 feet of narrow bark. Unlike some chairmakers, he wove the seat in the same pattern underneath as on the top. He also turned the sap side of the bark down so the attractive diamond-shaped grain of the other side was up (some, like Aaron, split the bark in two, discarding the top half with its diamond grain; they preferred as smooth a surface as possible).

The top stretcher, or seat round, was smooth rather than eight-sided like the other rounds so as not to cut into the bark and weaken it. On the chair in figure 22, this round is curved like the slats for greater comfort and because "it looks better thataway," said Chester. To begin bottoming, he tied one end of a hickory splint to the curved round of the seat at the back of the chair on the left side as it faced him. He carried the splint across the round, took it under and brought it back up; tension held it in place. Had the splint been uneven in width because of knots, or too wide, Chester would have trimmed it with his pocketknife. His grandfather used to make the top front stretcher oval rather than cylindrical to prevent the bark splints from drawing toward the center of the seat front and bowing in the front stretcher. Chester did not do this, first because of the extra time required, and second because his weaving was so tight that the splints did not draw together (as I write this, two decades later, the fronts of chairs he made for us in the mid-1960s still have not bowed in).

In figure 22, the warp of the splints going from the front to the back of the chair is slightly loose near the front; at the back where he has begun the woof, the seat has tightened. Also apparent is the pattern of three under and three over. "I use a three-weave on the inch stuff, I use a two-weave on the two-inch stuff, an' on the half inch of real nar' I use the four-weave. On the *real* nar' I use the five weave." The only chairmaker to do so, Chester inserted short pieces of bark at the back of the seat and at the front between the posts; this improved the appearance.

Since a single strip of bark was not long enough for the whole seat, Chester had to join several strips. On the splint already in the seat he cut a small notch on each side near the end. Then he cut a hole in the end of the next strip that he would use. He slipped the notched splint through the hole in the other splint. This notch lockin' always holds. Most craftsmen, and even Chester when he made cheaper chairs of wide splints in a two-weave pattern, did not splice the splints but merely overlapped them.

The final steps in constructing a settin' chair or a dining chair were to use a rasp to file the edges and tops of the four posts, and then to place the chair against a windowpane or on top of the kitchen table to ascertain whether it was level (fig. 23).

Chester made rocking chairs in much the same way as he

10 *Opposite*, Aaron, another local chairmaker, shaves the rough outer bark from a hickory, using a drawing knife. **11** With a pocketknife he peels off the inner bark he will use in weaving chair seats. **12** The strips of bank are rolled into "hands." **13** Like most chairmakers, Aaron removes and discards the top half of the inner bark; Chester, however, used all of the inner bark, finding the diamond-shaped pattern that others removed attractive.

14 Chester "hewin' out the slats" for a settin' chair.
15 Cooking slats and posts to make them pliable for bending. 16 *Opposite*, in "mortisin' the back posts" each mortise required about twenty-five strokes with a hammer and chisel. 17 Checking the angle at which to drill stretcher holes.

18 *Opposite*, determining the
proper length for the slats.
19 "Layin' off the rounds" or the
"postees"—that is, marking the
stretchers or legs for
ornamental notching.
20 Assembling the back of a
settin' chair. Chester used a
maul so as not to scar the wood;
he judged the fit by the
sound.   21 It took ten to fifteen
minutes to carve each peg;
Chester used twelve pegs in a
settin' chair, about forty for a
rocker.

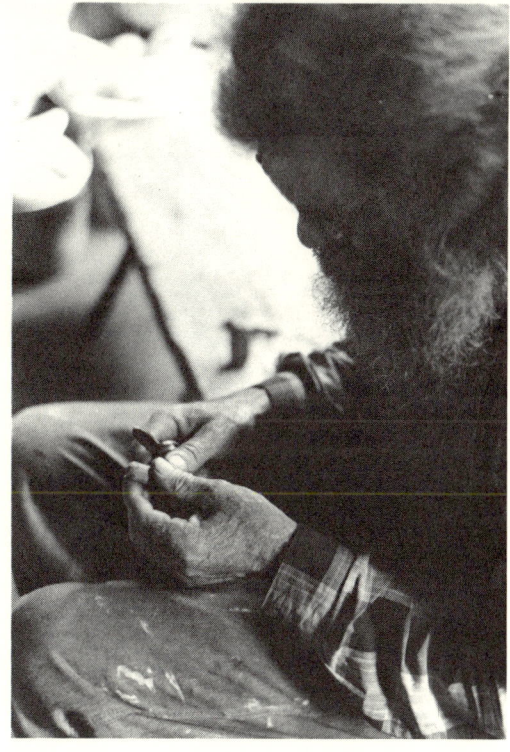

22 Chester bottoming a chair. He used notch locking to hold the
strips of bark together; most chairmakers tied them.

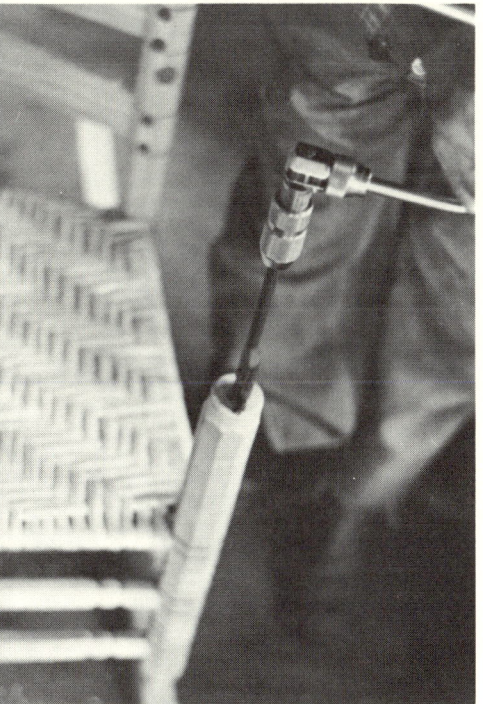

23 To be sure the chair was level, Chester placed it on a table.   **24** Using a special bit, Chester shaped the top of the front post into a tenon to fit into a hole in the underside of an armrest.   **25** Driving the armrest into the mortise on the back post.

26 One of about ninety pegs carved in the same pattern for an elaborate rocker made in 1962. Each peg probably took thirty to forty-five minutes to make.

constructed other kinds of chairs, although the armrests and rockers had to be dressed, shaped, and added to the chair. The longer the back posts are in relation to the front legs in a rocking chair, the greater the tilt. Whether Chester added the rockers first and the arms second or vice versa did not really matter. To assemble the arms, he had to shape the top of each front leg into a tenon, using a special bit (fig. 24), measure to establish the length of the armrest, drill a hole on the underneath side of the armrest to fit onto the top of the front post, and drive the piece into the back post with a hickory maul (fig. 25).

In later years Chester used pegs prolifically. Most dining chairs and many settin' chairs he made in the mid-1960s have at least forty pegs. Each standard peg required ten to fifteen minutes to carve; fancier pegs could take thirty to forty-five minutes each (fig. 26). Rarely were these needed structurally. The chair held together because the ends of slats and rounds were more seasoned than the posts that shrank around them, the foot of a post was drier than the rocker it was driven into, and the tops of the front posts contained less moisture than the armrests attached to them. It was a matter of controlled seasoning in working wet wood. Sometimes Chester used a peg with a bigger head at the top of the chair in each end of the slat. "Sort of a trademark, I guess."

CUSTOMERS AND CHAIRS

Chester's workshop was inside his home—and around the yard. Formerly a coal company office and weigh station, the building consisted of one room on the upper level in which seven family members slept (eight in 1966) and three rooms—kitchen, living room, and workshop—on the lower floor. In 1967, when Chester built a workshop outside at his wife's insistence, the inside workshop was turned into the kitchen, and the kitchen became a dining room. It was also in 1967 that Chester painted the new dining area a dark bluish purple with maroon trim and the kitchen in horizontal bands of red, yellow, and shocking pink, which he set off with red curtains. Ruth insisted that the kitchen cabinets be white enameled steel rather than wooden ones that

Chester could have made. She replaced his chairs in the living room with modern, factory-made reproductions of early American chairs and sofa.

Most of the words in the two signs adorning Chester's house are misspelled. One person in the area thought this was intentional. While Chester tried many ways to attract attention to his chairmaking business, purposeful misspelling was not one of them. "That's the first 'un I ever made; done a bad job on it," he said. "Messed it up so you can't hardly read it." What Chester lacked in spelling knowledge he more than made up for in skill at chairmaking. His business acumen was less well developed.

With Chester's help, we located many of his earlier chairs on that first trip in August 1965. He could recall who had bought his chairs over the years, how much he had asked for each chair and what was in fact paid, what the chairs were constructed of, and the reasons for some of the chairs' unusual features. What struck me at first was the great variety of forms. The attitudes of some customers also surprised me—manifested in their treatment of the chairs and the prices they had offered Chester.

One of the first chairs I found, but certainly not Chester's earliest work, was in a laundromat in a small town near Hazard. A folding chair of red hickory, it was one of fifty that Chester made in 1949 (fig. 27). He sold them for $1 each to the owner of a traveling movie theater, who sold all but this one chair when he gave up the theater business. "Those are beautiful chairs," he said. "I told my wife I shoulda kept one of them for a souvenir." He sold this one to me for the Museum of History, Anthropology, and Folklore at Indiana University.

In 1953 or 1954, Chester made several chairs with seven or eight legs. Dave Harley, the owner of a hardware store in town and the purchaser of several of Chester's works, said the eight-legged chair in figure 28 was crude (it had not been sanded), but he was struck by its oddness. Although he did not need more chairs, he bought this one and ordered a seven-legged chair as well (fig. 29), keeping both chairs in his basement most of the time—which is where they were before I photographed them—but sometimes in good weather leaving them on the porch—

27 Chester at work on fifty folding chairs in 1949 (photo by Ruth Cornett). He sold them for $1 each to the owner of a traveling movie theater.

which is where they were in the months after I took pictures of them.

The shininess of these two chairs results from Harley's having varnished them. Chester neither sanded nor varnished his chairs, but several people who bought them did, finding the resulting form, the gloss itself, or both, appealing (as well as protective of the chairs).

The McIntosh chair, varnished and kept indoors, exemplifies the value of good care in comparison with its mates. Chester made this settin' chair about 1955 (fig. 30) as part of a set of four that he sold for $3 each. McIntosh sold three chairs to a neighbor for $4.50 each. McIntosh's wife varnished the remaining chair, which was kept in the bedroom and seldom used. (After I photographed the chair, McIntosh began leaving it outside in front of his grocery store home for passersby to see.) The neighbor painted his chairs blue and left them outdoors. After a decade of weathering, the seats had disintegrated, the joints had

28 Chester's first eight-legged chair, made in 1953 and sold for $2 or $3.   **29** Chester made a seven-legged armchair in 1953, which he sold for $5. The following year he made six more.

30 The McIntosh chair, a sassafras settin' chair made about 1955, has some of the characteristics of a dining chair.

loosened, and the chairs squeaked when sat in. McIntosh would not sell me his chair, but I was able to buy one of his neighbor's chairs for $5 for the museum at Indiana University.

The absence of notching, the presence of relatively wide feet, and the rather exaggerated angle at which the back posts bend backward and outward in the McIntosh chairs presage traits of some chairs Chester was yet to make. Although Chester called the McIntosh a settin' chair, the seat is unusually high. The chair is 32½ inches tall; the seat is 17 inches from the floor (as opposed to the usual 12 to 14 inches of a settin' chair). Because of its height and the fancy slats, the chair is a cross between a characteristic settin' chair and a dining chair.

"That's a beautiful chair there," said Chester, who, however, also thought it was a technical failure as the settin' chair he intended it to be. "The only thing I like about McIntosh's chair is

the backs. It'd be all right for a dinin' chair but not a settin' chair."
He went on to explain that the curvature in the back might be
appropriate for a dining chair but would not be comfortable in a
settin' chair. "Cause a settin' chair, you're gonna do a whole lot of
settin' in it," he said. "An' it takes a real comf'table back in it.
Course, a dinin' chair, you don't set in them too much."

I liked the chair. The fit seemed fine, but then I am of larger
build than Cornett, McIntosh, and most others in this area. The
chairmaker Hascal, whom I got to know in 1967, criticized the
"openness" between the bottom slat and the seat, and he remarked on the presence of a stretcher in back below the seat (as
on the sides and front). "The slats are too high. There's too much
space between the seat and the bottom slat," he said. He allowed, however, that "it's got pretty slats and pegs. If it had one
more slat at the bottom, it'd been perfect." He repeated, "It's a
neat lookin' chair, all right." Then he commented, "It has that
extry round, but that's nothin' to criticize a chair over—it don't
hurt no more than it helps." Chester was one of the few craftsmen or perhaps the only one to include the extra stretcher in
back, which he said increased the chair's strength.

Contrasting in some ways with the McIntosh chair is a red elm
settin' chair dating from 1954 (fig. 31). Although the back posts
are bent between the first and second slats and there is a single
large peg at each end of a slat, the chair differs in that the slats are
narrow and the posts and rounds are small in diameter. Chester
attributed this to the size of wood he had available. At 36½
inches, the chair is 4 inches taller than McIntosh's; the bark
splints are 1¼ inches wide—only ¼ inch wider than the splints
in McIntosh's chair.

The red elm settin' chair sold for $2. Claire Wilson bought it
and several other settin' chairs and bar stools to furnish her
tavern. She eventually sold most of them at a higher price, but
she kept one—both to sit in and to use as a stepladder when
painting (there is white paint dribbled on the back of the chair
and on the seat). That she could stand on it, she said, demonstrates how sound the chair is.

Also about 1954 or 1955 Chester made a love seat (fig. 32) and a
rocking chair (fig. 33) that he sold to a man nearby, who later

31 A red elm settin' chair made in 1954 and sold
to tavern owner Claire Wilson.

moved to Lexington. The furniture stayed with the house, which
the owner rented to "Smitty" Smith and his family. Like the
McIntosh chair and some others made at this time, this rocking
chair has large button-headed pegs. The chair's back flares outward and backward; the front posts also curve outward. Painted
light green by the owner or a tenant, the chair and love seat are of
mulberry with hickory pegs. The armrests are relatively thin,
contoured somewhat to fit one's arms and pegged into the top of
the front posts. Chester shaped the wood entirely with an ax,
not a drawing knife. Smitty remarked over and over again that
the chair would not tip over, which he demonstrated by rocking
backward with great force. Twenty and a half inches apart at the
front, the rockers are only 4¼ inches apart at the back. This was
one of Chester's favorite chairs.

In the early 1960s Chester made several "high chairs," most of

32 A mulberry love seat (painted light green), made in the mid-1950s.   33 A mulberry rocker made about the same time, using only an ax and hatchet.

34 Chester called this sassafras chair, built about 1961, a "high chair." It was sold to a tavern owner who used it as a bar stool.

which were used as bar stools in taverns. The one in figure 34 is of sassafras with hickory pegs. The chair has slender posts (about 1¼ inches in diameter), no notching, back posts that are bent outward, and front posts that are flared at the top for the sitter's convenience in getting in and out. The arms are pegged from the top. The overall height is 47 inches, with the front posts 37 inches tall and the seat 28 inches from the floor.

The owner of the tavern who has this chair has or had other chairs by Chester. One has cross-hatching on the front legs. Another chair, which he had sold, was "one of my most inter-estin' chairs," said Chester, who mentioned it several times. It has square rather than eight-sided posts, very wide slats, and diamond-shaped pegs. "I b'lieve that settin' chair is the most beautiful settin' chair I ever made."

I was able to obtain for the Indiana University Museum of

35 Sassafras rocking chair is one
of four made by Chester about
1961. It sold for $18.

History, Anthropology, and Folklore several high chairs that a
man in Hazard had bought from Chester for $7 each. One with
armrests is of black walnut, another without armrests is of
sassafras. The owner had kept them in the basement of one of his
rental houses; they were dusty and splattered with paint. He
never used the chairs, he said, having ordered them only as an
act of charity because he knew Chester could use the money. He
donated them to the museum, along with a bench made of
mulberry and hickory bark.

The owner of a laundry in Hazard purchasd a rocking chair
resembling some of the other kinds of chairs that Chester made
about 1961. Of sassafras, this chair is 42 inches high (fig. 35). The
rockers are 34 inches long and 1⅜ inches thick. The seat is 17
inches deep; it tapers from a width of 22 inches in front to 17

inches in back. The arms are 2¼ inches wide, ¾ inch thick, and 18½ inches long. The rounds or stretchers are 4 inches apart.

Because it has five slats, Chester called this a medium-back rocker. The armrests are contoured on the inside rather than on top. As in many of his other chairs at the time, the posts are relatively thin (1¾ inches in diameter), the front posts bend outward slightly, the top three slats have been pegged at each end, and there is no notching—although the crisply defined stiles (flat faces on the front of the back posts) and the peaked slats add a decorative touch.

Chester had asked $40 each for a set of four; he finally accepted $18 or $19 apiece. The buyer, who said he really did not want them, gave three to employees and a relative; he kept only this one, which he shellacked and left on the front porch most of the time. "It's sort of an honor to have a chair like that [i.e., hand-made], I guess," said his wife. "I guess I should take better care of it." She said it "sets good" and probably would last a lifetime if cared for properly.

Another chair I found at this time was Chester's first two-in-one rocking chair, which he had built about 1961 (fig. 36). Constructed of white walnut with black walnut pegs, it represents the first use of pegs whose color contrasts with the wood of the chair. It also is the first chair in which Chester used *double* pegs at the end of each slat. And it marks the first noteworthy use of notchings corresponding to turnings.

The person who bought the chair managed an auto franchise in town. He did not want want any of Chester's chairs (his wife had been the sole purchaser of furniture in their overfurnished home). He finally relented because of Chester's persistence in returning with this rocker. Asked the lowest price he would take for it, Chester said $50 (originally he had requested $300). The buyer sent it to Lexington to be sanded and varnished; when he showed me this chair in his bedroom he remarked on the beauty of the chair's finish, which had cost an additional $50. In regard to the chair itself, he was puzzled as to why there were four rockers.

Every chair had a story about it. Chester commented on each piece of furniture, remarking on some circumstance under

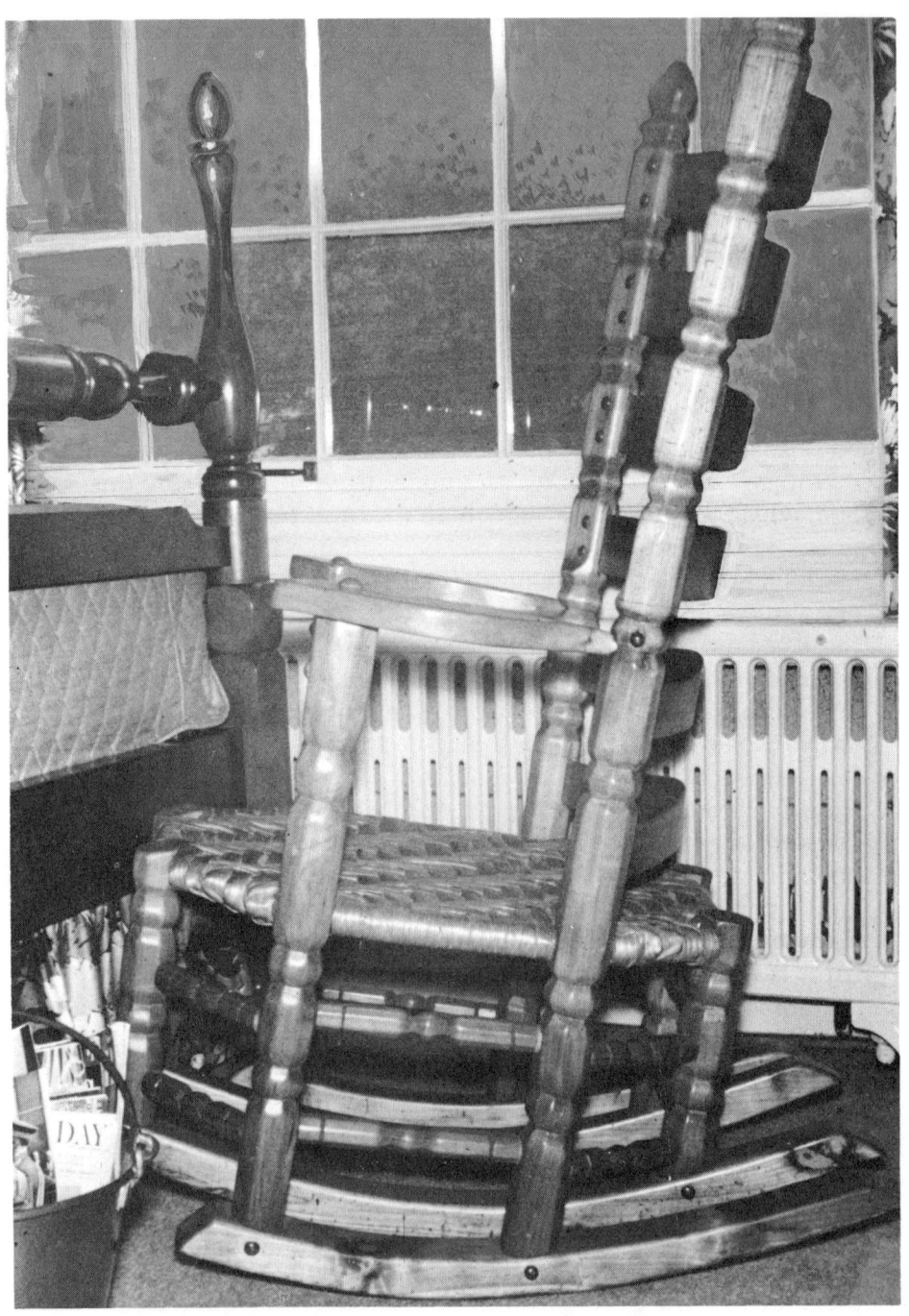

36 Chester's first two-in-one rocking chair (late 1961) sold for $50.

which it was made or purchased, identifying the wood or woods used, describing construction techniques or problems, giving some reasons for specific features, and occasionally passing judgment on the work. Customers usually referred to the approximate date or other matters attending the purchase (including perhaps the price paid or their relationship to the craftsman). Customers also mentioned uses of the chair and sometimes expressed opinions about the object or its maker. Their comments and actions, as well as the recurrent themes in their narratives, told something about the perceptions, attitudes, and concerns of those who purchased the chairs.

Many customers did not have the money to buy, or would not spend it on, old-fashioned furniture handmade by a bearded, barefoot craftsman. The chairmaker developed a large variety of types of furniture he could offer, experimented with novel designs or features to alter the appearance or improve the comfort of a chair, and sought a wealthier clientele whenever possible.

When we met him in August 1965, Chester had a detailed price schedule in mind. At that time he said he would make an ordinary mule-eared settin' chair for $12.95 (he had rarely received as much as $4 each for such chairs). He priced a dining chair with four slats in the back instead of three, and the seat 17 to 19 inches from the floor instead of 12 to 15 inches as in settin' chairs, for $18.95, although he had never made such a chair. A more expensive dining chair with notchin' or decorative elements and knobs or finials, he said, would be $29.95. He wanted $59 for a rather plain rocking chair with four slats. A five-slat rocker would cost $69 (the highest price he had ever gotten was $18 or $19). He asked $79 for a six-slat rocking chair with a brace in the back for greater support (he had made one recently that he called the Abner chair). He wanted $89 for a larger rocking chair with a "better rock," a seat of narrow hickory bark splints, seven curved slats, and extensive ornamentation.

He also said he would make a two-in-one rocking chair with seven slats, eight posts or legs, four rockers, and woven hickory bark seat for $269; the most he was paid for any of the four chairs he had made like this was $75 and the least was $30. For $500 he would construct a bookcase rocker with eight posts, four rockers, leg rest, and woven back and seat. He had made one of these for which he received $100; eventually he was to build a second one which he would sell for $169. He could make other kinds of furniture and musical instruments for different amounts.

These Sears and Roebuck prices, as several people called them, were not very meaningful before 1965 because no one accustomed to bartering ever paid Chester much for his chairs, and the prices meant little after the summer of 1965 because people who read newspaper articles erroneously thought he made only seven-slat rocking chairs, so they ordered only this type at the current price (which later increased and differed according to the wood, walnut being most expensive). It was also impossible for other people and for us at the time to conceive of the difference in chairs correlated with the various prices.

Nevertheless, pricing seemed a dominant concern. The brief article in the *Louisville Courier-Journal* mentions the family's dependence on Chester's $50 monthly check for "an injury suffered in World War II" and dwells on the amount of effort and time to make a big rocking chair, "which takes a month to complete" and for which Chester asked $70. "Visitors to his workshop near Dwarf, in Eastern Kentucky, usually offer much less and frequently leave empty-handed when Cornett refuses to drop his price. During the winter he sold only two chairs."

This was the second article about Chester. In March or April 1965, Gurney Norman published a lengthy piece in the *Hazard Herald* called "Rare Hand-Made Furniture Produced by Bearded Chairmaker." The article begins, "There was a time, long ago, when Chester Cornett would have held an eminent position in his community as a man with a genuine talent for making fine things with his hands." The author remarks on Chester's tools and construction techniques, emphasizing the absence of glue or nails in chairs. Several times he contrasts handmade chairs with their factory-made counterparts. In a long paragraph he describes visitors expecting to pay "ten and twenty dollars" for a chair that Chester "has invested a month of patient labor in." The prospective purchaser, writes Norman, "gets back in his car empty handed, or perhaps, as a compromise, with one of the smaller sitting chairs" selling for $12, "feeling a little incredulous that someone would ask over twenty dollars just for a rocking chair."

One of the first to do so, Gurney Norman took particular interest in Chester. He bought a large rocking chair at the full amount the craftsman requested, and encouraged Harry Caudill, Wendell Berry, and other writers to purchase furniture. He was instrumental in bringing the press's attention to Chester, which attracted a client base from outside the area.

"But are they 'just chairs,' pieces of anonymous furniture to sit on and otherwise ignore?" asks Gurney Norman in his article. "Most of the few people who buy original Cornett chairs think not," he writes. "They have more important reasons for wanting to own one. They buy them because they know there is no other chair in the world like theirs and because they know they can last a hundred years and longer and grow more valuable all the time."

He continues: "They buy them, too, because they know that Cornett chairs are among the last such hand-made furniture our society will ever produce and that their creator is perhaps the last of a long line of craftsmen that reaches farther back in time than we can even imagine.

"They would not say a Cornett chair is 'just a chair,' " Norman concludes, "any more than they would say a great painting is 'just a picture.' "

Gurney Norman had likened Chester's furniture to the world's great easel paintings. Two years later, a customer in Kansas City, Mary Carey (a friend of my wife's with an extensive collection of Zuni and Navajo jewelry) would remark that Chester "truly is an artist in his craft; he reminds me of a saint who gained sanctity by doing the common things uncommonly well." Both Norman and Carey recognized—even emphasized—the aesthetic aspect of what otherwise seems to be a utilitarian object. Some of the local residents, I discovered later, also appreciated the formal excellence of the chairs.

I found this attitude rare in the literature, however. Most commentators considered "country furniture" a weak imitation of their high-style counterparts, better known in the history of American decorative arts. "Folk art" embraced easel painting and sculpture for the most part, and occasionally quilts, duck decoys, and decorated pottery. Chairs were notably absent from the list. Crafts tended to be described in terms of technology and subsistence livelihood. Researchers focused on the objects, not their makers. Curators and folklorists alike were quick to assert that traditional technology was rapidly disappearing.

It was ironic, I thought, that the museum specimens I was able to obtain through purchase or donation reinforced some of these notions. Often abused, the chairs were not exactly sterling examples of the chairmaker's art. When he bought some power tools in 1967, Chester donated his well-worn vise bench, drawing horse, and slat presses to the Museum of History, Anthropology, and Folklore. The director of the museum then mounted an exhibit of "vanishing industries" of "a bygone era." The only saving grace, perhaps, was the inclusion of a rocking chair and a settin' chair that Chester had made in 1965 which went directly to the museum without having seen service or abuse.

After a week and a half of observing Chester at work and seeking earlier examples of his chairs, I had four hundred slides. I had filled several notebooks with information and had taped some of the interviews. What would I do with the material?

Had I wanted to, I could have typologized these chairs and others that had been reported historically throughout the South and East. As researchers were then doing with traditional houses and outbuildings, I might have postulated the origins and distribution of chair types over time and space, treating the objects as diffusible entities that changed according to certain "laws." Had I done this, I would have been following the precedent of earlier historical-geographical research on folktales and ballads, using what had been venerated as "the folklore method."

I had data on the values and ways of doing things of some people in the hills of southeastern Kentucky. Was chairmaking related to other values and to behavioral norms? Could I use it somehow as an index to Appalachian culture?

Did the material I had about economic matters imply the existence of a system of bartering? If so, how did this relate to other institutions? And what were the effects of industrialization, migration, and other social processes on chairmaking?

Art historians had written extensively about the styles of epochs and great masters. They tended to identify periods of development, postulating origins in earlier trends and conditions. Could I do the same with chairs?

In sum, I could have studied traditional chairmaking in southeastern Kentucky as a diffusible entity and source of information about historical conditions and processes, as an element of culture and index of sociocultural processes, or as an aesthetic phenomenon. Each approach was well established in scholarship; each typified a different discipline at the time.

But there seemed to be an alternative approach to art, survivals, culture, and institutions per se. Chairmaking had its aesthetic dimension; chairs and their construction did indeed exhibit continuities and consistencies through time and space; and the makers and consumers existed in some sort of relationship and held particular attitudes and values affecting the objects produced. Expressiveness, traditions, and immediate circumstances of manufacture and use—these seemed to be important to chairmaking, at least according to the information I had recorded.

Such issues could be pondered later, however. A more immediate concern was that of returning to Chester's home in late November 1965 to pick up the rocking chair that I had ordered for the museum at Indiana University and to get the two sassafras settin' chairs I had purchased for my wife and me. I also wanted to locate and photograph more of the chairs Chester had made earlier, and talk to customers. While there, I placed an order for a rocking chair like the museum piece. I was to return for it the following August.

Chester and I corresponded between my visits in November 1965 and August 1966. In several letters, he mentioned a "strange rocking chair" that he had started work on immediately after we had left in November. Little did I know that this "two-in-one, bookcase rocker, masterpiece of furniture" (as he later called it) would become one of the focal points of my inquiry, that it would introduce yet another element to consider in analyzing chairmaking, or that explaining how and why it came to exist would encapsulate the method of research that I seemed to be gravitating toward.

TWO

The Masterpiece
and the New Design

When we saw "our" chair in Chester Cornett's workroom, we gasped. We had ordered a rocking chair with seven slats and a seat of hickory bark splints, similar to the one we had purchased from Chester for a museum (fig. 37). The only similarity between what we had requested and what we got was that the chair crowding a corner of the room had rockers—four of them!

This "strange" chair, as Chester called it, which he presented to us as ours, is made of solid oak with black walnut decorative trim at the top. The heads of its walnut pegs are carved in a pattern of ridges and grooves (fig. 38). It has eight legs and four rockers. Because it has twice as many legs and rockers as usual it is a "two-in-one" chair. Five panels forming the back and sides create a strong feeling of enclosure. Shelves on each side of the chair are supposed to hold books. Beneath the lowest shelves are storage units; the seat lifts up to reveal storage space below it.

"Now what's it s'posed to be?" asked a visitor to Chester's workshop shortly after we had arrived. Chester informed him that it is a rocking chair that holds books—hence, a Bookcase Rocker. "That's nice, real nice," said the man, without much conviction.

All of us were uneasy. Chester knew this was not the chair we had ordered. My wife and I doubted we could afford it, really wanted it, or would ever appreciate it fully. The visitor was as surprised as we were at the nature of the chair. After an embarrassing pause in which none of us could think of anything to say, the man asked, "How much time you got involved in that?"

Chester explained that this chair was one of the few he had made for which he did not have to cut timber in the hills and

37 Sassfras rocker with black walnut pegs made by Chester in November 1965; the author purchased it on behalf of a museum and ordered a similar one for himself.

dress it entirely by hand. Despite its complexity, the chair required less time than one might expect. During most of his productive career, said Chester, "takin' it from the stump, it takes one week to make a settin' chair and a month to make a rocker." Most other chairmakers can produce the same kinds of chairs far more quickly through the use of different construction techniques and more modern tools. This chair, made of wood purchased from a lumber company, required a month or so to build.

There was another pause. The man finally said, "Boy, that's excitin'," and hurried out of the room.

Trying to understand what had happened, I reflected on the correspondence between Chester and me the past few months. "I have Bin this month Workin day and nite on a Big Rocker," Chester had written to my wife and me in late December 1965, a

38 Chester's Bookcase Masterpiece (August 1966), which he presented to the author instead of the seven-slat rocking chair that had been ordered.

few months after we had met him and photographed him at work. Although not typical in southeastern Kentucky, big chairs were scarcely remarkable for this craftsman. He had been known for several years as the maker of rocking chairs at least five feet in height with seven or more slats, thick posts, and plenty of room in the seats.

"This one is Made so different that hit dont look like iney chire that I Ever made," he insisted. "They are somtin strange about this Rocking chire   I don't Reley no what hapin   I just startied workin on hit   Seems to Be sometin Kidin me   so strang."

We had been mildly curious about the piece of furniture to which he alluded, but not having seen it, we were not as perplexed as Chester. We knew that while he had made some unconventional chairs they were, well, *chairs;* and a chair is a chair, so to speak. More puzzling at the time was Chester's own bewilderment about the process of manufacture. Our impression had been that he fully conceived of a chair before he began construction; the requirements of useful design usually preclude spontaneity.

The chair disturbed Chester, as was apparent in a letter written to my wife's sister shortly after he had sent a letter to us. "This one is a strang [chair]," he repeated to her. "I Reley dinton in tin to Make hit this tipe   Sem to Be somtin new about Ever day has got to Be Adied   Hit is so hevey now that I can't hardly lift hit." All of Chester's big rockers are heavy. There was no description of the chair, only the same reference to an unsettling feeling in Chester: "This Rocker is Reley strang   Neve sen iney thing like hit in my hole life   hit Reley looks like my Master Pece of furniture." He concluded his remarks about the chair with the promise that "i will send you ale some pictures of hit sometime   A Bisinis man in New York wants some Pictures of hit and I gess they will by hit."

No one in our family received photographs or further details. In another letter, dated 3 April 1966, Chester mentioned in passing that he still had the chair. There was a hint that the businessman had chosen not to buy it. "Still have the Maste Pece," wrote Chester, "and Lokes like I will get to keep hit."

Curiously, he had not remarked upon the rocking chair he was supposed to be making for us. Except for a brief statement in late spring that it was finished, we received no word at all about the rocking chair we had ordered. Nor did we learn more about Chester's strange chair until we arrived at the end of August, 1966, to pick up our rocker and confronted his "masterpiece" (fig. 39).

"That's a chair, hain't it?" asked one of Chester's neighbors to whom I showed photographs later. "New one on me. Yes sir, that's pretty—all that little stuff up here," he said, pointing to the decorative detail along the top of the chair.

"It looks like a privy to me," said a close acquaintance of ours.

"I think it looks like a throne," remarked another friend.

Most people who have seen the chair said nothing at first sight, perhaps because of shock, and little afterward, owing to mixed emotions. But two other craftsmen in southeastern Kentucky declared the chair a work of art because of the elaborate construction and the extensive ornamentation.

"I think it's pretty," said the chairmaker Hascal. "If I had that chair, I'd set it up in my living room and set things in it. Put ivy vines on it, you know, to make it look kinda like a cliff."

"I think the people that bought that chair bought it for the looks," replied Beechum, the other craftsman, after a moment's reflection. "Now if I had that chair I wouldn't let nobody set in it. I'd fasten that to the wall and put whatnots in it." Beechum also noted that the four rockers seemed to "fit the design of it" and looked "all right on the chair," although he had complained earlier that the extra rockers and legs on some of Chester's other two-in-one chairs are "kinda dangerous" and that "a man could hurt hisself on them things."

Another man who knows Chester well examined a stack of photographs in search of Chester's chairs, which he claimed he could recognize easily. He made many mistakes, confusing works of Aaron with those by Chester and failing to identify many of Chester's earlier chairs because he had focused attention on ornamentation rather than on form and technique. But when he spotted the Bookcase Masterpiece he proclaimed it Chester's chair, owing to the pegs and the strange design.

"It's kinda pretty," he concluded.

"Maybe," I granted, "but it's not very comfortable to sit in."

39 Chester seated in his "strange rocking chair" (photographer unknown).

"Well, I think it's pretty and probably more for lookin' at than to set in."

The man's remark about the chair's being just something to look at might have troubled Chester. On one occasion I showed him pictures of a stool and a chair made by Hugh, who worked in a coal mine and dabbled at chairmaking. "He ain't no chairmaker," said Hugh's neighbor; "he jest pranks around with it."

"That's completely handmade but that back's bound to a been worked out on a bandsaw or a jigsaw," noted Chester. Hugh copied the stool, which is of northern European design, from a picture in a magazine and used a jigsaw to form the back. But the stool is poorly made, uncomfortable and unstable.

"Looks to me like hit's jest somethin' to look at," Chester remarked. "But I al'ays said, some'un or other that's made oughta be useful."

Other craftsmen felt the same way; that may be why the

Bookcase Masterpiece posed a problem for them. In this area most handmade chairs are rather plain and simple in appearance. Their simplicity facilitates their use and corresponds with the values of some people—the absence of ostentation in home furnishings. Even Chester said of one of his other complicated works, "It's too expensive for a poor man like me." But this so-called chair is a bookcase that surrounds one and moves with one's own motion, a throne that rocks, a privy that won't sit still, just something to look at, or an anomaly whose purpose cannot be divined. Characterization of the chair depends on who examines it and on what they associate it with, given their past experiences. Ornament and exaggerated attention to appearance override utility, thus confusing the issue.

Both Hascal and Beechum declared the chair a work of art to be chained to the wall and not sat in. That was their first impulse. But, like Chester, neither could quite accept it; it was confusing for a utilitarian object such as a chair to serve no practical purpose. They came upon this rocker unexpectedly while flipping through about thirty photographs of different chairs. For a moment they said nothing at all. It seemed that as chairmakers they had suddenly lost their frame of reference as they stared at this creation. After stating initially that the chair is a work of art just to be looked at, these men had second thoughts. No, if Hascal and Beechum owned the chair themselves they would not just look at it but use it in some way, perhaps to hold "pretties" or "whatnots." Pretties are useless (although not worthless) things, such as flower and pinecone arrangements, found objects, and the miniature corn sleds Beechum made. Whatnots are objects whose purpose is not immediately apparent or small, practical items too attractive or expensive to be used often. Either way, whether it was a work of art to be gazed upon or an ivy-covered cliff or whatnot holder, the chair was not conceived primarily as a chair.

What was Chester's attitude toward his "two-in-one, bookcase rocker, masterpiece of furniture" ?

"When I first saw it, I liked it pretty good," he said. But after having lived with it for eight months and having endured the puzzled stares and inane questions of neighbors and customers, he was less sanguine.

"I'm kinda like other people," he said; "hit don't look right someway."

He suggested adding a leg rest in front, as he had done on a couple of other chairs, and black leather upholstery on the seat, back, and sides. Even so, "It don't look like it b'longs here yet; I b'lieve it come here too early or too late, one."

"If you don't like it," I asked him, "why do you call it your 'masterpiece'?"

"Cause, uh, it is. I never made nothin' like it in my life. There ain't nothing in the world like hit. That's why I call it my 'master-piece'."

Chester's remark is a bit misleading. There were, in fact, design precedents for the chair in his forty-year career as a chairmaker, although at the time we knew of only a few of these. Reference to the earlier works alone, however, does not explain the masterpiece's unusual qualities.

Regardless of one's opinion of the chair, attention to the object at this moment leads us to the important issue of how Chester conceptualized form. In addition, the chair exemplifies the way in which even designing and making useful objects may be a mode of expressive behavior. Furthermore, the construction of this chair is significant in that it represents, in some of its aspects, a rather rare occurrence in the production of useful objects, which usually involves direct customer stipulation and the designing of objects that serve practical purposes—that of an object's being developed in form and design without the completely conscious control of the producer.

Chester was by nature planful in his work. He would never "just throw a chair together" or let the design develop of its own accord. Yet he wrote that he did not know what was happening to him or to the chair during manufacture. Apparently he had begun to depend upon intuition and sensation to guide him through much of the construction so that he could not, to his great distress, predict what he would have to do to the chair each day after he had begun work on it.

What happened during this time? What were the compelling forces over which Chester felt no control? Why did he make so strange a chair?

The factors accounting for the creation of this chair may never be fully known, because I was not with Chester during the month or so in which he built the chair. In addition, he did not tell me much about the circumstances of manufacture because of our mutual embarrassment. Some beginning points, however, are how he conceptualized form, what he thought the nature and uses of a chair should be, and what relationship existed between Chester and the customer for whom he built the chair.

We have the distinct impression from Chester's comments in letters and conversations that he had intended to make a special chair for us as a gesture of appreciation (and at no extra cost). He said as much when we were with him in November 1965—despite the fact that we repeatedly asked for an ordinary rocker.

Chester seemed to feel greatly indebted to those who helped him. He retained a deep reverence for Gurney Norman, the young journalist at the *Hazard Herald* who published an essay about him in the spring of 1965. This article resulted in a photo essay in the *Louisville Courier-Journal* in June 1965, then a piece in the *National Observer* in December. It eventually led to other articles in regional and national publications—all of which provided many additional sales for Chester at higher prices, which at the time he said he wanted. Gurney Norman encouraged friends to purchase Chester's chairs at the current asking price, having bought one himself. And he took Chester back to Pine Mountain to visit his birthplace, sixty miles south of where Chester was then living on a busy highway.

As a gesture of appreciation for the help that the young writer had given him, Chester presented him with a settin' chair. For several months he considered making some miniature settin' and rocking chairs to be used as paperweights. But sometimes Chester's vision was blurred so that he could not make out small details. He never built the model chairs, although he mentioned them often as something he was going to do to express his thanks to Gurney Norman for befriending and helping him.

We learned later that Chester had constructed at least one other chair whose features expressed some of his feelings. Of black walnut—an expensive and pretty wood—the chair has many notchings. Even more striking are the hearts that he carved in the slats. He made the chair for his daughter Brenda in

40 An oak settin' chair made by Chester in August 1965 for a museum.

1961, about the time his wife left him in a mountain hollow and moved to the highway for several months.

The settin' chair that Chester made in August 1965 on our first visit was unusual in its own right (fig. 40). He knew it was destined for the museum at Indiana University. He made it "special" by using small double pegs of black walnut in each slat to contrast with the white oak of the chair. He also curved the top seat round in back for greater comfort. Neither trait was common on such a chair at this time.

I noticed, too, that the seat on the museum's rocking chair (fig. 37) is of narrow bark, which Chester did not often use. The armrests are curvilinear. They seem to invite a person to sit in the chair. It is easy to imagine them as arms, crooked at the elbow, with hands extended—open and welcoming.

The two chairs we had ordered for ourselves in August and picked up in November were supposed to have been simple settin' chairs. Instead, Chester made dining chairs with knobs,

41 Some designs used by Chester: *left,* chair with single pegs (about 1960); *center,* redbud chair with black walnut double pegs and slats notched at ends (about 1961); and *right,* sassafras chair with black walnut pegs (November 1965). The first two are settin' chairs; the last is a dining chair.

notching, double pegs, and narrow-bark seats (fig. 41, chair on right). He asked only the settin' chair price, saying that he had wanted to make special chairs for us. We insisted on paying him the full amount for dining chairs, however.

We spent several days over Thanksgiving with the Cornett family and also searched for earlier chairs that Chester had made. Before we left on 28 November with the museum's rocking chair and our two dining chairs, we placed an order with him for a rocking chair. It was to be of sassafras, like the dining chairs, and patterned after the museum's rocking chair.

It was about this time that we learned Chester's wife was pregnant. The family named the girl, born in late spring 1966, LuAnnie Jane—the first name for a relative and the middle name for my wife. After our visit in August 1966, Chester wrote to us on 11 September: "We awal shere Enjoied you all So much   after you left we just walked around and around for a few days   funny nothin never Bothered me this way Before   hit are somtin like a famliey having some one in a familey levin for a new home . . . are somethin." And Ruth told me in 1967 that when we had left the preceding August, "Check hated to see you go. He went out there an' sat down by the side of the house an' didn't hardly move all day."

It seems likely, therefore, that Chester wanted to create a chair with some special qualities as a way of repaying us for the attention and the orders for several chairs he had received. He also may have wanted to make a chair befitting his self-image as a master craftsman. Certainly he mentioned in one of his letters the recent publication of an article in the *National Observer* that inundated him with queries about his chairs, much to his dismay and confusion, but also perhaps his pleasure.

"Lettres Went to Comin in froum East South North West Wantin to no if they Culd But a Laddre Back Rockker and they said they Engoid Redin About me in the natin advzer news papre   I never herd of this news papre. . . ."

Just like the chair he had commenced to build, "Ever thing is so strang   try to ancer Ever Lettre and tele thim that I dinton have iney [chairs]." The only chair under construction was the strange one, and so, "I tole thim about this one and to day I got a lettre from New York Bisnis sain they had made arrangement with [a local bank] to go in to [H]azard and see thim at the Bank   they said send thim some pictures of the Rocker and hit sise   I will haft to get a Poride Camery I gess."

One of the first requests for chairs following the appearance of the *National Observer* article in early December came from Martin Loughhead in New York City. He wanted to purchase a full year's production from Chester plus any chairs he had on hand. Chester tried to explain to him about the Bookcase Masterpiece he was working on; Loughhead agreed to buy it for $300. He sent a check for this amount to a bank in Hazard and made arrangements with the executive vice-president of the bank to handle the transaction. This much is clear from statements made by Chester, in addition to information in the letter from Loughhead dated 22 December 1965, which Chester still had in August 1966.

Before he would close the deal, Loughhead wanted a picture; he could not visualize the chair from Chester's remarks. He also asked Chester to sign a contract binding him to sell a year's production of chairs to Loughhead. Chester bought a used

Polaroid camera, took pictures of his masterpiece and sent photos to Loughhead. Perhaps because he was suspicious of the man's motives and because he felt Loughhead was not offering enough money for a year's supply of chairs, Chester demanded $479 instead of $300 for the Bookcase Masterpiece. The businessman refused to buy it or pay any greater price for a large quantity of chairs. After their disagreement, Loughhead ordered a seven-slat rocking chair, but to my knowledge Chester never made it for him. Within the next year, two other business firms, one in California and the other in Indiana (an insurance firm), offered to buy a year's production of furniture, but Chester refused them both.

Chester carved an inscription on the walnut inserts at the top of the Bookcase Rocker, Masterpiece of Furniture. Beginning at the far left panel as one faces the chair, the inscription reads: "Old, Kentucky / Made / Buy / Chester / Cornett's / Hands / Engle Mill." Engle Mill is the area north of Dwarf where Chester lived at this time. Engle Mill is in Kentucky, but did not represent to Chester's way of thinking, as I realized later, *old* Kentucky. But where he then resided was where he made chairs, which had been described as "old-fashioned" in design and construction. Moreover, he had learned these traditional ways of doing things while he was a youth living on Pine Mountain—a place that *did* represent old Kentucky ("Now I was born in old Kentucky," he had told me on 21 August 1965).

Of all the chairs I saw that had been made by craftsmen of the Cumberlands, only this one had the maker's name emblazoned on it. Why it bore Chester's signature is a matter of speculation. The chair seems to have been well along in construction when Chester received Loughhead's letter of inquiry and responded that he had only this one. The walnut inserts would have been among the last elements made for the chair (probably during the time of the negotiations with Loughhead), although not necessarily the last to be conceptualized. Perhaps they were advertisements for him. On the other hand, maybe he had in mind all along to inscribe the inserts, since I had complimented him and praised his work many times. A chair originally intended to be a gift might well bear a message from the maker to the recipient.

After his disagreements with the businessman in New York, Chester still had the Bookcase Masterpiece. All the orders coming in as a result of the nationwide attention were for seven-slat rockers and modified settin'/dining chairs, because only those types were described and pictured in the article.

During the late spring Chester indicated to us in a letter that our red oak rocking chair (we had ordered sassafras) was ready; we could pick it up anytime. Apparently he had once again decided to sell the masterpiece to us at the cost of a seven-slat chair.

For the first few days we were with him in August he refused to consider more money for the chair. He said repeatedly that if we did not like it or want it, he would make the chair we had ordered ten months earlier. We finally overcame our initial shock and managed to suggest that we thought the masterpiece was a brilliant creation. By the time we left in early September, Chester had agreed to accept at least $200 from us (equal to my monthly fellowship check, which is one reason our enthusiasm over the chair was slow to wax). Later, we ordered another chair, this time one that would have only four legs and two rockers.

The eight-sided post that Chester had shaped by hand since giving up the turning lathe in the early 1950s became one element in the design of the masterpiece. Other features have precedents in the several eight-legged chairs that Chester made in the mid-1950s and the two two-in-one rockers that he built about 1961. But Chester's masterpiece most closely resembles his third two-in-one rocking chair, the Dolph rocker (fig. 42).

Wherever I asked about Chester's chairs, people enthusiastically directed me to the mayor's chair, referred to also by his name, Dolph. It was in the basement of his department store when I saw it. Made of black walnut with hickory rounds and bark, it dated from late 1962 or early 1963. Chester claimed it required five hundred hours to construct.

The chair is 44 inches high. The back panels are 34½ inches in length, and each is about 6¾ inches wide. The lids of the basket armrests lift up to reveal storage space for knitting or books; each is 13 inches deep and 4 inches wide. The outside rockers are 3½ inches from the inside ones, which are 7½ inches apart. The octagon-shaped seat is 22½ inches at its widest. A footrest extends from just beneath the seat for a distance of 16 inches; it is 6¾ inches wide.

Chester used nails on the armrest baskets and some other pieces, which he later lamented having done. But at the time he did not have the proper kind of pegs, or enough of them, and the rounds were so small in diameter that he feared he would break them trying to drill holes for pegs.

Most people seemed impressed with the chair's uniqueness. A few I talked to also said it was the prettiest chair they had ever seen or that Chester had made. They seemed to respond especially to the juxtaposition of colors and textures—the light-colored woven hickory bark against the dark walnut posts—and they marveled at how something that looked so bulky could be so light in weight, and how structurally sound it seemed to be despite the large area covered by bark.

Dolph paid Chester $100 for this first bookcase rocker. I heard that Dolph intended to present it to John F. Kennedy (widely known to be an aficionado of rocking chairs), ostensibly in gratitude for his program of economic assistance to Appalachia. But then the president was assassinated.

Chester had built several other two-in-one rocking chairs since 1961, but all of them had been made from logs he had hewn himself; Chester would cut the timber in the hills or obtain culls from a sawmill, split the logs himself, and hew the planks into posts and slats with a hatchet. To my knowledge, the masterpiece was the first rocking chair made of pieces of wood purchased at a lumber company. It required different techniques of construction, for it is almost impossible to hew lumber that has been sawed and kiln-dried. This is because the wood has already been cut partly with the grain and partly across the grain; a hatchet or drawing knife will not follow the grain well, if at all.

The panels in the back of the masterpiece were unaltered boards Chester had bought from a lumber company. The two-inch-thick posts appear to have been planed eight-sided at the mill, rather than shaped with a drawing knife; but Chester did carve the finials by hand, probably using a hatchet. He had the lumberyard mill the rockers, sawing them out of larger planks;

42 Chester's third two-in-one rocker and first bookcase rocker (1962 or 1963), of black walnut with hickory bark, is known as the Dolph chair or the mayor's chair.

Chester beveled the edges with a saw and a rasp, rounding off the sharp edges. The seat consists of three planks pegged and glued together and then hewed out with a hatchet.

The chair is of heavy red oak (the decorative trim and pegs are black walnut). It stands 50 inches high. It is 36 inches wide, and the 2-inch wide rockers are 39 inches long. The shoulder space between the shelves at the top measures 18¼ inches. The inside corner of each shelf is rounded off; in addition, Chester curved the inside edge of the middle and lowest shelves, and even carved out this edge on the middle shelves.

The lowest armrest shelves, which are hinged to the sides of the chair, lift up to reveal storage space below, as does the seat.

On the top edge of one storage shelf is carved the word "Book" and on the other is inscribed "Case." There is no mistaking, then, their purpose: to hold books. (Chester had said the baskets on the Dolph chair were for books, and he called it a bookcase rocker; other people told me the baskets were for knitting or books, or both.) However, books on the shelves of the masterpiece will fall off when the chair rocks, making the shelves impractical for this purpose.

Chester had to glue and peg the masterpiece together. As in other Cornett chairs from that time, there are more pegs than are structurally necessary. The chair has about two hundred pegs. Several have decorated heads. In November 1965, I had expressed amazement to Chester at the decorated pegs in the two-in-one rocking chair owned by Phil Banks (figs. 26, 92, and 93); Chester had carved the head of each of the eighty or ninety pegs with grooves and ridges. "Ain't too many people notices that," said Chester. Many misunderstand the nature of the pegs, thinking they are bolts, while others ask how "those little round things are stuck on the chair," he said.

Is it possible that such a chair as the Bookcase Masterpiece is the result of spontaneous creation? Spontaneity of sorts is often involved in chairmaking. The details of an object may not be clear in the craftsman's mind, the material itself may require some revision of the mental image, or the hand cannot possibly carry out precisely the idea inside the producer's head.

Consider another chairmaker, Aaron, whom I met later. At times he preferred not to plan some of the work in advance, particularly the decorative elements. Rather, he enjoyed visually imagining the decorative field. Sometimes, too, he manipulated the raw materials until design elements emerged, chiseling posts rotating on his homemade electric lathe, selecting patterns that pleased him, and then duplicating the decorative elements on the other chair parts before constructing a chair (the planful operation). On finding a pattern acceptable to him and attractive to customers, he continued to use it until compelled by boredom to alter the visual appearance of the chair again.

On one occasion, Aaron made a drawing of patterns for slats and posts, but he gained no satisfaction from sketching designs and trying deliberately to translate them into wood (although two other chairmaking brothers I heard about followed this procedure). Aaron's seemingly spontaneous manipulation of raw materials was limited to decorative details, however. He did modify the overall form of a rocking chair, reducing the number of stretchers as well as changing from vertical panels in the chair's back—reminiscent of commercially made chairs—to horizontal slats (figs. 111-113). He altered the back to divest his chairs of any resemblance to factory-made chairs, rendering them "traditional" and "handmade."

If he had had his choice, then, Aaron would have done nothing but turn posts to create new decorative elements. But since economic survival depended on building chairs, he could not spend all his time at the lathe turning designs for the pleasure derived from this simple act. Like Chester, he was still a chairmaker who had to construct utilitarian objects serving a practical end. Before the actual manufacture of a whole chair, Aaron knew what it would look like, what size the finished chair and its separate parts would be, and what decorative elements it would have.

Not every chair turned out quite as Aaron envisioned it. As Aaron remarked about one of his rocking chairs, "It ain't the prettiest one I ever made," by which he meant that the grain and the color of the pieces of walnut did not match as he had expected, although the chair's form and ornamentation corresponded to his initial conception.

THE NEW DESIGN

Normally Chester, like Aaron and other chairmakers, had not only the product but also the tools and techniques to be used rather well in mind before beginning construction. A look at Chester's notebooks for orders reveals that he and his customers agreed in advance on detailed specifications, as in the following order:

Paid in advance $75.00 for
a rocking chair like _____'s
in solid black walnut with
hickory bark woven seat.

Front posts bent outwards
Seat size—inside measure—
Front = 21"
Sides = 16"
Back = 18"
High back with seven slats
Rockers = 2½"
balance same as chair I saw here

Ordinarily the customer would have received a chair made according to these specifications, but in this instance Chester had to alter another six-slat rocker to make it a seven-slat one so he could fill the order within a reasonable length of time. This brings me to the subject of the New Design chair (fig. 43), which probably helps explain how the Bookcase Masterpiece developed.

Late in the evening on 1 July 1967, as we sat on his front porch, Chester told me that several of his chairs had appeared to him at night just before he went to sleep and that later he thought about the forms and designs until they were well formulated in his mind. He had imagined his first eight-legged dining chair several months before he actually made it, and more recently he had even conceived of a way to make a table with eight serving places and in the center a lazy Susan. If he made such a table with a revolving platter, he said, "A body wouldn't have to say, 'Pass me this, pass me that.' "

I asked him about the Bookcase Masterpiece. "I've been a-thinkin' about that kind a chair for five or six years," he replied. After making his first two-in-one rocking chair about 1961, "I said the next one I was gonna make it outa solid walnut an' put a place on it for books and a pipe rack and also a place under the seat for books. I thought I could make a chair like that with a removable seat of hick'ry, but it wouldn't work on accounta the side pockets wouldn't a had nothin' to rest on."

On the following Friday, 7 July, as Chester finished converting a six-slat rocker into a seven-slat chair, the germ of an idea sprang up in his mind and in a sudden flash of inspiration he knew that he could make yet another kind of chair. A more complete image of this new design came to him that night as he lay in bed in a semiconscious state. He was unable to sleep all that night, he said, for this design was the first major new one he had thought of in two years—since the masterpiece.

Two days after his dream, Chester explained the new chair to me in detail. It was to be a rocking chair consisting of alternating pieces of dark and light wood. Initially his mental image was of a chair with one post dark, the other light, and one armrest and one rocker dark and the opposite member light. But he rearranged the details in his mind as he spoke so that he saw a chair in which the posts were made up of sections of wood alternating in color with each other and with the slats; the arms and rockers were of laminated wood, with alternating light and dark layers; pegs contrasted in color with the wood they were driven into.

He could probably make the chair out of scraps of wood so it would cost him nothing for materials, he explained excitedly. (As it happened, however, there were few scraps he could use so he had to cut up some good pieces.)

To join the separate pieces of post to one another, he would drill a hole perhaps an inch deep in the top and bottom of each piece and insert about 2 inches of doweling in one hole. Then he would connect the light pieces to the dark ones, fitting the dowel on one piece into the hole in another.

The only features he was uncertain of were the arms and the rockers. Would he glue and peg the thin pieces of wood together horizontally, or vertically, before he carved the arm and rocker forms out of them? For a while his mental construct was without arms and rockers, until finally he decided they should be horizontal for greater solidity. But during actual manufacture he made them vertical for appearance's sake (fig. 44).

What about the finials? In his mind they, too, would be made from pieces of wood alternating in color. But as yet they had no clearly defined form. No matter, he thought; he could turn them on his newly acquired turning lathe. He could make them any shape that happened to develop without definite planning. Or, as an alternative, he could make them octagon-shaped without ornamental turnings. He preferred the former, but he left the image of turned finials fuzzy in his mind at this stage. Later he

43 Chester's New Design rocker, which came to him in a dream, is made of alternating pieces of sassafras and black walnut.

44 Laminating pieces of walnut and sassafras for the armrests of the New Design chair.   **45** Turned finial that Chester chose not to use on his New Design chair.

turned some finials from the laminated wood, only to throw them away (fig. 45). Instead, he used simple carved finials of solid walnut.

In Chester's first mental image the seat of the chair was of ordinary woven hickory bark, but he later decided this was not in keeping with the rest of the chair. No, he would have to have a checkerboard pattern, he explained, which he could easily make by using fresh hickory bark for the woof and bark soaked in the creek until it turned dark for the warp. Eventually Chester used very narrow bark of light color; he did not weave a checkerboard pattern after all, because he was appalled at the poor quality of older bark that he had. He felt that the fine chair he was con-structing should have only the best quality bark and of the narrowest width.

46 Six-slat rocker made by Chester in early 1967; later that year he transformed it into a seven-slat rocker (*opposite*).

The New Design chair, like the Bookcase Masterpiece, was unusual as a whole, but half a dozen or more experiences contributed to the design's generation. The essential technology was based on the way Chester had devised to transform a six-slat rocker (fig. 46) into a seven-slat one (fig. 47). He had made a separate section consisting of two pieces of post about nine or ten inches long with a slat between them and finials at one end. He reshaped the finials of the six-slat rocker so they became dowels about ¾ inch in diameter. Then he affixed the separate section to the top of the six-slat rocking chair (fig. 48). That night he had his dream.

Chester had been trying to think of some way to use waste pieces of wood he had been buying at a lumber company, beginning with the manufacture of the masterpiece. In early June 1967, he had settled on a design for a bedstead with a checker-

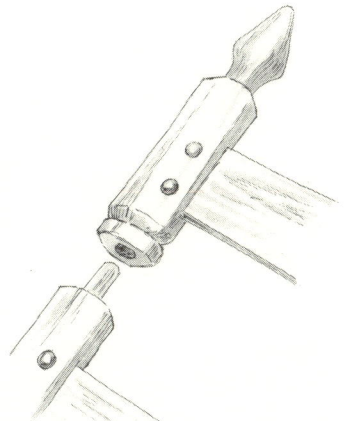

47 Seven-slat rocker (photo by Chester), originally constructed with six slats. **48** The method Chester devised to add a slat to a rocking chair.

board veneer of black walnut and sassafras squares, about 2½ inches wide, glued and pegged onto a supporting frame. He gave up the idea because of the time and work required, although he did make a small trivet by way of illustration. And in the late spring of that year he made his wife a dining table of alternating pieces of walnut and sassafras. He had intended the table to be entirely of sassafras but, as he did not have enough sassafras boards on hand, he used a few pieces of black walnut.

The use of contrasting pieces of dark and light wood was an old idea. In the first place, the hickory bark seat of a chair contrasted with the wood when red oak or walnut was used. Second, on many earlier chairs Chester had used the white outer wood of black walnut for decorative trim, particularly on the arms and on the slats, which often had a band of white at least ½ inch wide along the lower edge (figs. 49 and 50). Third, when

49 A baby rocker of black walnut with hickory pegs made by Chester in August 1965. Note the mushroom finials and the use of contrasting colors of wood for decorative effect.
50 Chester used bands of lighter color on the slats of this black walnut rocker made in August 1966.

making a stool of black walnut, most chairmakers, Chester included, usually chose hickory (a very light-colored wood) for the rounds because of its durability. Chester's first child's rocking chair was constructed this way; so was a black walnut settin' chair he made in the spring of 1964 and sold to a man in Rising Sun. Fourth, since at least August 1965, when he constructed the museum's settin' chair, he had been pegging chairs in a color that contrasted with the color of the chair's posts and slats (usually sassafras pegs on red oak or black walnut chairs and black walnut pegs on white oak or sassafras chairs).

The idea for a checkerboard seat came from two other experiences. Early in the summer, June 1967, Chester and I had gone to a small town a few miles away to try to find someone who would sell Chester hickory bark for seats. We met another chairmaker named Verge who told us that he and his son Hascal and the chairmaker Aaron had made a chair for President Kennedy (presented to him by the dean of a local academy and by state politicians to attract attention to themselves and the school). The chair was of spotted walnut. To accentuate the decorative quality of white spots on dark wood, the men wove a seat of light and dark hickory bark in a checkerboard pattern. They took the light bark fresh from a hickory tree and soaked other hands (or bundles) of bark in creek water for a month, turning it black.

Chester had recently done much the same thing in rebottoming an older chair that a customer had brought to him for repair. Chester salvaged some of the old bark, using it along with fresh splints.

The New Design was not perfect, as Chester realized after construction. The pegs were not properly seasoned—they were dowels, purchased at the lumber company, that Chester had glued into the posts. Eventually some of them fell out (fig. 51). The back was too tall and too heavy for the chair. None of the joints was really secure because the many peg holes and the holes for the rounds removed much of the hickory dowel inside the pieces of post and because these pieces were not properly seasoned but were held in place with glue. Two of the joints broke, shearing the back of the chair from the seat.

Chester said that if he made another chair of this sort he would

51 Some of the pegs on the New Design rocker fell out; Chester had used dowels from a lumberyard and glued them in.

turn a projection on the end of one post section, drill a hole in the end of the other post section, and insert the projecting piece into that hole. This would make the joints stronger. In addition, he would make arms and rockers of solid wood but alternating in color—one rocker dark, the other light; one arm light, the other dark. He also would put a brace behind the chair, extending it from the back of the seat.

As the idea of the New Design developed into an actual chair (we paid Chester $150 to make it because he would have had no other opportunity to construct such a chair at that time), Chester made alterations in his mental image for technical and aesthetic reasons.

IMAGINING AND CONSTRUCTING
THE TWO-IN-ONE, BOOKCASE ROCKER

The Bookcase Masterpiece must also have required revisions and construction of unpredicted elements. But the spontaneity was not "art for art's sake" so much as it was pragmatic and serendipitous solutions to technical problems.

Whether or not Chester intended the Bookcase Masterpiece for us initially, an image of it probably came to him in a dream, just as the New Design had. He also would have imagined specific design elements, then puzzled about how to make them. Having mulled over the forms and ways of realizing them, he assumed the chair was well planned. He began construction. Not having built a chair quite like this one, however, he encountered problems of structure, comfort, or appearance that he had not anticipated. He had to imagine solutions to these problems by reflecting on analogous situations he had heard about or had experienced before, or learned by trial and error. If he were inspired to make a unique chair for us, then his original construct probably had features that he knew or thought awed or pleased us. From what we remarked on in wonderment—perhaps in combination with what he projected onto us—these features would have been complexity of design, two-in-one chairs, and decorated pegs.

He likely would have imagined a chair for us with some traits he thought appropriate through association or transference. For example, Chester could scarcely read and write. He knew I was a student, studying to be a professor. I read books. I hoped to write a book (which is the way I described a dissertation). In addition, I smoked a pipe. In one conversation some time after he had made the masterpiece, he envisioned me in the chair, remarking that it was for a person like me to sit in, surrounded by books (which the shelves are supposed to hold) and smoking a pipe.

He may have imagined initially a two-in-one rocking chair resembling the Dolph chair—one that would hold books. He would have begun construction with four posts in back and a corresponding set in front to which the four rockers would be attached. The chair would differ from the Dolph rocker in being made of wood panels rather than woven hickory bark backs. For reasons that I did not understand at the time, Chester was becoming increasingly preoccupied with the concept of solidity; panel backs would indeed be *solid*—heavy and enduring, seemingly impenetrable.

How would he add the "baskets"? He designed extensions to the sides of the chair, adding four more posts and panels. One way to hold them in place more securely was to glue and peg shelves to them, which also would be in keeping with the notion of a bookcase. But the shelves had to be shaped so that they were neither blocky in appearance nor a danger to a person backing into the chair to sit down. Since the volume above the seat between the two columns of shelves is only 18½ inches wide, space for the upper torso was minimal. The middle shelves squeezed the sitter's arms. Chester shaped these shelves, cutting away wood under them along the edge next to the sitter, which allows the sitter to move his arms away from his body somewhat.

How could he attach the boards to the posts on the sides and in the back? He mortised or had the mill rout a channel in a crosspiece at the top and bottom into which he drove the ends of each panel. He carved a tenon on each end of each crosspiece, inserting it into a corresponding hole in the post (as on the Dolph chair).

The panels of woven hickory bark on the Dolph chair are straight across the top and bottom (fig. 42). They seem to work visually by repeating the rectangular forms of the baskets and the panels below the seat. Moreover, they are relatively close to the mushroom-shaped finials that cap the tops of the posts.

But by 1965 Chester had begun to elongate the finials. He also was beginning to shape the slats so that the top center formed a rounded peak (figs. 37 and 41). Although he responded to customer demands, on occasion compromising between what they expected and what he wanted to do, Chester tended to continue to use a design element that he had recently developed. Perhaps he wanted to see where he could take it. As Chester told me on 17 August 1965 about his technique of notch lockin', "A body get to doin' something, he just don't wanna change."

If he had let the masterpiece stand as it was with only the wood panels between the posts, there would have been large empty spaces above the panels because of the length of the finials. He filled these spaces with semicircular inserts reminiscent of the rounded, peaked slats in recent dining and rocking chairs. He had scalloped the edges of the walnut inserts; this rhythmically repeated the decorated walnut pegs whose heads he had carved in a pattern of grooves and ridges. He inserted spires and inscribed a message in the semicircular inserts.

The actual sequence of conceptualization and construction might have differed from the order suggested above. Perhaps he first had an overwhelming desire to carve his name on a chair, or maybe he envisioned the inserts in isolation, letting the form of the chair follow later. He might have divined how to attach the baskets and shelving before he ever assembled the eight central posts and four rockers. Whatever the sequence of images, concepts, and steps in building the chair, it seemed to him quickly and disturbingly to take on a life of its own.

Chester said the masterpiece is a two-in-one chair because it has twice as many posts and rockers as an ordinary chair. It is a bookcase rocker because it has shelves and storage space for books, and it rocks. It is a masterpiece, he said, because of its uniqueness.

Although nearly every element of the chair has a precedent in Chester's forty-year career as a craftsman, each feature has been elaborated or even carried to an extreme. The chair culminates Chester's chairmaking endeavors; each major element extends a concept previously developed. It is a masterpiece in the original meaning of this word. To be conferred the status of master in the guild system, a craftsman had to present to others a piece that demonstrated his skills and capabilities—his mastery. The two-in-one, bookcase rocker, masterpiece of furniture testifies to what Chester could accomplish through a lifetime of learning. If the masterpiece has become "just something to look at," it is not because it is useless, but because its form transcends our experiences, transmuting the commonplace into something uncommon indeed.

The particular method of creation varies from one situation to another. It depends in part on the craftsman's skills and capabilities. It may be affected by the problem that needs solving. An individual without orders to fill may have occasion to experiment with new designs as Chester once did when he sawed a crosshatch pattern on the front posts of a settin' chair and as Aaron enjoyed doing as he turned posts to see what would emerge from his chisel work. The manufacture of useful objects, however, requires some degree of planning. Also, one may have to produce the object according to customer specifications, a situation that inhibits spontaneity.

For all the variety of ways in which craftsmen might conceptualize and actualize form, there seem to be only a few fundamental cognitive and behavioral processes. As discussed earlier, these include envisioning in a flash of inspiration a form or parts of a larger form, puzzling about how to actualize the form, and imagining (and even mentally testing) ways to achieve objectives. Alterations occur during the process of execution. Intuition and serendipity frequently accompany the manufacture of the object. This is particularly so when the craftsman sets aside matters of utility and allows expressiveness and personalization to dominate.

Whatever the constraints imposed by customer expectations and the manufacturer's skills, knowledge, and abilities, the craftsman both plans and does not plan what he will make. Chester's New Design was not exactly what he wanted. His Bookcase Masterpiece was not what we had requested or expected, although apparently Chester wanted it for us. Both chairs were at first dreamed, then developed into more detailed mental images, and finally brought forth as actual objects, albeit with spontaneous modifications during manufacture.

One reason the New Design was conceived at all was that several people, including Chester himself and a local newspaper publisher who promised him "a good write-up" if he made another unusual chair, expected Chester to be innovative in his chairmaking. Hence, Chester was open to suggestion, if not actually seeking ideas or inspiration.

Despite its faults, the New Design chair certainly exhibits imagination. Some techniques of construction and elements of design were traditional in the sense that other craftsmen used them. Some were traditional in that they exhibited techniques and designs employed by Chester's forebears or developed by

Chester himself in earlier years and perpetuated to the present. Both the New Design chair and the Bookcase Masterpiece existed and had some of their particular features because of the customers who inspired, influenced, or otherwise affected the craftsman. In sum, the chairs demonstrate that the aesthetic impulse existed even in a utilitarian form serving practical purposes.

There must be more to understanding Chester's Bookcase Masterpiece than knowing the tools and techniques of construction, the cognitive process of envisioning form, and the relationships between this craftsman and some of his customers. After all, no one had ordered this chair, yet Chester felt compelled to build it.

What did chairmaking mean to Chester? What did the forms he built express? What did he aspire to be and to do? Although he had several objectives and numerous aspirations over the years, much of what he planned, hoped, or expected, said Chester, "ended up the wrong way." Reflecting on his life in later years, he sometimes saw himself as "a man of constant sorrow." The next chapter explores Chester's life and some reasons why the things he made possessed certain traits.

THREE

Man of Constant Sorrow

"You know, I had it all planned and all; studied about it an' studied about it. When I come home on the furlough, what I was gonna do was take my wife back with me when I went back to the service," said Chester Cornett, who did not have a wife at the time. The year was 1944 and Chester was, as he sang in a song of his own composition two decades later, "a soldier boyee, a long, a long ways from my ole Kentucky mount'n home."

"I guess I was cravin' a woman, if the truth is known," he admitted. "I was 'bout thirty years old, hadn't never been married before, an' didn't know too much about a woman a-tall."

Chester was sitting on the edge of his chair, head bent forward and hands cupped together between his legs. "I was shore gonna get married now. I had it all planned out to get married, but I was tryin' to plan whether to take her back with me or not." As he stared at the rotting boards of the porch he shook his head back and forth. "It all ended up the wrong way," he mumbled.

Much of what happened to Chester—at least what he planned for himself—ended up the wrong way, according to him. He attributed most of his problems, including poverty, marital discord, mental and physical illness, and the retardation of his sons, to experiences in the 1940s when he was plucked from the protective mountain hollow where he was born and reared and dropped onto one of the fog-shrouded islands in the Aleutian chain for "two years, seven months, and twenty-eight days."

But Chester's problems really began when he was a child. He was a loner who kept to himself and spent most of his time making things, partly because other people would have little to do with him. He tried to help his uncle build chairs when he was young, but Chester was a slow worker and his uncle was an impatient man. "Linden used to swear at me when I was a kid if I didn't get that bark when he shot it through there."

His uncle and brother sometimes took advantage of him, Chester and Ruth implied. "Kenton never did have to work," complained Chester's wife about her brother-in-law; "somebody else [meaning Chester] always kept him up." As for his Uncle Linden, "you couldn't put any faith in him," Chester admitted to me once in a moment of candor; "you couldn't depend on 'im." On one occasion, while Chester was in the hills peeling bark, his uncle and brother took all his chairs to town and sold them for forty cents each to buy liquor. Another time they took the money that he had been sending home to his mother while he was in the army, said Chester, so they could get drunk and then pay the fine after they had been thrown in jail.

After their mother died, Kenton tore down the cabin that Chester had built for her when he was about twenty; finding the first two chairs that Chester had made on his own, he apparently sold them for a few dollars. At any rate, for several years Chester had been asking about the chairs but his brother would not give him any straight answers. Those chairs—his first—had become special to Chester in later years.

Because he was born on 4 September 1913, Chester said, "Thirteen is my lucky number; I never worry about Friday the thirteenth." But as Chester told me several times, "I never work on Sundays 'cause it's bad luck an' I got enough a that."

Chester attended school for only a few weeks at a time, finally reaching the fourth grade when he was seventeen. He felt embarrassed in the classroom because of his age and dropped out of school to make chairs full time. He did not learn to write until he was in the army and retrieved discarded letters to copy.

"I was borned on Kings Creek, Letcher County," he said in August 1966, as we drove deeper into the hills of southeastern Kentucky in search of the graves of his mother and her father, Cal. It was Chester's third trip "home" in two decades. He had insisted on returning the year before with the journalist Gurney Norman to find the burial sites of his kin and to stand once again on top of Pine Mountain above the fog and far from the noise of cars and the sight of people. And he had been in the area half a dozen years earlier trying to find his runaway wife.

"Is that where you were raised, too, on Kings Creek?"

"Nope. Left there when I was a boy. We went to Poor Fork. My dad and mom, they separated when I was a little bitty young un, 'bout eight years old, I guess. I was just startin' to school on Poor Fork when they separated.

"Dad got the four kids," said Chester; but he never kept them. "He give the schoolteacher money to buy us clothes with. All I got was an ole hat out of it." Chester laughed nervously.

"Two weeks later Dad got us and walked back to Kings Creek to his mother's. Grandma put up with us about two or three days when here comes Mom. Grandma made Dad give Mom the two least uns and Grandma took the two biggest uns. Mom had a time raisin' us two little fellas," said Chester, referring to himself and Kenton.

"Then when I was 'bout ten years old Dad come up and got me and took me home to his other wife. I stayed three or four months, but they had three kids and she had two of her own an' I was right in the way. Then Dad took his wife and kids to homestead in Oregon and then he up an' left the land, woman and chillun there. He left them jest like he did Mother."

The upshot of Chester's remarks was, "I couldn't say which— Letcher County or Harlan County; I was mostly raised up 'twixt both them counties."

There was no rancor in Chester's voice as he reviewed the events of his youth. It was a straightforward narrative occasionally punctuated with a nervous laugh at the most serious points. The war, however, left a bitter taste in his mouth. It also left him with an undiagnosed skin disease. "Been botherin' me ever since that winter when I was overseas," said Chester about the patches of redness under his beard and hair and over much of his body. "That last winter I was over there, buddy, it got down to sixty below zero."

He laughed, but not because he found it funny. "The Aleutian Islands. An' I b'lieve my soul I got frostbit one way or another an' it never will be right no more.

"Or maybe it's them shots they give me or somethin' or other.

They give me so many shots I always think 'at they caused it. Some people can't take them shots, they're elergict to them. It hurts 'im. An' I al'ays felt worser ever time they give me one of them shots."

Again the nervous laugh. "Don't b'lieve in 'em myself. That's the reason I won't get these chillun vaccinated or anything on accounta when Donny was a little baby they started him in on takin' shots in town at the health department an' he got in such a shape he had to quit. Couldn't give him any more shots."

Donny was Chester's oldest son, who could not walk or speak but lay in bed making buzzing sounds. When he was a child he seemed all right, but as the years passed his condition deteriorated. So, too, did the health of Chester's second and third sons when they reached their teens. Chester did not know why three of his sons had become mentally retarded and physically crippled. He tended to blame himself and the war, though, because the boys were "nervous" and so was Chester, and Chester's nervousness was worsened by his army experiences. He spent several months in an army hospital and was finally given a 30 percent certified disability discharge because of his emotional state.

"Know what caused it?"

"The nervous condition? Zactly what really caused it was the isolation over there in the 'Leutian Island, really 'bout what caused it. I al'ays really was kinda nervous on the edges since I was a child. But I don't know just what if it wasn't the [isolation] over there in them 'Leutian Islands. You know, there was nothin' much over there, not a thing."

Chester also claimed to have weakened eyesight, a cataract, impaired hearing, a disease resulting in a strange taste in his mouth and missing teeth and general aches and pains caused in some way by his military service in the Aleutians. "That's where my eye started botherin' me—that last year I was over there. 'Bout every year it takes a spell and starts botherin' me."

He also worried about his hands, which he said had been "bothered" by medicine given him in the army. "I'll betcha one a these days my hands'll get completely stiff," he said, flexing the fingers on his right hand but staring at two fingers on the left

52 Chester, about 1944, when
he was stationed in the Aleutian
Islands.

hand which would bend only far enough to form hooks.
Chester's paternal grandfather had been crippled with arthritis
as a young man and could make few chairs.

When he was in the army Chester was trained for nothing in
particular but did everything in general. "First, they have you
doin' one thing an' then another'n." Mainly he peeled potatoes,
cleaned latrines, washed pots and pans, greased army vehicles,
and stood guard duty late at night in the snow that covered the
ground from September to June. "No matter what the company
commander tells you to do, you got a do it."

And that was what Chester did for more than two years
without a break. No wonder he was "cravin' a woman." But his
wife, Ruth, was third choice. They scarcely knew each other and
seventeen years separated them in age, but they had grown up
in the same general area. They had one other thing in common:
both were despondent when they decided to marry. By counting
on his fingers Chester ascertained that they had first met in

September or October of 1945 and were married in Hazard shortly afterward.

"I married oncet before I married Ruth. Didn't last, though," said Chester. "I come home on a furlough after I come back from overseas. They give us a furlough to come home and I got married." He laughed again because he was serious. "That's as long's it lasted—two weeks.

"When I went back in the service an' they put me in the convalation hospital there in Fort George Wright there at Washington, kept me till October the twenty-seventh [1944], I was give a discharge. I come back home an' the first place I went was, I got a taxi out a Cumberland an' went up to her house an' she'd backed out on me.

"I was tryin' to get her to live with me for several months afterward," said Chester about his first wife, Sarah. "Couldn't get her to live with me no more. I met Ruth an' we come to Hazard an' we took a notion to get married. She'd been married, too, before. She already had a young un. It was just a baby somewhere aroun' a year old." The child's name was Annie Mae and her father had deserted the mother and child.

"Why did Sarah turn her back on you? Was it because she was only fifteen and you were over thirty, or was it that her mother just didn't like you?"

"I don't know. But I al'ays thought it was the mother's fault the reason she wouldn't live with me. I think all her mother was after was 'llotment from the gov'ment. When I went back in the service I made her out a 'llotment and the gov'ment paid her $50 a month. She just drawed about two checks. I b'lieve that's what her mother was after an' she found out I was bein' discharged an' comin' home, why she talked Sarah out a livin' with me then. I really didn't love the girl when I married her."

"Why did you marry her?"

"I just married her too quick. I just been over in the 'Leutian Islands all that time an' I just—I knowed her all my life an' ever'thing—but I never thought a bit 'bout marryin' her than I did a flyin' when I come home on my furlough. I didn't even think about it."

Sarah spread rumors to the effect that Chester was a poor lover (maybe even impotent). Chester claimed he had no previous sexual experience, but as he said, "You could tell she'd been pranked around with 'fore I ever pranked around with her."

Chester had intended to marry his first cousin. The initials M.W. were tattoed on his arm; although the ink had faded over the years the memory was still strong. "I's figgerin' on marryin' her when I come home on furlough," said Chester, "but she was two or three months pregnant an' she wasn't but about, uh, sixteen. An' she thought enough of me she wouldn't marry me."

I asked Chester what he would have done had she not told him.

"Boy, I guess I'd a blowed up all over the place if I'd a married her an' found that out later. She might a been 'fraid to marry an' then I'd a found out. . . . I guess I'd a whipped 'er maybe. . . . I don't know jest what I would a done."

It was at this point in the conversation that Chester said everything had ended up the wrong way. "I was in bad shape when I come home on a furlough. That last winter was when it hit me. My eyes bothered me. I was in a bad shape when I come home from a furlough. An' when I went back after my furlough, doctor sent me to a convalation hospital at Fort George Wright in Washington. I stayed there till October 27, 1944. I'll never forget that date."

Nor would Chester forget his experiences in the early 1940s and later. In the late spring of 1965 he composed a song entitled "My Old Kentucky Mountain Home" which ostensibly related to 1944. It is set to the tune of "Man of Constant Sorrow," which is not surprising in light of the song's content and something that Chester told me later.

In June 1967, two years after he sang his song for my wife and me, I asked him his favorite songs. "I'd rather hear 'Pretty Polly' better'n any song I've ever heerd b'fore," which I knew him to request musicians to play. "Next, I like 'John Henry.' But the most touchin' song I've heerd is 'Constant Sorrow.' An' the best person I've ever heard sing that song is Robert Fields who used to live on Kings Creek. You couldn't keep from chokin' up to hear him sing it."

Robert Fields had been a neighbor. Chester was recalling the times when he lived on Pine Mountain and heard Fields sing this plaintive song of "the place where I was born and raised." The song expresses the emotions of a man who has always had troubles, who has left his home and who will probably not return or see his "loved companions" unless it be in the afterlife when "we'll meet on the beautiful shore."

The song that Chester sang for my wife and me on 21 August 1965, as he plunked on his homemade banjo into the face of which he later scratched "My Old Kentucky Gourd," is as follows:

I was born and raised in old Kentucky mount'n home.
Now I'm a soldier boyee, a long,
A long ways from my ole Kentucky mount'n home.

Fer, oh, fer o'er the deep blue sea,
Whar the sun hardly ever shines,
I get to wonderin' about my ole Kentucky mount'n home.

Whar the sun shines so brigh',
Whar the whippo'wills are so lonely and lonesome,
And I wonder if they ever think of me.

At night when I lie down a-lookin' up at heaven,
With a prayer in my heart,
To God I pray if thy will,
Oh, ift thee go through this war,
So that I can go back to my old Kentucky mount'n home.

Whar the sun shines so brigh',
Whar the whippo'wills are so lonely and lonesome
After the war is over.

Now the war is over, so I thank God in heaven
That I'm now on my way
Back to my ole Kentucky mount'n home.

The place where the sun still shines so brigh',
And at night the whippo'wills are so lonely and lonesome
Place whar I was born and raised.

Four years later Chester would use some of the same phrases and images in letters to us after his wife left him for the third and final time. But in 1965, when he first sang the song, I misunderstood and thought that it had been composed twenty years before, a few months after Chester's service in the army.

My confusion stemmed largely from assuming that, because he lived in Kentucky when and where I met him, he was in his "ole Kentucky home." Little did I realize the difference between the state and a state of mind. Consequently I asked, "Were you thinking about makin' it up while you were in the war?"

"No. No. No, I just thought about it, sayin' 'this war's a-bein' a long ways from my ole Kentucky home'—*mountain* home," he emphasized. "I just mumbled that, studying about it, you know, an' so I just took a notion about four months—it's been about four months countin' from now. I had that five-string banjer an' I just got to beatin' on hit, an' kinda thought up that song. It's not been over four months ago. I ain't got it completed yet—all of it—just a few verses of it."

"And this is the only song you know?"

"That's the only song I know. And, uh, hit's a quar song."

Just like the Bookcase Masterpiece he would build a few months later, Chester's song was "queer" or "strange." In other words, it was of great significance to him.

"Now the story in the song relates to when you were in the Aleutian Islands?" I asked him at the time, taking the song's content literally.

"That's right. The sun hardly ever shines up there. It'll be, uh, sun'll peek out a minute an' all at once here comes a rollin' fog, just rolls 'er away."

In the years that followed, Chester sang the song only twice to other people, at their request, and he never added any more verses to it. He did not have to add anything; he made the Bookcase Masterpiece.

Still curious about the song, though, I asked Chester two years later, on 24 June 1967, "That song you made up, how long was that on your mind before you made it up?"

"That hasn't been but about three years ago. I thought about it a lot. You know, you hardly ever see a morning here in Kentucky but what you don't have sunshine. That is, now, *back up on top Pine Mountain where I was raised at. Always the sun shines bright in* the mornin'. And, uh, that's where I really made that song up, based on that country back in there [emphasis added]."

Chester never returned to Pine Mountain to live after the war. When his first wife, Sarah, spurned him, he headed for Hazard to marry Ruth. They lived many places, near the highway and in hollows, but always kept sixty miles of twisting road between them and Pine Mountain.

"Down in these valleys," said Chester, "you know, early mornin' it'll be fog, but there in that mountain you look down an' see the fog down under thar. Just like lookin' out over an ocean. . . . You can look out over that fog thar early in the mornin' when it's kind of a cool night, an' that fog's all settled down thar in the valleys an' you can see back over the top of it—just see the backs of them hills over in there's all you can see. Just like lookin' out over an ocean." He laughed again, but the laugh was edgy.

"You'd like to go back there an' live someday?" I asked.

"Yeah, I'd like to live back in there an' go back in there where my gran'pa is [that is, Cal's grave]. Course, all them buildings is burnt down an' gone now. If I could lease that, I'd go back in there an' build that back jest like it was when me and Mother had it. Don't guess they'll ever lease it to me. It b'longs to the wildlife—act'lly, guess it b'longs to the state."

Obviously, the words of the song express the loneliness and despair of a man who longs to return home, a man who is so afraid he will never again see his "old Kentucky mountain home where the sun shines so bright" that he asks for divine assistance to see him through the present trouble. One can understand the way in which a southern mountaineer, or anyone else for that matter, never before away from home and kin, would react to being in the army on some desolate island in the midst of a war. There would be shock and fear and a desire to return home, and then withdrawal and an idealization of life in the past before the disruption. In such a situation a man might well compose a song expressing his feelings as a way of dealing with his grief and of adjusting to his loss.

Chester did not compose the song until twenty years after the end of World War II, however. This suggests that he never fully adjusted to the events at that time but continued to be disturbed by them, that present vicissitudes could be traced to this major turning point in the past, or that history had become a symbol and its recollection a ritual.

The setting of the song is generalized. No specific war is mentioned, and the narrator does not identify his present location, only that it is a very long way from his home. As Chester intimated, the early morning fog in the valleys where he then lived separated him from Pine Mountain like an ocean—and like the sea during World War II.

Apparently, a global conflict among nations was not the only war Chester had to struggle through. He had other battles to fight after World War II, but as soon as he won one of them, he had to confront another.

That there were additional problems after 1944 to which Chester attempted to adjust was evident in his behavior in the 1960s. Many of Chester's letters and conversations, his body image, some of his chairs, and the song indicated that he identified at times with an earlier age and isolated himself from his problems and from other people who might have caused those difficulties, or who certainly would generate further frustrations for him. By isolating himself socially and geographically, Chester apparently felt he could reestablish and maintain his stability. Interacting with other people often upset him, and external pressures were partly responsible for his losses, requiring the expenditure of much emotional energy, which in turn enervated him physically.

As a function of his dislike of interacting with other people, Chester attempted to erect protective barriers, real and symbolic. As part of the process of grieving, sometimes he developed a nostalgia for and an idealization of the past when he was free of other responsibilities, was living among his own kinfolk, and had not suffered the hardships he later encountered. To isolate himself in 1965 or 1966, Chester would have had to live in a secluded hollow on top of Pine Mountain, far away from the highway in the valley where he then resided. There on the mountain he could be in full control, and there on the mountain could be found his most pleasant memories, made more golden by the passage of time and by comparison with the

53 Chester in the late 1940s.

unhappy events that occurred in the quarter century after he left the mountain.

What else happened after the war? First of all, Chester married a woman whose values, aspirations, and needs differed from his, and with whom he frequently was in conflict. It was at Ruth's urging that they moved to town and that Chester attempted to find a "decent" job instead of making chairs. So Chester tried his hand at several occupations, but employment at each task lasted only a few days or weeks.

"When I first come back from the army, why, uh, I got a job in the Blue Diamond coal mines. I don't know just how many shifts I did work up there. I never was used to that, never could work in a mine, but I thought I'd try it. Them fellas was makin' good money when I first come back from the army. Doctor couldn't hardly decide whether to let me go to work or whether to not. Finally I talked 'em into lettin' me have a paper and sign it lettin' me go back to work." After all, Chester had a wife and child to support, and an apartment that he could not afford, so he had to have a job whether or not he was fit for it emotionally or by training. He loaded coal onto a conveyor belt.

"How long did you work at that?"

"I don't know how many shifts. . . . I didn't work a week I don't think. Might a worked a week at it. Couldn't take it. I'd get them cramps in the back of my legs. . . . I got so sore I couldn't go down a hill to save my life. Had a go down back'ards.

"That's the first job I undertook. Then I signed up on that unemployed. Then I got me a job workin' for that newspaper up there, workin' as a janitor an' a caster. I'd do a little castin' work and a little janitor work—I'd have to sweep the floors. I was just a handyman around."

"You enjoy that?"

"Nope."

"Why not?"

"I don't know. I never was used to that type of work. But *I's always could do anything, you know.*"

Chester worked as a janitor for four or five months but was fired because he did not always appear on Saturday when the Sunday paper was printed. Then for a few months he had a job in the Pepsi-Cola bottling plant loading cases of soda pop onto a truck and sweeping floors. He quit.

"What did you do after that?"

"We lived over there in Hazard, had an apartment over there—two-room apartment—an' I had a work at somethin' so I signed up on unemployed an' in just about a week or two I got a job with the power company settin' light poles in that there 'rural areas,' puttin' up power out in the country—what they call 'rural'."

Chester's job was to help carry the heavy transformers. "Sometimes you'd have to pack 'em hunnert, two hunnert yards to where they'd go on a pole." He enjoyed being outdoors for a change, but it was simple-minded work requiring nothing but manual labor. Often he was on the job for ten or twelve hours because of the distances the workers had to travel, and of course he had to punch a clock. There were also financial problems.

"We had a move out of that apartment. I didn't make much money then, 'bout seven dollars a day it paid. An' the only apartment I could find was fifty dollars a month an' I couldn't pay that much. So I bought a few pieces of furniture an' moved out on Main Lott's Creek," said Chester, who then tried to laugh about it. "I started makin' chairs when I moved down on Lott's Creek. I couldn't get a ride back and forth an' stay on my job an' I had a give it up."

"Have you been a chairmaker ever since then?"

"Been 'bout twenty years an' I've done nothin' but that. Boy, we've seen it pretty hard sometimes. I've worked many a time all night long and packed it off the next day just to get enough to do us a day or two." Again, Chester tittered nervously.

"Did you ever think about getting another job?"

"Yeah, I tried to get a job around a few times. I'd get burnt out a few times tryin' to make chairs. Bad job, I'll tell you. I've heard it all my life, a chairmaker never has nothin'." He laughed again as one does at a bad joke just to be polite. "I've heard that all my life, a chairmaker never has a thing to set on. That's about the way it is here, ever' time I get one made pretty an' I wanna keep it I al'ays sell it—somebody talk me out of it."

Chairmaking was the only occupation at which Chester was skilled and the only work he enjoyed, for it provided the opportunity to develop and present to others the images with which he was chiefly concerned. During the many days and nights I lived with the family in 1967, I saw Chester wander around the yard from one piece of work to another, usually oblivious to the presence of others, preoccupied with the visions in his mind to which he was trying to give physical shape. Often he did not realize that cars had driven into the yard or that someone was standing in his shop or that others were talking to him, and he gave little attention to his relationships with the world outside himself or with his wife.

"A body gets to doin' somethin' an' he just don't wanna change," said Chester in explanation of why he is a chairmaker, echoing a remark of two years before regarding why he con-

54 Photo of Chester by his wife, about 1960, when they lived at the head of Combs' Branch. Chester was making a chair for his young daughter.

tinued to use the technique of notch lockin' when nobody else did. "My wife," however, "don't think much of this here chair-makin' business."

For many people whom I met in this area, Ruth included, handicrafts were too much a reminder of an older way of life, characterized by poverty and deprivation, which they sought to escape. This was one reason that some of Chester's nephews and younger cousins who learned chairmaking from him preferred to work in coal mines or to pump gas at a service station instead of building furniture. Ruth eventually replaced handmade furniture in their home with the more desirable plastic and chrome table, chairs, and cabinets, and with Early American–style sofa and end tables (which soon fell apart). After all, "A body has a right to have somethin' aroun' that you kin enjoy. The other stuff wasn't fit to set on."

"I understand you haven't always been happy with Chester as a chairmaker," I said to Ruth late one evening as we sat on the porch enjoying a few moments of cool air after a summer storm. "Sometimes you thought he oughta be something else?"

"I don't know. Sometimes I thought he ought to be, I guess." She chose her words carefully. "But that's what he's always liked."

"You have anything particular in mind you think he oughta do?"

"No, he thinks it hisself more so than I do," she said and then chuckled for my benefit. "He thinks that I think he oughta get out an' work." Smoke drifted lazily from the end of her hand-rolled cigarette and hung in the air until a sudden gust of wind blew it away.

"She gets tired a-lookin' at me day after day after day after day," said Chester, who tried to laugh it off. "I bet that's it."

"He thinks that," Ruth mumbled.

"Well, it does. People *ought* to be away from each other at least oncet a year awhile. Man an' wife should. Body gets tired a-lookin' at one another year after year after year. . . .

"I *'magine!'* he added quickly. "Hit never bothers me much, though," he said in all honesty, for he paid little attention to what happened around him. "But it bothers her. I'm sure it does."

"I couldn't go away and stay an' work," protested Ruth who struggled to care for three retarded children, a young son and daughter, and an infant girl.

"No, I never said that. I said it bothers you 'cause it—we—have to look at one another all the time. I said it never bothers me, but it does you. That's what I said," repeated Chester, growing a little threatening as he raised his voice for emphasis.

We were huddled very near one another because the porch was small and because we could scarcely hear ourselves above the noise the children were making inside the house. The breeze had died in infancy, the heat crept in again, and the air felt sticky and close.

I noticed perspiration trickling down Ruth's neck like a small rivulet, picking its way among the parched channels of what had once been rich and fertile ground. "You get tired of looking at Chester?" I asked her.

Ruth laughed, rather sadly it seemed to me, and eyed her husband. "No, I don't get tired a-lookin' at 'im."

"I can go away and stay a night or two an' you're pretty well pleased t'see me come back." Chester's eyes struck mine. "When I went down to Lexington—stayed down there with Lester a few nights—she was pretty glad to see me come back," he boasted as he clapped a hand on the arm of his chair. Lester was their third son who slipped on the ice and broke his hip the day before Christmas in 1966; a few months later he could not walk at all. A bone in his leg deteriorated at the same time that his mind began to crumble.

"I guess that was the first time I'd stayed away from home in a long, long time," said Chester. His remark was like an echo from the distant past, for we all knew that Ruth had twice run away from their stormy marriage, leaving some of her children behind in her haste and hiding from Chester for six months the second time.

Ruth's temper broke. "I b'lieve he thought I art t' went up an' stayed wit' 'im, but I didn't have no chancet to go an' stay wit' 'im. They wouldn't a let me kept the baby in thar," she snapped. "An' he had a better way t' go 'n I did." Her eyes flashed. "I wouldn't care to go down thar an' stayed wit' 'im if I'd knowed they could get 'im t' walk a-tall, but I don't see no chance t' it."

Chester was stunned for a moment. "Well," he said slowly, "I'm gonna hafta take 'im back if he don't start walkin' by July the tenth or whenever it is." He did not know the date because it was Ruth's responsibility to care for the children, not Chester's. After a pause to recover his sense of indignation Chester turned on her sarcastically and accusingly: "Now, of course, if you don't want 'im to walk I won't. . . ."

In fact, Chester never took him and Lester never walked. Chester rigged a contraption to lift him off the ground to free his limbs, but he had to beat the boy to get him into it, and then Lester dangled helplessly, sobbing and flailing his arms and legs, for he could not understand what he was supposed to do. Both of them finally settled for a wheelchair.

Ruth tried to discern Chester's feelings, and she was concerned about his welfare—although Chester often refused to believe it—as was evident in her comments about Lester's crippled condition. "Jest like I say, Mike, hit'd be worth more to Check to git him t' walkin' than all that work out thar, wouldn't hit? Stay thar an' make chairs . . . ," she said derisively. "You know, in just a few days, if he could get 'im t' walk, it'd mean a whole lot to 'im. It would Check and it would Lester."

To Ruth, Chester was simply "nervous," which said everything and nothing at once, but she refused to elaborate on her diagnosis. "He jest gets excited. I'd jest rather not talk about hit. He wouldn't like me to talk about hit."

Chester apparently did not have the patience or understanding or compassion to help Lester overcome his fear of walking again, to encourage him to exercise his legs; and Lester's mental and physical state had degenerated to the point that he could not and would not help himself. Although six years younger than Donny, who lay in bed and made buzzing sounds, he was rapidly approaching a similar condition. Whatever it might have meant to Chester if Lester could have walked again, it was less important to him than his chairmaking.

CALLING TO OTHERS IN THE DARKNESS

Chester's responsibility was the making of chairs, and nothing should interfere. Why care for the children, tend a garden, saw firewood, fetch water, buy groceries, share experiences with his wife or even spend time hunting raw materials?

From Ruth's point of view, Chester's seeming disregard of other duties proved that "Check, he always wants the easy way out." But to Chester his work impatiently awaited him, and his task in life—his goal, his reason for existence—was to create things and give his ideas to others who seemed, unfortunately, not to accept or appreciate them. As he trudged through the streets to town one day, I saw him mocked and aped, and I felt the sting of barbs aimed at him. Sometimes it seemed that chairmaking, instead of being his salvation, was really a cross for Chester to bear.

Chester had put much of the blame for their marital dishar-
mony on Ruth, who had, he felt, neglected him, made fun of
him, rejected him, and in all ways possible hurt him by her
words and actions. One cause of his nervousness or irascibility,
however, was other people and anything that might divorce him
from the one thing he loved.

"I can't stand big, big crowds," said Chester. "At times I can
put up with 'em pretty good, but [at] times I feel like runnin' and
hidin'." A crowd usually consisted of one or more strangers.
Several times when we were with other people whom Chester
did not know, his hands shook and his eyes looked frightened;
he coughed and shuffled his feet, and circled about like a caged
animal. Only when he was working on a chair did he seem to be
at ease; only when he held a drawing knife in hand like a scepter
was he in control of the situation.

Often he remarked, "Traffic just aggravates me to death," but
since the early 1960s he had lived on a major highway exposed to
strangers from the outside world. He was especially annoyed by
people who stopped at his house to stare or take pictures. "Some
ask you to take a picture; some of 'em just steal it. They honk
their horn and get ya t' run out, then bing! they snap a picture,
and whoosh! off they go. Them people aggravate me t' death.
Guess I won't get to do nothin' all summer."

Why live by the highway, then? Mainly because of Ruth's
demands. At first they lived in town and then in a hollow for two
or three years. Ruth insisted they move to the highway, which
they did, but after two years Chester could not take it any longer
and moved the family to another hollow. When isolated, Ruth
"don't git no chance to visit people," which she needed, so she
ran off for a week to live in a shack near the highway until
Chester agreed to move there permanently. Shortly afterward,
Chester grew a beard and discovered the basic technique for
making armchairs and settin' chairs with seven and eight legs.

In the mid-1950s Chester's will prevailed and he and Ruth
moved back to a hollow for half a dozen years. Eventually Ruth
ran away for six months, but Chester finally tracked her down at
the home of some relatives near Cumberland. Ruth agreed to
return. After one of the children was born when Ruth was home

alone on a snowy night, without even a midwife in attendance, she said that that was enough isolation.

Ruth forced Chester to move near the highway again in the early 1960s, after which he grew a beard again and began building chairs with a strong sense of enclosure epitomized by the two-in-one rocking chairs.

Chester was the consummate artist. He could create a world of his own in which he was in total control—sometimes. Unfortunately, people and some forces in the world external to his own were not easily held in check. He reigned supreme over his old hand tools, which were rather an extension of himself. He even employed such expressions as "controlled shaving" to describe the power he had in using the drawing knife when working a piece of wood, and "controlled seasoning" to refer to his manipulation of the aging of raw materials. He was able to use a knife or an ax with such skill and precision that one is unaware that the pieces in a chair have not been sanded.

New objects seemed to arouse fear in Chester, perhaps because they concealed unknown dangers and maybe even a life principle of their own that Chester could not dominate. For example, in the spring of 1967 Chester bought a gasoline-powered tiller to make gardening easier. Neither of us understood how it worked; Chester could not start it himself, and he put the belt on improperly. We got the engine running, but Chester did not exert enough pressure to hold the plow in the ground as the blades turned. When it started bucking in the air, Chester dropped it and ran for the house. Eventually he had to pay a fourteen-year-old neighbor boy to plow the garden with his machine.

Chester had used power woodworking tools briefly in the early 1940s, and in 1966 he spoke with enthusiasm about buying some equipment to make his work easier and to enable him to make cabinets, tables, and chests. In 1967, with an FHA loan, he was able to purchase a lathe, a drill press, a jigsaw, and other tools. But the scream of the saw terrorized him as much as the snorting, bucking plow. As he ran a board over the saw, he screwed up his face; with tongue clamped in the corner of his mouth and with shaking hands propelled by rigid arms, he

55 Chester uses his router on the drill press for decorative notching (June 1967). **56** He shapes an armrest, made on a jigsaw, with an ax; the thin shavings indicate the craftsman's control.

57 Chester cuts a walnut plank from the lumberyard on his new electric saw (bandaged fingers indicate earlier mishaps).

pushed the plank into the blade. After a few minutes' work Chester's shirt was stained with perspiration. He tried to plane the board, but it jumped out of his hands. Chester looked at the board and admitted that it had a "whole lot a humps and bumps. Take a whole lot a experience to cut without 'em. I'm nervous anyhow."

"Spect I'll cut my hand off one of these days," he muttered. One Sunday while he was sawing firewood with his electric saw, a small block of wood broke off the plank and shot upward at Chester's face. He threw his arms up and the block cracked a knuckle. Wild-eyed and trembling, Chester ran to the house, doused the wound with turpentine and tried to wrap his finger in a rag, but he could not hold his hands still enough. While Ruth bandaged his finger, Chester rocked back and forth on his feet, moaning low in his throat.

Later in August Chester got his beard tangled in the drill press. The event so frightened him that he defied fate, risking his future as a chairmaker, by cutting off his beard and long hair. "I b'lieve I'm broke up now. I'll never get another order. I said I'd never get it shaved off."

Chester was no longer sure it was wise to buy the electrical equipment. Nor was Ruth, who remarked about his nervousness when using the machinery. "I don't know what in the world is gonna happen if I die. I still have to pay for it," lamented Chester. "I never thought of that 'til too late."

The equipment was a financial burden. Chester could not make chairs faster, he did not find the work easier than it had been when he used the old equipment and techniques, and he had not been able to meet the challenge of control presented by the machines.

Chester also had tried—unsuccessfully—to impose his will on Ruth. A congenial environment for Chester was an isolated hollow where he was in control of his world, but Ruth needed other people. In addition, Ruth had what could only be described as "social mobility aspirations" manifested, among other ways, by her demand to reside near the highway or in town, which was more expensive and prestigious than living along a creek or on a ridge; by her rejection of Chester's furniture and her stipulation that their home be furnished with expensive factory products; and by her currying the favor of her older daughter, Annie Mae, and her son-in-law who, without children and with their impressive annual income of $5,000 a year from coal mining, were free to socialize, go to the movies, travel, and buy consumer goods at will.

Ruth's daughter dressed rather grandly, but Ruth wore rags without even a bra or a slip, much to Chester's moral indignation. When Chester criticized her appearance, Ruth retorted, "I jest wear what people give me." Chester, seeing Ruth's daughter as a threat to his own home, took steps to alienate her. He enraged the woman and her husband in an effort to force them to leave. During one of their visits Chester kept them awake by working on chairs in the house all night. He also accused Jim of theft, contended that Ruth wanted to run off with Annie Mae, and alleged that Ruth and her daughter committed the unforgivable crime of making fun of Chester behind his back and laughing at his appearance.

Chester desperately wanted Ruth to love him, but he also wanted her to be subservient to him; he wanted her to care for the children by herself and do the mundane chores while he immersed himself in chairmaking. He, in turn, seldom extended love to others, at least not in the form of affection, physically displayed. Sometimes he bought dresses for Ruth and pop and candy for the kids, but often he was subject to violent displays of temper, hardly in proportion to the provocation, during which he struck out physically at the children and verbally assaulted Ruth, whom he accused of plotting to leave him saddled with their offspring or even of mistreating them, especially the retarded ones.

In July 1967, for example, Clifford (the second oldest) had a muscle spasm in his neck, which for several days Chester, without evidence, maintained was the result of Ruth's having beaten him with a broom. I expressed my doubts and Ruth vehemently denied the charge, so finally Chester attributed the spasm to Clifford's unfulfilled sexual desires.

Whenever Chester talked with Ruth, the conversation soon developed into criticism of her and the things she did, such as her handling of the children, the meals she cooked, the way she dressed. Even Ruth's last pregnancy was entirely her fault. Chester wanted their marriage to be a pleasant one but mainly on his terms, which included his dominance and the submission of others. Chester yearned to believe that his wife loved him, but doubt, which caused him to challenge her feelings and demand that she convey her love verbally, disturbed his well-being. Frequently, he expressed fear that Ruth would leave him, which in fact she did.

Chester could not shape Ruth, as he shaved and trimmed the planks of wood for his chairs, into the image he had for many years sustained. It was Ruth who was to blame for their marital problems. She "has hert me so meney times," Chester wrote in 1969, and "is never goin to Chang her Way are hit semes to me that way." As far as he could discern, Ruth had no reason to leave him, despite a financial setback the last winter they were together. "Bisonis has Bin Bad this Winter But she had a nofe I no." If there was food on the table and a roof over her head, what more could Ruth ask for, Chester seemed to be thinking. It may not have occurred to him, or perhaps he refused to believe, that

58 Chester in August 1967, after shaving. He has injured his hand on the new equipment.

his freedom to travel and to be among other people, culminating in trips to folk art fairs in several places, reinforced Ruth's own feelings of deprivation and subservience.

Neither Chester nor Ruth always understood the other person or was able to resolve satisfactorily the mutual antagonism that sometimes arose because of a conflict in aspirations, values, and behavior. Ruth liked the company of others, but Chester pre-ferred to hide in a hollow. "Check, he talks about Pine Mountain all the time. What he sees in that place I don't know; if he ever goes thar hit'll be by hisself, that's fer shore."

Chester was satisfied—and at peace—only when he was at work. He engaged in chairmaking regardless of the absence of financial rewards or status. Ruth demanded a few of the con-sumer goods and modern conveniences, which they could not

afford, that were available to other women. She had to attend to
the home and care for six children, three of whom were retarded
and crippled. "Hit's jest like takin' care a three babies, an' Check,
he don't do nothin' 'cept make chairs."

"Check, he always wants the easy way out," so he detached
himself from family and the world to devote himself to objectify-
ing his images. But Ruth had to handle all the domestic responsibilities, and "Whar thar's jest one to wait on 'em, boy hit keeps
a body busy." And "Hit's a job t' keep up with you fellas, I swear
t' goodness it is; if hit ain't one a ya needs waitin' on, hit's the
other'n." The only solution open to Ruth, it seemed, was to leave
Chester to his chairmaking while she went in search of a better
life.

(Ironically, and unknown to Chester, Ruth wound up two or
three years later on the outskirts of Cumberland—near Pine
Mountain—having encamped with the children in a deserted
schoolhouse.)

RETURNING HOME

In a letter dated 4 March 1969, Chester informed us that a few
months earlier Ruth's aunt had visited the family and the two of
them had talked Chester into going with the aunt to a sawmill
where the woman left him. She then took Ruth and all the
children.

Chester wrote to us that "they dinton leve me very much this
time, But a Brokin Hart and Wered mind I Love my familey
very Much But she [Ruth] has hert me so meney times Cant
take much More. . . . I ame afraid she Will destroy thim kids I
cant do iney thing about hit. . . ."

A few weeks later he wrote that "hit Shere lookes Bad for
me gess Will Louse Every thing that I have in this Wourld for
the Way I fele will not Be Able to make hit much longer my
head is in Bad Shape and Semes to Be getin Worse Ame Getin
Totry whin I get up in the Morning." In the first letter he had also
mentioned a general malaise: "Have Bin sick and very Puney all
this Winter I ame all alone." As he said in the second letter,

"there is no one But God to ask for help and am Shere he is With me all the time and makes me fele Betre to no that he goin to Stay With me   he has the Pour that no man one this Erth Haze are have I."

Chester then mentioned offhandedly having been at work on several rocking chairs, which he would finish in the near future, adding: "thin I dont no   Just hoap God Can Help me   some Way shere   Wesh you were here   hit Shere is Afful Lonely at times."

Significantly, perhaps, he was writing to us on Easter morning. "Well to day is Ester Sunday and Shere is a Butiful day   Clere and Brite   Ame Sitin here trin to Rite this Lettre." At that point he used a phrase from his song and reiterated his hope that he was being looked after. "Shere hoape this Lettre Reches you all Happey and Well   as for me *Just Lonely and Lonsom* [emphasis added]   But Hopin that tomarow Will be a Betre day and a happey day are What Every God wats for me to have good or the same   Will say so long for now   your frind."

Most of the stages in the process of grieving over a loss are apparent in the letters.

• There is a feeling of shock at the event that has occurred and the gradual comprehension of the loss over a period of time, followed by an emotional release when the depth of the loss is fully realized.

• Chester sought an explanation of the loss first in respect to himself and his possible contribution, but he finally concluded, as one usually does, that it was not his fault, that even his financial failure was not the cause. It was Ruth's wantonness, and it was she to whom he directed his hostility and resentment.

• There is mention of physical distress, generated by emotional anxiety.

• Panic is obvious in predictions that Ruth would destroy the children and that he would lose everything in the world.

• Nostalgia for the past is apparent in his wishing that we were there and in his opening line in the first letter: "ame thinkin About you all to nite   Were goin thrue some ole lettres of Last yere."

• Finally, at the end of the second letter there is an apathetic return to life.

• Usually, of course, this stage of return would be followed by a successful readjustment to the loss and a reaffirmation of reality, although the process may take months or years to complete.

Half a year after Ruth left, Chester went into hibernation. He stayed in bed day and night for several months, getting up briefly twice a day to relieve himself and to eat from one of the cans of pork and beans with which he had stocked the cupboards. His only companion was a stray cat.

He had built himself a raft on the polluted water near his house, furnishing it with sofa, stove, refrigerator, and tools, for he contemplated floating down Stinkin' Creek, dumping his problems behind him like so many tin cans as he neared Pine Mountain. He hesitated, however, because he hoped Ruth might return or perhaps we might arrive.

While Chester was wrapped in his dreams one night, a tornado struck, picking up Chester's workshop and smashing it down on the little raft, which sank. Trembling, Chester called some relatives near Lawrenceburg, Indiana, to come for him immediately.

Later he claimed that these same relatives turned against him, leaving him vulnerable once again. He kept correspondence to a minimum and refused to accept mail orders for fear "they"— those who were "after him"—would discover his address. The few chairs he made were priced many times higher than in earlier years, and these the customer had to pick up himself.

Eventually, he moved to Cincinnati, where he lived in an apartment on Sidney, using a section of the basement as a workshop and completing the construction of chairs in his kitchen. His final chair, built in 1977, was a tall, eight-legged, two-in-one rocker—the kind, he once told me, that has slats so deeply curving that "it's just like somebody huggin' you."

From childhood Chester had difficulty relating to other people. He feared those inanimate objects that refused to be held at bay. He worried about the future of his children once they were not underfoot. He became concerned that his own health was

59 The last chair that Chester made (1977); he was then living in Cincinnati. The process was filmed by Herbie Smith and Elizabeth Barret. Photo by Clark Thomas, courtesy Appalshop, Inc. The inscription on the slats reads: Chester/Hand Carved/FOR THE FIMING/ THE APPLESHOP/MOVIEY CALED/Check the Chiremaker/ DIREXEDBUY/HEIRB SMITH/ELIZABETH BARRET/PRESIDENT APPLSHOP/PIN MOUNIN WOOD/MADE. I.N. N.OV.A, DEC 1977/ WITH OUR LORD,S HELP." And on the arms: "Chester Hand Made/ With Our Lord Help."

failing or that he might be injured. Because "there's too much meanness in the world not to have a gun," Chester cradled a loaded revolver in a box under his bed at night, then locked it in a suitcase during the day only to put it back under the bed again each evening.

Apparently nobody loved Chester, from his first cousin pregnant by another man to his first wife with her slanderous remarks to Ruth who had "hert me so meney times." Even his mother, no longer alive, whose hard edges had softened in Chester's memory, had bounced her boys from one relative to another.

When we took him back to Pine Mountain in 1966, we could not find the graves of his mother and her father. But Chester located the spot where the house had been and found the oak tree that was a sapling near the cabin door when he had left a quarter of a century before. It stood proud and high, deeply rooted in the soil.

Chester tried to put his arms around the tree but it had grown much too large for that. So he scratched a toehold in the ground at the base of the trunk and tucked his arms next to his sides with thumbs crooked under the straps of his new overalls. The sun splattered bits of light through the leaves, dappling Chester's face and shoulders as he stood like a sentinel on his mountain next to his tree.

Except for a rooster crowing on a hilltop a mile away, it was perfectly still. Chester felt the freshness of the air about him. He saw the highway far below where tiny people inched along in little cars. He heard voices faintly in the distance. He sank slowly and deeply into quiet reflection, his eyes glazing over as his attention turned inward to the only world that really mattered, the realm of images and ideas.

A fly buzzed nearby. Chester paid it no heed until it touched him, its incessant nagging finally bringing him back to the present. We wanted to go. Chester left reluctantly but the sky was graying. A cloud of fog had rolled in, blanketing the area below. We had a long way to travel that day to return home to Chester's family whom we had left behind in a valley far away.

In his song and in his dreams Chester was thrust into an

imaginary hollow on top of the tallest mountain in Kentucky, where he was surrounded by the familiar and controllable things of childhood, objects that he had recreated in his mind as he would have to reconstruct them in reality, because most of the tangible things in his youth—including his first chairs and the log cabin he built for his mother—had been destroyed.

But if he was unable to escape physically to Pine Mountain or into the blurred past, then for a few moments Chester could retreat into his fantasies or, as a way of dealing with the present, into the comforting enclosed space of his two-in-one rocking chairs.

More constructively, he could rebuild himself, just as he created strange chairs challenging his skill and his identity.

After his wife left him for the third time, Chester was shocked into realizing that once again he was engaged in a battle in which he was "lonely and lonesome," with no one at his side to help him through the conflicts of life or to guard the flanks and protect him from unseen enemies. Only with God's assistance, Chester said, might he be able to adjust to this most recent catastrophe, though Chester told me several times that he had never been devout (maybe God caused the oak tree to grow, but Chester had planted the seed).

Chester's appeal to the Supreme Being was weak, the plea of a man who was temporarily desperate, perhaps, but not of a man who could give himself up to someone else or relinquish all control to another power. Chester was himself a creator and a wielder of authority. As some people have said in print and in person, Chester was the "king of the chairmakers" and Chester knew it. He had believed it for years, and he had said as much in the chairs he built, but few would listen to his message.

After he moved to Indiana, and from there to Ohio, Chester again held his raw materials in a gentle embrace as he shaped them, once more using hand tools which were extensions of himself and with which he caressed his loved ones. He could express his feelings and emotions in the things he made, but he seldom displayed affection for people or for those things in the world that seemed beyond his control and inferior in importance to his immediate concerns. The more strongly he attempted to

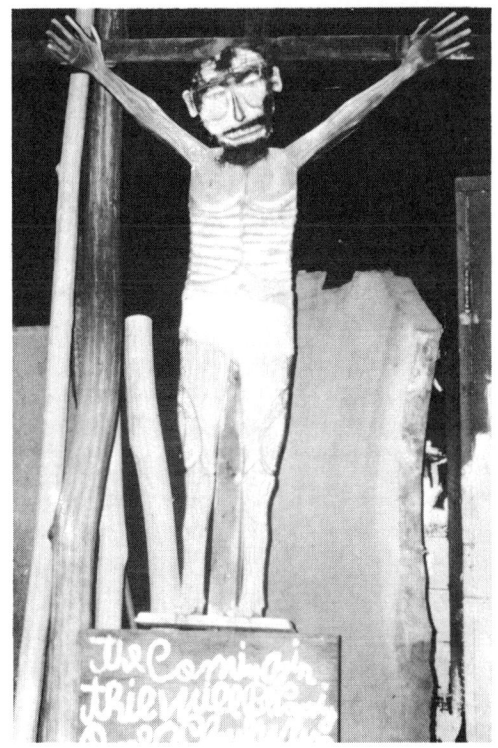

60 A sculpture of the crucified Christ that Chester carved after moving to southern Indiana. Photo by Willard B. Moore, about 1969.

dominate the objects in his environment, the more enslaved he became by them. Freedom was withdrawal. The day would come, however, as he mistakenly thought it had on several occasions in the past, when he might step forth in the world of men bathed in the glory of his brilliant creations. With his wife gone again for the third and apparently the last time, Chester had only himself and his work, with nothing to divorce the two.

And, of course, he had memories of suffering, which linked him to Jesus, as manifested in letters and in his sculpture in wood of the tormented Christ upon the cross which Chester erected in front of his house. Beneath this figure of the bearded Son of God, blood dripping from the crown of thorns, was a plaque with an inscription warning of the Savior's return as He descends from a cloud high above man:

The Coming Agin
thie will Be Coming
One A Cloud When
He Comes agin Les All
Be Redy to go Out And meet
HIM WHIM OR LORD COMES

While Chester's unique personal qualities were instrumental to his creating some remarkable objects, they also led him into situations he could scarcely handle. It is perhaps unfortunate that a man so sensitive to images, ideas, and the intrinsic qualities of raw materials was so aloof from other human beings and so indifferent to their feelings. But if he had been a different man, his chairs, too, would have been of some other kind.

Many features of the chairs he made were unique, of course. Not surprisingly, perhaps, some were glorified by Chester as "antique," allegedly reflecting an earlier (and presumably simpler and less troubled) way of life. But to understand how his chairs could be both innovative and traditional, we need to examine specific works in greater detail. The tools and techniques described in chapter 1, the process of conceptualization discussed in chapter 2, and Chester's values, aspirations, and experiences characterized in the present chapter are only part of the story of how and why he built the chairs he did. A crucial element to be considered in the next chapter is what his style was: how it developed, the models that inspired him but which he transformed, and his experiences as a chairmaker that help account for the kinds of chairs that he built.

FOUR

The Unique and the Antique

"The backs don't look flared," said Chester about two chairs made by Aaron (figs. 111 and 113).

It was a hot afternoon in August 1967. Chester was sitting in the shade of his porch, taking a break from work in order to plan his next step in the manufacture of a chair. I interrupted his thoughts by handing him a stack of photographs of chairs I wanted him to examine. His task was to group the chairs according to the individuals who made them on the basis of the photographs alone, without my telling him until later who the craftsmen were. He was also to evaluate them, discussing whatever points he found significant. He tackled the job with considerable interest and skill.

Eventually Chester singled out two rocking chairs by Aaron, one made in 1962 and the other only a few weeks before our conversation. Both are of black walnut. Neither the front nor the back posts on the two chairs curve outward, for Aaron did not find that element attractive on his rocking chairs; also, he was unable to bend the fragile wood the way Chester did. After criticizing the chair made in 1962 for its apparent lack of comfort and its plainness, Chester compared the two, noting that the posts were not curved. This disturbed him because he usually bent the back posts of chairs outward and backward to increase the comfort and improve the appearance.

"Only thing I think is better lookin' twixt them two chairs is the backs," continued Chester, pointing to the more recent rocking chair with horizontal rather than vertical boards in the back. "The slats make it look older, *more antique*, more like a rockin' chair oughta look."

After a brief pause Chester complained again about the legs in the back. "I don't like the posts straight like that," he said.

It is not surprising that Chester would find something to

remark upon in Aaron's chairs, for the character of the two men's work differed. Refinement and delicacy distinguish Aaron's later chairs. Posts are relatively small in diameter, the color and grain of one piece match those of its corresponding member, and the turnings are perfectly proportioned and distributed. Straight and curvilinear lines complement one another in a complex interplay of point and counterpoint. Executed with finesse, each chair is contained in space, a thing of exquisite beauty and proud workmanship, rather than awesomeness or haughty grandeur.

Many of Chester's works are bold, forceful forms that thrust upward and backward into space. Even when more subdued, they command attention as creations that state concepts and demand inquiry rather than objects whose workmanship alone is to be admired.

There are important similarities, however. Once they found their own voices, both craftsmen made declarative statements. They clearly articulated the components of each chair, sharply differentiating the stiles on the back posts and developing distinct fields of decoration. In addition, both wanted their chairs to be readily distinguishable from factory-made items. Aaron achieved this primarily through the use of horizontal slats and a preoccupation with detail; Chester, through the development of several features and construction techniques that he claimed were reminiscent of the past.

In the preceding chapter I suggested that sometimes Chester was nostalgic about the past and that he expressed this identification with an earlier time in several modes of behavior, including conversations, letters, and the song "My Old Kentucky Mountain Home." His body image harked back to an earlier age, as did some chairs he made to which he gave such names as the Old-Timer (figure 77) and the Abner or the George Washington chair. His comments about other men's works often dwelt on whether or not the objects exhibited an old-fashioned appearance and were made with traditional techniques. Chester remarked numerous times that the pegs, eight-sided posts and stretchers, and some other characteristics of many of his chairs are "antique." Preoccupation with them might have grown out of his idealization of the past in his efforts to cope with stress in the present.

But the situation is more complicated. When analyzing and assessing Aaron's chairs, Chester focused on two matters, not one. An ongoing issue was appropriate appearance in combination with maximum comfort. Straight posts violated his sense of propriety, although, if the truth be known, he did not always bend chair posts. Old-timiness was sometimes of concern. While he associated horizontal slats with chairmaking in the past, Chester made chairs with panel backs or woven hickory-bark backs; he did so in later years even when voicing a preference for slat-back chairs. Moreover, some traits of his chairs that he conceived to be antique were peculiar to him.

Several questions arise. How does a characteristic mode of construction or execution in chairmaking develop? Why do a craftsman's products sometimes exhibit discontinuities and inconsistencies? What unique traits in craftwork must be taken into account if we are to understand why objects possess the qualities they do and to apply the concept of style in meaningful ways?

MODELS, PREFERENCES, AND PREDILECTIONS

"When I was about the size of Billy," said Chester in reference to his youngest boy, "I was makin' chairs outta cornstalks. I made little horses and I made little people. Used to make little dolls outta rags and use empty shotgun shells for boots." Somewhat to Chester's chagrin, his four-year-old son was not interested in doing any of these things.

I asked Chester why he had become a chairmaker.

"Well, I don't know. When I was a boy big enough to make anything I was always makin' somethin' or other outta cornstalks—little log cabins. I built 'em outta cornstalks— things like that that I couldn't . . ." He never finished his sentence but said, "I guess I just inherited it from other ancestors. They was all makin' chairs by hand, makin' ever'thing by hand them days. They even made the shoes they wear by hand. Just about ever'thing they made it, couldn't buy 'em them days, you know."

Chester's maternal uncle, Linden, and Linden's father, Cal, made chairs, as did Chester's paternal grandfather, Pike, and

Pike's brother Hiram. But Chester differed from them in his identification with and dedication to the role of chairmaker. Pike made only a few chairs, mainly for his own use, and the other men worked rapidly, lacking the patience to "shape 'em out by hand" the way Chester did because making chairs meant making money. Economic incentives were important to Chester, too, but his primary concern seemed to be that of fulfilling to the best of his ability the requirements of useful design, especially those of access and appearance.

"Them days they made 'em awful small," complained Chester about the chairs of his kin in the past. "They jest barely made 'em big enough you could set in 'em; then you'd be settin' partly on the rounds. And the rockin' chair was almost completely square all the way around; the back and the front was about equally the same size them days. The rockin' chairs they made in them days you couldn't rest in one hardly—they didn't space their backs in 'em, they didn't put the right bend in 'em to rest your back."

Typical of the work of his grandfather Cal, for example, is a settin' chair of maple and locust made on a foot-powered turning lathe about 1925 (fig. 61). The chair is small. Stiles are present but ambiguous in nature; there is little curve to the slats and none to the posts, and there are no shoulders on the ends of the stretchers. Such traits suggest speed in production with minimal attention to other considerations. In appearance, the chair is a closed form, its simple rectangles suggesting stasis rather than tension or movement.

Contrast this with one of Chester's earliest settin' chairs, which he whittled from white oak and locust about 1935 (fig. 62). Chester made a chair that is taller, deeper, and wider. He curved the slats and bent the back posts backward and out. He cut the stiles sharply, differentiating them forcefully from the rounded form of the posts. He built the chair with a total of twelve rounds instead of the eleven common in the works of other chairmakers. A dynamic quality infuses this chair. An energetic thrust in the curving, biomorphic lines gives it vitality. Most of Chester's chairs seem to grow upward from the ground like organic forms boldly pushing outward into space in an emphatic declaration of presence.

61 Settin' chair made by Chester's grandfather Cal about 1925 was sold for $1, but Chester bought it back in 1966 for $5.   **62** This settin' chair, which Chester made about 1935, was whittled with a pocketknife.

Chester attributed the shortcomings of his ancestors' chairs to inadequate financial remuneration. "They had ways a bendin' 'em, you see, same as I do. They, uh, but most of the sales they'd get 'cause they'd be straight an' they'd sell 'em cheaper. An' the bent chair that was curved in the back postees [of which I never found an example], they'd be more expensive, they'd charge more for them. Them days they didn't get over two to five dollars apiece for a settin' chair," Chester concluded. "An' maybe three to six dollars for a big rockin' chair," though none of his ancestors made rocking chairs as large as Chester did. "They couldn't get more for a rockin' chair or a settin' chair them days like they can these days."

What Chester did not note was that he received about the same amount of money for his chairs, too, until the 1960s. Although there is the implication that Chester's kin could have made chairs of higher quality, greater comfort, and more attractive appearance if they had been able to obtain higher prices for them, it is more probable that they were limited to customers unable or unwilling to pay more than a few dollars for a chair and that they were interested primarily in economic gain, building chairs that met but rarely exceeded the minimal requirements of useful design. Chester was different, and so were his chairs.

"The chairs that I make is completely differ'nt, all the way round, than what they used to make," he said. "I can put in the wide bark, or the nar' stuff or the real nar' stuff. They had one reg'lar size they'd make." His kin, he said, "would never fool with makin' a little bitty nar' chair," that is, a chair whose seat consisted of very narrow hickory bark splints. For Chester, however, a bottom of narrow bark in a chair "really makes it comf'table to set in and it really makes it purtier." These two qualities—comfort and beauty—were of great importance to Chester, although he did not like some of his own chairs because in his view they are neither comfortable nor attractive.

"Chairs they made them days," said Chester, "the back postees—I call 'em—they come straight up, an' they tapered off and get really small up at the top, an' nine times outta ten they turn on the turnin' lay a little knob up thar on top." An example is a chair made by Chester's great-uncle Hiram about 1905-10

63 Rocker made by Chester's
great-uncle Hiram (about
1905-19); Chester restored the
rockers and seat in 1967.

(fig. 63), whose seat and rockers Chester repaired in 1967. It has
barrel arms, a few turnings nicely placed on the arms and on the
front posts above the seat, and small, rounded finials at the top.

Several of Chester's earliest rockers are interesting by comparison. The oldest chair of Chester's that he and I could locate,
built in the early 1930s (fig. 64), was a panel-back rocker made of
square pieces. He was to use spokes under the arms in the 1960s
on his two-in-one rocking chairs, and he made other chairs with
square posts, as in 1963 (fig. 65), because they are easily and
cheaply made and could find a buyer quickly at a low price.

"Why was the first chair made with square posts?" I asked
Chester. "Easier to make thataway. You gotta take more time to
make it to eightsquare, you see, an' I guess it just come easy to
make it thataway. The first chair I ever made was completely
foursquare—the postees," he continued. "Course the back

64 The rocker on the porch, one of Chester's first rocking chairs, was made in the early 1930s.
65 A "cheap chair"—made with nails—is of a type Chester built because he could sell it more easily.

wasn't slat back, they was panel back: two crosspieces and then one big center piece in the back and two little nar' pieces on each side next to the post was the first chair I ever act'lly made by myself."

"Did your uncle make one like it, too?"

"No, no, I just thought that up my own self a-makin' that. You take a square post thataway, an' put slats in it—called a 'slat back' you know—hit don't look right a-tall to make the back look like that. To make it look right, for a foursquare post, you got to have a panel back, you got to have two crosspieces an' one big piece in the center an' two nar's on the side of hit."

"Were the pieces bent?"

"The two crosspieces were bent. If they wasn't bent, they was carved out to fit your back the way I made 'em."

On Hiram's chair, however, the slats are just barely bent and the posts not at all.

"Were the posts on your chair bent, too?"

"Yes sir, I bent the back postees down 'twixt the seat an' the back of hit. The postees was gen'lly hewed out in a crook or bent, but I always bent 'em 'twixt the seat an' the first crosspiece in the back. That's where I bent 'em at or carved it out to fit 'em."

He remarked again on some of his own principles of composition and construction which he sometimes violated, as in a rocking chair he made in 1935 (fig. 66).

This white oak rocker has barrel arms like Hiram's chair. The posts are not bent and the slats are not curved, despite Chester's contention that he always bent or curved both. The seat is bigger than in Hiram's chair, however, and the armrests are placed higher, which is typical of Chester's work. There are more slats than are usually found on chairs made by other men, which again is common in Chester's creations. And obviously Chester paid close attention to the decorative quality of the chair, especially in the front, the position from which it is usually viewed.

Although the slats and posts are not bent (perhaps because of the many turnings), this chair is consistent with Chester's other work in

• emphasis on comfort in other ways, especially the greater number of slats that are closer together and the wedge-shaped

66 This white oak chair, made about 1935, shows Chester's concern for comfort and his interest in decorative detail; each of the many sets of turnings is slightly different from every other.

seat (note how close the rockers are in back compared with Hiram's chair)
- a concern about appearance, not only in the turnings but also in the notching of slats in each corner
- experimentation (the many turnings of different kinds)
- the conceptual statement that the chair makes

The few turnings on Hiram's rocker are well placed and pleasingly repeat each other; the chair is "nice." But Chester's chair seems to call out for explanation. There are many different kinds of turnings on the front posts, the back posts, the stretchers, and the arms. Rather than settling on one form and repeating it throughout as Hiram and other craftsmen did, Chester experimented with variations on a theme, exploring the very notion of turnings.

A panel-back rocker that Chester made about 1942 and sold for $2.50 (fig. 67) indicated how experimental his work could be. The back posts are square but the front posts have been turned and ornamented.

In Chester's words, the chair is "a mixed-up proposition" because it consists of maple panels, four-sided back posts, turned oak front posts with extensive ornamentation, hickory rounds, and hickory bark seat. He claimed he did not have enough materials on hand to make the chair of one wood or one design, but he proceeded anyway; I did not meet any other chairmaker who would have done so. In fact, Hascal identified the chair as Chester's because of its unique composition and construction. The only criticism came from Chester himself. He thought the bottom stretchers were too close to the rockers (as in Hiram's chair).

Chester made many other chairs in the next thirty years, all of them possessing a quality peculiar to him which few people were able to describe: a propensity for the unusual and an adeptness at chairmaking were the tendencies suggested most often.

One of his rocking chairs may epitomize Chester's preferences and predilections in creating form. It is a mulberry rocker (with matching love seat, figs. 32 and 33) that Chester made about 1954 or 1955 using an ax rather than drawing knife.

The slats on the rocker curve deeply, the posts thrust back and out, the dramatized proportions call attention to the chair. The large pegs dominating the stiles proclaim durability. The curving armrests invite touch. The chair bespeaks comfort. This work makes a statement about the concepts "rocking chair" and "rocking," for the rockers are only about four inches apart in back.

"It's got great balance and it just fits your back perfect. Been in use here about ten years," said Smitty Smith, the tenant in the house of the man who bought the chair. The chair "sets good," he said. He was impressed most by the fact that it would not tip over because the rockers are extremely close together in back. He demonstrated this several times by rocking forcefully in the chair, unsuccessfully trying to tip it over.

67 A panel-back rocker consisting of maple panels, ash back posts, oak front posts, hickory rounds, and hickory bark seat was made just before Chester was drafted in 1942.

"Now that man ain't foolish," said Smith. "I don't know how much education he's got, but he sure can work with wood."

The chairmaker Verge remarked, "That looks like a comf'table chair to set in an' I like the looks of it. It don't have no rings," that is, turnings (a decorative element that seemed superfluous to Verge). His son, Hascal, disagreed. "I wouldn't make one or have one like it. I don't like them square posts or bent posts," which Chester preferred to turned pieces. Beechum, who was working with Hascal in a chair shop, told me he liked "that rocker but the arms are a little high," a trait typical of most of Chester's work. It was also Beechum who identified the chair as Chester's, citing several elements common in his chairs.

"I think Chester made that rocker," said Beechum. "Way the posts is bent, an' it's wide in the front and nar' at the back. Way he's got them pegs in there, and all them rounds, and the posts and rounds has got eight sides." Beechum's characterization of the chair points to several key elements in how Chester built chairs, which may be why this chair appealed to Chester.

In August 1966 I asked Chester what his favorite rocking chair was. "My favorite chair in a rocking chair would be—the one I like best—I don't know just which one it was. But it's not the one I've got now, an' it's not the one I made the mayor. I b'lieve that the chair that I like best'un myself is the one you looked at, took pictures of at Smitty Smith's."

"Why do you like it the best?"

"I like the shape of it, the way it's made. It's my favorite chair of any of the rest of 'em."

"Do you think it's better made than the rest of them?"

"No, no, it ain't no better, but I just like the design of it. I like the shape of it, the design. It's no better than the others but I like the design of it."

By "design" Chester meant not merely appearance but fitness for use, too. In 1955 he made four sassafras settin' chairs that he sold to McIntosh, who sold three and kept one (fig. 30). The chairs are unmistakably Chester's handicraft. The feet are shaped so they will not puncture a linoleum floor and the slats are notched at the ends to produce a striking decorative effect. As in many other chairs of Chester's, there is a large peg at each end of the slats and the back posts curve backward and outward at a rather exaggerated angle. Chester told me in 1965 that "that's a beautiful chair there," but it is also a technical failure, for the seat is too high and the posts are not flared outward far enough to provide the comfort he felt was required in a settin' chair.

Dedicated to his craft, Chester wanted to build chairs that accomplished as fully as possible the purposes for which they were designed and produced. He often photographed himself sitting peacefully in one of his chairs after constructing it. His interest in the creative act seemed to wane until the job neared completion, but "then I can't hardly quit 'til I find the balance on a chair." He would spend hours looking at the finished chair, touching the slats and arms and stroking the finials and stretchers to feel the smoothness of the wood beneath his hands, and sitting in the chair before the splints dried so the seat would have proper "swag," as he called it, and thus would be comfortable.

EXPERIMENTATION

During the latter part of the 1950s and at times in the 1960s Chester produced many other settin' and rocking chairs as well as counter stools that consistently exhibited a strength of character, clarity of form, and economy of line, but he tried other designs and techniques of production, too, gaining somewhat different effects. I never felt close to Chester, or comfortable around him. Whether or not he was aware of this I don't know. But I was greatly impressed by his artistry. What fascinated me most, I suppose, was that for Chester the manufacture of each chair posed problems whose solution completely absorbed his attention. This quality is essential to understanding much of what he made and why he made these things in a particular way.

Often the dilemmas were self-generated. It was not enough for Chester to find a pleasing design for the feet of his chairs and employ it regularly. No, he made the feet large so they would not poke holes in linoleum rugs, but then he thought he should spend a lot of time shaping them by hand so as to reduce their visual bulk. This self-imposed task required more labor than desirable, given the lack of financial rewards. Then he made the feet even more pointed than previously, which involved more work than simply leaving them straight. (The pointed feet did produce a strong visual impact but also took a toll on linoleum floors.)

The same observation about self-imposed requirements could be made in regard to the finials on rocking chairs. "I turned 'em on a turnin' lay all kinda differ'nt shapes, an' after I've turned 'em on the turnin' lay I have done some carvin' on them to make 'em look more like an *antique* or some'un or other on the ends of 'em—do a little hand carvin' up on 'em."

A settin' chair Chester made about 1960 with wide feet is unusual in that he incised the front posts with cross-hatching using a saw (fig. 68). The back posts are plain. Why? Chester just wanted to decorate the chair, justifying the decision to himself

68 About 1960, Chester incised the front posts of this
chair in the hope of selling it at a higher price.

by saying that he might be able to get more money for it. After
spending two days incising the front posts, he quit. He did not
receive a higher price anyway.

Another settin' chair, made about 1961, to which Chester
referred several times as "one of my most interestin' chairs," had
square posts, very wide slats, thick feet, and diamond-shaped
pegs prominently displayed. I never saw the chair because the
man who had bought it sold it to a tourist several years before I
came to the area.

"I b'lieve that settin' chair is the most beautiful settin' chair I
ever made," Chester said.

"Why did you make it?" I asked him.

"I jest took a notion to make the pegs like that to see what it'd look like."

Other chairs, too, can be appreciated as the result of Chester's having taken a notion to make them in a certain way just to see what they would look like, in the process extending concepts of materials, construction techniques, structure, comfort, or appearance and thereby testing the limits to which he could take a chair.

In the early 1960s, for example, Chester cleared some "swamp willers" from the creek near his home, thinking he might be able to make a chair from them based on the design of a factory-made chair he had seen earlier in the home of a customer (fig. 69). The form is different from that of other chairs Chester made at the time, although the chair is unmistakably Chester's.

He was not entirely pleased with the product, owing to the technique of construction. Chester disliked chairs that are loose at the joints and squeak, which distracts the sitter—chairs that "have what I call the rickets, and cry." Because Chester nailed the willows in place, and because the owner kept the chair in his living room near a large heating vent in the floor, the chair dried out during the winter. Each spring, however, the owner set the chair on his lawn, hosed it down with water, and let it soak overnight so that it did not squeak until the following winter.

Of all the chairmakers I met, Chester had the greatest respect for his raw materials. He carefully shaped the posts and rounds with his drawing knife, removing tissue-thin strips as he followed the grain of the wood and working around the knots to preserve the integrity of the material. This procedure is particularly apparent in a sassafras high chair used as a counter stool in a tavern, which Chester made about 1961; there are slight irregularities in the surface of component elements, such as the lowest stretcher in front (fig 31).

The front posts as well as back legs are flared outward, which was done to improve the chair's appearance and to facilitate access. Sometimes Chester flared the front posts at the bottom, as well, in order to "make your espensive chair look a leetle bit better."

On other chairs Chester inserted the arms below the stiles; on this stool the armrests are affixed to them directly. There is no

69 Chester made this rocker of swamp willow in
emulation of factory-made chairs (about 1960).

evidence of progression and development, for the placement of
the arms depends on the nature of the chair and the height of the
back. The back of the counter stool is low, but the arms must be
rather high if they are to function properly. Chester liked the
stiles, which are attractive and add to the comfort of certain
kinds of chairs, but if they had started between the top slat and
the middle slat above the arm they would have looked absurd.

New features or forms produced by experimentation, upgrad-
ing, or adaptation of design to use might appear almost any time
during the craftsman's career. This confounds attempts to describe and explain an individual's style.

Consider the chairs in figures 64 through 67. The chair from
the early 1930s, one of Chester's first rocking chairs, is panel
back with square posts. A chair he made a few years later (fig. 66)

is slat back with turned posts. Not yet aware that Chester made panel-back chairs on other occasions, including three decades later (fig. 65), but having seen many slat-back chairs, I assumed that there was a progression from panel-back to slat-back chairs.

"When did you change the design to the slat-back chair?" I asked him as we talked about his early panel-back rocking chair.

Chester said, "In the chairmakin' business you make all kinds of different chairs an' different types of backs." I thought he had not answered my question. For two years I organized his works sequentially on the basis of what I assumed was a steady evolution in style. When a chair exhibited what I surmised to be both early and late features, I thought of it as a transitional work; even so, many chairs did not make sense, especially when their dates of manufacture conflicted with the "stylistic evidence."

Eventually I realized that Chester, in fact, had answered my question; it's just that his response was not what I was looking for or could appreciate at the time. My perspective had been that of easel painting and of sculpture, not craft work. After telling me that *in the chairmaking business* a craftsman knows a variety of designs that he makes whenever the need or desire arises, he added: "I've made different types of chair seats. Chair seat like that a chair you're settin' in there is a different chair." He was referring to a settin' chair with a panel bottom rather than a woven hickory bark seat.

Like other chairmakers, Chester was pragmatic. He knew many chair designs, including different types of backs as well as seats, and employed them when called upon to do so or when he thought they would find a willing buyer. For example, in a letter to a customer dated 10 November 1966, Chester writes that he is nearly finished building the chair the customer had ordered. He enclosed a Polaroid snapshot of it and also a picture of a different chair he had just completed. He concludes his letter: "If there is iney thin that you dont Like about the Rocker I Will Wate one Weak Befor I Crate hit Let me no if you are satfide with hit There are *a lot of difernt dezins*" [emphasis added]." Seven days later, Chester wrote to the man, "I ame sendin some *more Pictures of differnt dezines* that I have the Prises of [emphasis added]."

In sum, experimentation led to the conceptualization of different forms. Knowledge of varied designs meant increased sales. Although the chairmaker had his own preferences, and certain underlying propensities and proclivities might inform his work, a particular design—especially an older one—could appear at any time.

CUSTOMER PARTICIPATION

A peculiar mixing of design elements in four chairs made in the early spring of 1967 resulted directly from customer influence (fig. 70). A man in North Carolina wanted walnut dining chairs similar to dining chairs that Chester had just made (fig. 71). The finials are elongated, the slats curve upward toward the center, and there are double pegs in the ends of slats. But the customer also found an earlier chair of Chester's attractive (fig. 41, center). This is a redbud settin' chair—not a dining chair—which is not as tall as a dining chair and has stiles on the back posts.

Lacking other information, and on the basis of these three sets of chairs, one might assume a steady progression from a period of settin' chairs with stiles and no finials (the chair made in 1961) to a transitional period of dining chairs with stiles (the North Carolina chairs of 1967) and a later period of dining chairs with finials and no stiles (1966-67). One would not know from their appearance the order in which the chairs were made or the direct part played by the customer directly in the execution of what, in fact, was the most recent design.

"Boy, that's a nice chair there," said Beechum in reference to the California rocker, which Chester made in 1967 (fig. 73). Built of red oak, it was Chester's second version. This chair was influenced indirectly by the customer; the first (fig. 74) was directly influenced by him. Together the chairs illustrate several ways that elements of design originate, and how they develop or change.

Having seen an article about Chester in *Appalachian South*, Willard Moore (then living in Berkeley, California) wrote to Chester in the fall of 1965. Moore had a set of four dining chairs. They had spindle backs and pointed finials, and the seats were caned rather than woven of hickory bark splints (fig. 75). He wanted a rocking chair reminiscent of the dining chairs.

70 Black walnut chairs and table made in the spring of 1967 (photo by Chester).   71 Walnut rocker and dining chairs made by Chester in late 1966 or early 1967.

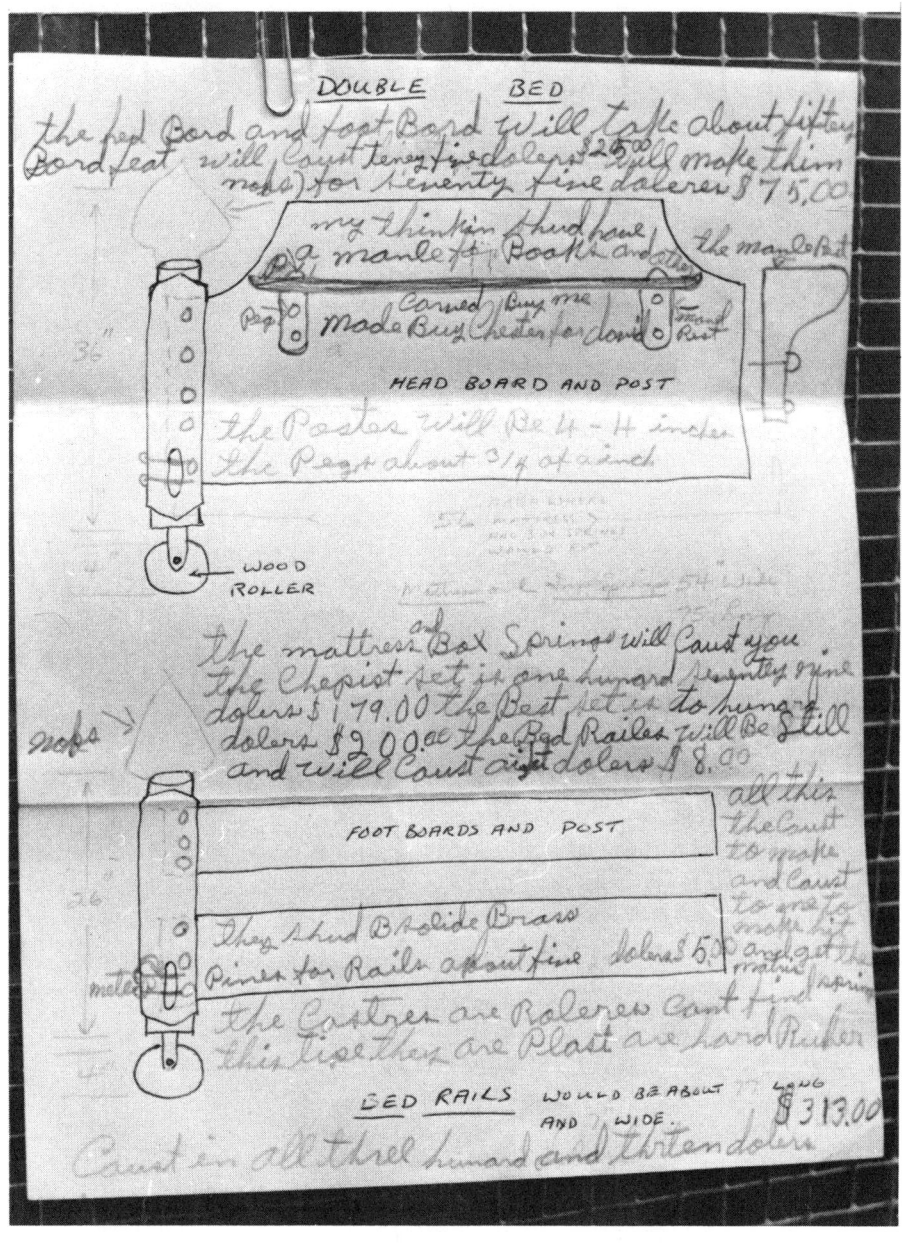

72 One page of an eight-page letter from a North Carolina customer detailing the furniture he wanted made; the page also contains Chester's comments.

73 Chester's second California rocker was made of red oak in late spring 1967.   74 The first Moore rocker or California rocker, made in 1966 (photo by Chester).

75 The California customer's dining chairs had cane seats similar to the one in the background of the photo; he wanted Chester to build a rocker to match them. Chester transformed his customer's design into his first (*left*) and second California rockers.

Moore's specifications included seven curved slats that were not shaped or peaked in the center, elongated finials, armrests that were not shaped, but rather wedge-shaped, and a seat with a hollow space in the center in which the hickory bark was to be woven on the model of a caned chair. "As I *recall*," Moore wrote in a letter to me later, "we sketched a plain ladder-back rocker. Chester's rocker has curved back rests [peaked in the center], much fancier than we requested. However," he concluded, "we *like* Cornett's design better than our own and we're delighted that he made it as he did!"

"What a suprise to here from you all and to get a sail to Boot," Chester wrote to him on 18 November 1965. "Well I shere wold like to Bild *the Rocker that you desined your self*," he said [emphasis added]. "Hit will Be a Butfule Creation I ame shere."

Two months later, on 16 January 1966, Chester wrote to Moore thanking him for the drawing he had sent of the rocker that he was requesting. "I Reley wanted to *make somtin in a new Fashon* and this one is hit [emphasis added]   I ame shere this Rocker is going to Be a Butey in Every Way are is one my mind."

Chester was interrupted many times; he did not complete and ship the chair until a year after Moore ordered it. On 10 November 1966, Chester sent him Polaroid photos of the chair "so you Can see what you Will Be Getin   hit is along way to California and if you wernt satisfid With hit Would Be aful   I Want you all to Be Pleased not Wored." Chester begins his letter with the statement, "think you very very much and you Cornett's Rocker are Moore Rocker *after all you dezined hit ho ho* [emphasis added]."

When I was with him, Chester called the chair the Moore rocker or, more often, the California rocker, "On account a Mr. Moore in California designed it."

Chester did not follow all of Moore's specifications, however, or follow them exactly. Chester was not acquainted with cane-bottomed chairs; he did not know from Moore's sketch how to weave the hickory bark he used (rather than caning) *within* the framework of the seat. Therefore, he made a frame of four wide boards and wove the hickory bark splints *around* this. In addition, he made curvilinear armrests rather than the wedge-shaped ones that the customer had sketched; Chester's form rhythmically repeats other curving elements that serve as counterpoint to the straight lines. Finally, Chester shaped the slats.

In the second version, a year later, Chester made the slats simple horizontal bands (the way Moore had drawn them), which he found more in keeping with the overall design of the chair. Chester might have peaked the slats on the earlier chair to add visual contrast to a work whose straight lines were too pronounced or perhaps to explore further a design element that he had recently developed and was unwilling to relinquish.

Another difference between the two California rockers is that the back posts on Moore's rocker are tapered at the bottom to a point where they join the seat. This repeats the elongated finials. In comparison with the later one, in which the finials are more square and the tenons at the bottom of the posts less apparent, the back of the earlier chair seems to hover above the seat.

The chairs differ also in the size and shape of the front and back stretchers. The doweling in the first chair is the same thickness throughout. On the later chair the front and rear stretchers are bulbous in the center, providing a visual anchor.

In effect, Chester reversed the peaked slats and the straight stretchers on the first chair, making them the straight slats and bulbous stretchers on the second chair. The two chairs look very different when viewed from the front.

The posts of both chairs are square, as in the rocking chairs Chester made in the 1930s (figs. 64 and 67) and in the panel-back chair he built in 1963 (fig. 65). Chester bought the wood for the California rockers from a lumber company. He could not shape pieces eight-sided with a drawing knife. He did manage to shave the sharp edges, however, which he did not do on the other foursquare chairs. Although Chester had said that a chair with square posts should be panel-back, the two versions of the California rocker are slat-back, in part because this is what the customers ordered.

The Moore rocker, then, owes its overall design directly to the customer's influence, as interpreted or transformed by the craftsman. The second version of the California rocker was influenced indirectly by both Moore and the man in Lexington who ordered it. Chester made the slats of equal width as Moore had sketched them originally; he also made the stretcher bulbous, which may have corresponded to the large central turning on the front stretcher of many older caned chairs and which Moore might have drawn. Chester built the second chair because the customer requested it, having selected it from Polaroid photos of different chair designs that Chester could make.

As large and as heavy as the Moore rocker must be, the second version is larger and heavier, and the back and seat are wider. The overall height of the second California rocker is 58 inches from the floor straight up to the end of the finial (the back, which is at an angle, is actually 62 inches, but it loses 4 inches in height when measured perpendicularly from the floor). The top slat is 4¼ inches wide and the bottom one is 4⅝. The rockers are 39 inches long; they stand 22¼ inches apart from outside edge to outside edge. The seat measures 22½ inches deep by a very wide 28 inches. One reason for the large scale of the chair is that the man from Lexington who ordered it weighed over 300 pounds

76 A chair that Chester rebottomed in 1967 at a customer's request, salvaging some of the old bark and adding new bark.

(he did not, however, follow through on the purchase; weighing in at 200 pounds, I bought the chair).

REPAIRS AND REVISIONS

In 1967 Chester repaired a chair his great-uncle had made around the turn of the century. The seat had disintegrated and the rockers were worn and broken. Chester replaced both after the customer had brought the chair to him. Although other chairmakers commented favorably on other aspects of the chair, they objected to the new seat. "The bark's too wide for the chair," said both Hascal and Beechum.

Chester once rebottomed a chair that someone had brought to him, salvaging some of the old bark and adding new bark (fig. 76). The resulting seat alters the overall appearance of the chair. Over the years, customers sanded and varnished, painted, abused, and otherwise altered Chester's chairs. Through use and alteration, the durability, appearance, comfort, or utility of a chair may be enhanced or diminished. Whatever one's opinion of the results, the chair is not what was originally envisioned.

77 Chester made this counter stool of sassafras in 1955; ten years later he added double pegs at the ends of each slat.

Sometimes Chester "revised" his chairs. In one instance he did so to inform customers of the kinds of chairs he preferred to make at the moment. On another occasion the motive was less apparent but may have related to his need for stability and protection when he was beleaguered by personal problems.

According to both Chester and the customer, Chester made the counter stool in figure 77 about 1955. Strangely, it has double pegs at the end of each slat, a feature that Chester did not use until several years later when he made an effort to attract a wealthier clientele and had begun to associate pegs with antiquity. At first I thought that either Chester and the customer dated the chair incorrectly, or that Chester erred when he told me that he did not use double pegs until 1961. Both hypotheses were highly unlikely.

What, in fact, had occurred is that Chester revised the chair while repairing it. With the publication of the article in the *National Observer* in December 1965 came daily queries, which both delighted and distressed Chester. Inquirers wanted to know what kinds of chairs he made. He bought a Polaroid camera to take pictures of the Bookcase Masterpiece for Loughhead. But he had no other recent chairs on hand to photograph, and photographing earlier chairs meant that he would be suggesting to prospective customers designs, or elements of design, that he did not necessarily want to duplicate.

Enter the counter stool. The owner, who ran a small grocery store about a mile down the road from Chester's home, brought the chair to Chester for repair. Not only did Chester replace some of the worn stretchers in front, but he also substituted double pegs for the single peg at the end of each slat (compare the chair in fig. 34). Then he took some Polaroid pictures of it to show prospective customers both the type of chair he could build and a feature that he now preferred.

In 1967 Chester repaired and revised another chair, but not to photograph it for the benefit of customers. Having made the chair about 1960, he had kept it for his own use. The rocker, of mulberry and hickory, had rather thin arms pegged from the top into the front posts (fig. 78). Originally, there had been six rather narrow slats in the back; in 1961 Chester cut several inches off the height, removing the top slat, as a customer had done to another chair that Chester had built. The back posts were bent high near the top of the chair. The chair had no notching or other ornamentation. Chester had put a single small peg in the end of each slat.

The seat of the rocker had disintegrated from exposure to the elements. When Chester rewove the seat with relatively narrow bark, he completely rebuilt the chair (fig. 79). He used the same posts. He also used the same rounds, but shortened them, making the chair more compact. He changed the armrests to very thick, curvilinear forms (as on the Moore rocker). He put in very wide slats, peaked in the center, that almost touched one another. Finally, he installed new pegs at the ends of the slats; these he carved in a pattern of grooves and ridges.

The smaller size of the chair, the wider slats, and the thicker arms made the chair more secure in its compactness, more

78 A mulberry and hickory rocker that Chester made about 1960 and kept for his own use was remodeled twice. He had removed one of the original six slats in 1961.   79 In 1967 Chester redesigned the seat, slats, pegs, and arms.

protective visually than the thinness and openness of the original design. And the large decorated pegs made the chair appear more "antique."

THE ANTIQUE LOOK AND THE HILLBILLY IMAGE

In midsummer of 1965, shortly after he composed "My Old Kentucky Mountain Home" and a few months before he built the Bookcase Masterpiece, Chester made a maple rocking chair with very thin posts, little more than an inch in diameter. Allegedly the posts were thin because he had no more substantial material. To strengthen the chair, Chester added a brace in back, reminiscent of Windsor chairs, which he claimed never to have seen. Chester also mortised the posts all the way through; thus, the slats and rounds extend through the posts, projecting half an inch beyond (similar to the chair in fig. 80).

"Some people called it the 'Washington chair,'" said Chester, "cause it looked like somethin' George Washington mightta set in. But I call it my Abner chair. Called it that b'fore I ever made hit."

Why call it an Abner chair? What was the source of the design?

"Oh, I got that outta the Abner comic strip an' comic books an' these here newspaper comic strips. I made it like Abner furniture I seen in pictures in the comic strip."

"How long ago did you see these pictures? " "Well, it's been about twelve years ago since I saw that picture in the paper, I guess. Li'l Abner settin' in this chair, way it was made and ever'thing. If you notice the furniture an' ever'thing they have is, have all these pieces stickin' all the way through. The furniture in the homes, you know, is thataway—picture frames."

Chester's characterization was not quite accurate. The furniture he alluded to, pictured in the Sunday editions of the *Louisville Courier-Journal* in the years 1952-55, did not have the slats and rounds extending through the posts. Rather the pieces projected beyond the posts because they had been haphazardly nailed to the backs of the legs, and the picture frames had been slapped together at odd angles with ends overlapping.

"This chair I made, I called it an 'Abner chair.' Ever' piece

80 A chair of simplified design and construction made in late 1965 or early 1966 has slats extending through the posts, a feature that Chester used in his Abner chair.

about it went all the way through—back slats went all the way through the postees, the pegs all the way through, the rounds all the way through—they went all the way through the postees an' stick out on the other side. And, uh, it had postees that come through the rockers, come all the way up through the armrests. That's where I thought that Abner chair up."

Chester's chair was made differently from Al Capp's drawings, of course, because Chester would never construct an object crudely. What is of more interest, however, is that a dozen years before Chester made the Abner chair, his wife left him in an effort to force him to live near the highway. At that time he began growing a beard, gave up using a turning lathe, and made his first eight-legged settin' chair. In the early to mid-1960s similar events transpired, but with greater intensity, when Chester's wife left for a longer time and they lived on the highway longer than before.

Chester had a beard and long hair after 1963, when Ruth and he moved to their house on a major highway. Other men in the area were clean-shaven and wore their hair short. By 1965 Chester was dressing in overalls, as farmers had done earlier and as a few of the older mountain men still did, whereas most men his age and younger wore belted trousers. He also went barefoot most of the year, although other men wore shoes or boots.

Chester cultivated a hillbilly image in the 1960s, ostensibly to sell his chairs or to hide a skin ailment allegedly contracted during World War II and aggravated by shaving. But the idea of a beard and long hair had occurred to him a decade earlier when the L'il Abner comic strip first attracted his attention and captured his imagination. Apparently, Chester wanted to look like the stereotypical mountain man who does old-timey things like making chairs by hand.

"The long hair's one thing that draws their attention more'n anything," he said. "Now you take some kids, they ain't never seen a beard. There's a whole lot a people over in Hazard thinks I b'long to some kinda church organization or club or somethin'. I've had a lot a people ask me what religion I had; I don't b'long to any church organization."

He hid behind a beard for a year or so in the mid-1950s when he moved near the open highway, but for much longer in the 1960s.

"I kept on a-wearin' hit this time on accounta hit helped my business," he explained.

"I think hit looks plumb awful," complained his wife.

"I betcha a dollar I'd cut my hair and shave hit off an' I'd lose what orders I got," countered Chester. "Somehow I think that. I might be wrong. Ever'body says, 'No, man, don't you shave that off.' They kin buy furniture off most anybody. There's a lot a people that'd buy the furniture off me jest to get a picture of me. Like the artist in Washington, D.C. I think they bought a chair jest so's they could take some pictures of me," though in fact the customer made only a small deposit on a chair which she never picked up or paid for. Chester eventually altered it to a seven-slat rocking chair, a process that gave him the technique necessary to create his New Design chair.

"If I shave an' the furniture warn't pegged," he concluded, "people wouldn't buy the chairs off me."

Economic concern is surely important in accounting for Chester's appearance, but so is identification with the past. Chester asked two writers in early August 1965 to take him back to Pine Mountain to find the grave of his mother's father, Cal Foutch; at his insistence I took him there in 1966 and 1967. Chester had a framed portrait of his maternal grandfather and grandmother on the wall of his living room (fig. 81). In the portrait Cal, like Chester, has long hair and a beard. One of Chester's neighbors mistook the portrait of Cal for Chester, or so Chester told me several times. I have seen another small, torn photograph of the grandmother with a pipe in her hand and her feet bare.

Regardless of the financial rewards that might have accrued from Chester's behavior and dress, he had adopted the appearance of the mountaineer at those times when he was most remote from a mountain hollow. He seems to have found spiritual kinship with the Yokums and other stereotyped hillbillies of Capp's, basing his behavior and some of his chairs on the comic strip. Chester purposefully posed as an anachronism in the modern world to promote his art and help him adjust to his losses. Ironically, some of his problems were exaggerated as a result of the additional attention he attracted to himself.

Other ironies and seeming paradoxes are evident in Chester's chairs and in his comments on them. "People like the pegs the best," said Chester. "They want the purtiest and espensivist stuff they can git." Yet he also admitted that many people did not know what the pegs were; some thought they might be large nails or bolts, or perhaps bits of wood glued onto the chair. As Chester had noted, "There's a whole lot a people that never even seen a rail fence; they don't understand this handmade stuff." For example, in 1965 Chester told me, "A fella stopped the other

81 A portrait of Chester's maternal grandfather, Cal, from whom he learned chairmaking, and Cal's wife.

day while I was a-gettin' ready to cook some wood and he asked me if I was a-gonna eat it." Still, Chester contended that if the chairs were not pegged they would not sell, as "people like it, and it makes the chair look better; holds the slats, too."

Only two pegs, one at each end of the top slat, are structurally necessary if a chair is made in accordance with the principle of differential seasoning of the parts. Forty to two hundred pegs are a bit excessive, although some of the chairs Chester made in 1967 of wood purchased at a lumber company required the use of a few more pegs because the wood was already seasoned. The pegs on older furniture made by other craftsmen are hidden from view, rather like the pins in the backs of Aaron's chairs. Pegs in most of Chester's chairs since the mid-1950s were visible; sometimes they were highly exaggerated in size, shape, number, or visual appearance. By the early 1960s there were two small pegs at the end of each slat, and beginning about 1964 Chester made the pegs of a wood that contrasted in color with the wood of the chair, except in cheap chairs made with nails or in chairs that the customers specified were to be solid walnut, a demand that Chester took literally. If Chester had really wanted the chairs to look antique, then he should have limited the pegs to two per chair and hidden them.

Chester also thought the tall rocking chairs, which he occasionally built after about 1962 or 1963, were old-fashioned in appearance. Again, they are unique, not antique. The mountain-style rocking chairs made years ago by other craftsmen are less than four feet high, whereas some of Chester's chairs are six feet or taller. No one made such tall chairs in the past, for, in Chester's words, "A rockin' chair in the house, if you ain't got much room, is right in the way. You can't hardly get around 'em." Few houses in the area or cabins in the mountains had much room.

Two other traits that Chester considered to be antique are the octagon-shaped posts and rounds, and the notches or incised lines that correspond with turnings. Neither quality is old-fashioned in the form manifested on Chester's chairs—although both are reflective of stages in the traditional process of turning chairs on a lathe.

On the legs of some chairs made in the past by other craftsmen one finds a few incised lines; they were not put there solely for decorative effect or out of nostalgia for the past. "Well, they do that so the mark will stay stationary there," explained Chester. "Don't matter whether they would sand it or whatever, the mark wouldn't disappear so they could see it right off. *An' hit really looks nice on a chair*—pencil mark or a mark caused by a chisel or a knife. You kin see it right on it. Those marks is put there while it's still in the turnin' lay. But I put my marks on there—used to—with a pocketknife. I jest marked an' rolled the post around on my legs."

Chairs that Chester made in 1966 and 1967, especially, had pencil marks all the way around each post at the places where holes were to be drilled, and Chester left them there. "Looks more handmade thataway," he said. Other chairmakers like Aaron erased or sanded off the pencil marks, but Chester had emphasized a trait he considered old-timey to such an extent that it became characteristic of him.

The eight-sided posts are not found on antique chairs either, but are peculiar to Chester's works from the mid-1950s through the 1960s. Chester's grandfathers, great-uncles, and other "ole-time chairmakers" did make posts eight-sided sometimes, using an ax, before turning them on the foot-powered turning lathe. Customers would not be likely to see this, of course, unless they were present during construction.

"You can't turn a square piece on a foot-powered turnin' lay," said Chester. The chairmaker would have to "split 'em out, then hew 'em out—you'd have to straighten 'em out with an ax—into eight-square finish with an ax, an' then you'd center that with a compass to find the center." At that point the post was turned on the lathe and chiseled into a cylindrical form.

Chester's first chairs were neither eight-sided nor turned.

"When I started makin' chairs I made 'em foursquare on accounta I wasn't strong enough to turn that turnin' lay myself. And the turnin' lay b'longed to my grandfather an' he, uh, he didn't like for the boys to prank with it, he was afraid they'd tear it up."

Chester made and occasionally used his own lathe, but it was cumbersome to handle, difficult to repair, and tiring to operate. It was virtually impossible for one man to wield a lathe effectively while turning posts and rounds. "It kinda gives your leg out an' makes it ache. You run it maybe four or five hours a day, if you've got a whole bunch of stuff to turn, it really gets you. It takes two big men to pedal one of them things all day."

"The last turnin' lay I made," said Chester in the mid-1960s, "hit's been about fifteen years ago." The power wheel broke. He could find nobody to weld it properly, he said, "an' it jest kept givin' me trouble, an' I jest quit plumb foolin' with a turnin' lay of any kind."

So how did he make chairs?

"I just turned loose an' started makin' it nothin' but hand-made—ever'thing by hand." That was about 1953, around the time when Ruth left.

During the years that followed, Chester developed in his own mind a distinction between handmade chairs with octagon-shaped pieces made with a drawing knife and homemade chairs produced by hand on a turning lathe. Both types differed from factory-made chairs, whose pieces were sawed by machinery in a factory, then glued, nailed, and screwed together.

"That ole man's a genius considerin' what he has to work with," said Hascal. "A man needs planers, jointers, and everything else to make chairs." Not Chester. All he needed, and all he ever really wanted, was a sharp instrument in his hands so that he could shape his raw materials as directly as possible.

CONTINUITIES AND CONTRADICTIONS

Perhaps the most interesting contradiction of all is that a man who tasted, smelled and felt the wood he worked with, and who wanted to be in contact with his materials, in 1967 bought himself planers, jointers, and everything else needed to make chairs. He made several chairs with the equipment, using the planer to shape eight-sided pieces of wood so the chairs would still be recognizable as his and would continue to be "old-fashioned."

He also used a router on the drill press to make notches on the

82 The New York rocker, one of
the last chairs Chester made
completely by hand (November
1966).   **83** A chair made in the
spring of 1967 after Chester
began using a planer and
router.

posts and rounds corresponding to the ornamentation he had previously cut by hand with a pocketknife. These uneven and irregular incisions with the router somewhat reduced the time and perhaps the labor of chairmaking, which Chester claimed was the reason for doing it this way. If rubbed with oil, the darkened notches were supposed to give the chair more of an antique appearance, which would make them "better lookin' " than those notched with a pocketknife.

To see the difference between chairs made before and after Chester obtained his new equipment, one need only compare the New York rocker (made for a customer in New York City in November 1966) and another one built a few months later (figs. 82 and 83, respectively). Chester hewed the wood for the New York rocker from a walnut log. He made the chair completely by hand, following the procedures I described in the first chapter. It is a bold form with sweeping lines. Chester made the second chair from wood he had purchased at a lumber company; he used his new planer to shape the posts and his router to add ornamentation.

Chester suffered many interruptions while working on the latter chair, which took him six or eight months to build. Two days before Christmas, his third son slipped on ice in the yard, fell, and broke his hip. Chester had to call on the services of a local mortuary to transport the boy to a hospital in Lexington. The mortuary charged $150 for the service, requesting Chester (who did not have the money) to make a copy of an eight-legged rocking chair with many decorated pegs that Chester had sold three years before to the owner of an automobile franchise across the street. Chester had other orders to fill. He did not understand why his son's hip was slow to heal or how to give him therapy. His relationship with Ruth, who had to stay with the boy in the hospital as well as care for the other children, was becoming increasingly strained. The machinery challenged him; he had not used such equipment since before the war.

Compare the details of the front posts and armrests on a chair made in mid-1966 (fig. 84) and on the chair that Chester made after he purchased new tools (fig. 85). The treatment of the wood on the earlier chair is more regular, consistent, harmonious. The

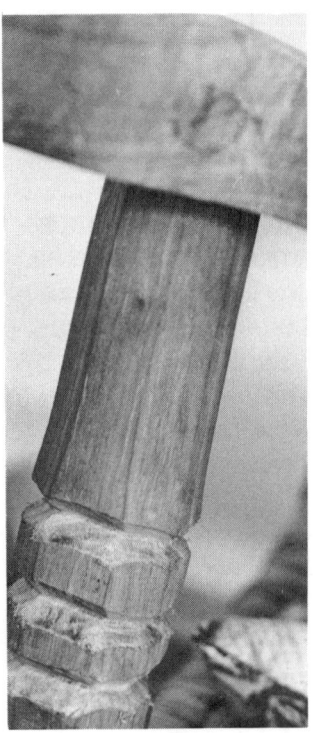

84 Detail of a chair similar to the New York rocker (but with straight front posts). **85** Detail of chair in figure 83, showing rough notching made with router.

ornamentation—almost understated—is sharply defined. Surface treatment of the later chair seems less clearly under Chester's control. The notching is rough, irregular.

The electrical equipment gave Chester the opportunity to produce the tables and cabinets ordered by outsiders that he could not make with simple hand tools. The equipment would also enable him to achieve a degree of standardization when orders became too numerous to fill by hand production alone. He hoped to reduce the hours of work as well. "Now it's a lot easier," he said. "That's what I always told ever'body anyhow. . . . On that machinery I wanna find out whether I can make a chair faster thataway or whether I can't. That's one thing I wanna find out. I still don't know. Hit's been thirty years since I used that machinery."

The equipment also would make possible the fullest expression of his art, or so he hoped. "Them shapers with bits can make all kinds a cuts and moldings and sash work and door-makin' and table shapin'," he said; "they's a wonderful thing, the shaper is." Unfortunately, Chester became increasingly "nervous"; seldom did he seem in command of the equipment.

The earlier clarity of line was no longer apparent in 1967 when he tried to use machinery. In contrast to the quieting stasis of his earlier ornamentation or the swiftly flowing lines of chairs with no notching at all, the irregularity of ornamentation on later chairs exhibits a feeling of nervous movement and visual excitation. Perhaps this reflects Chester's own inner turmoil at the time. If so, then maybe the feelings of uncertainty and loss of control were balanced by increasingly heavier chairs that stood tall and defensive.

At any rate, if Chester's chairs were really antique, they would be about 3½ feet, not 6 feet, high. To be truly old-fashioned, they would have three or four slats, not seven, nine, or ten slats that touched one another. To resemble chairs made in the past, they would not have pegs clearly in evidence, certainly not forty to two hundred, and the posts would be turned rather than left eight-sided, if they ever were hewed that way. To be antique, his chairs would not be constructed of four rockers and eight legs. It is even doubtful that they would have posts bent outward and backward—at least not to the extreme that Chester curved them.

All of these features were unique to Chester's works. They originated with various sources, including Chester's interpretation and transformation of elements in the chairs of other craftsmen, experimentation, and perhaps customer suggestion or at least reinforcement. Chester's style was conceptual and bold, in contrast to Aaron's, which was understated and delicate. But there seems to be more to understanding why Chester made things the way he did than the uniqueness of their separate features.

Many of Chester's chairs in the mid-1960s had to provide security and seclusion for his own protection from other people and from forces he could scarcely control, but they also had to be antique because of his nostalgia for the past. It mattered not that such chairs are unique rather than antique, for sometimes in Chester's mind they had be old-timers with walls, with high seats that "made you set away up high like a king or some'un," and with deeply curved slats that "hug you."

In the next chapter I examine Chester's search for financial and emotional security, his reclusiveness and desire for seclusion, and his struggle to maintain a sense of self-esteem. When considered in this context, the "two-in-one, bookcase rocker, masterpiece of furniture"—that strange chair that seemed to have a life of its own—becomes understandable at last.

FIVE
_____

Security, Seclusion
and Self-Esteem

"I was real sick that winter," said Chester. "I guess if a man gets to where he needs the money real bad, he has to give in to 'em."

He was referring to the sale of a black walnut two-in-one rocking chair and a walnut sewing rocker (figs. 86 and 87), both made in late 1963 or early 1964 and selling for $30 and $15, respectively. That sum of money was just enough for Chester to pay his rent and electric bill.

Chester had spent six weeks making the chairs. It was a cold winter day when he trudged through the snow on his way to Hazard, eight miles and two hills from home, hoping to convince the owner of a department store to buy the chairs. They were strapped to his back. Halfway to town Chester stopped at a roadside tavern to rest and warm himself. He met a man who offered to purchase the chairs for $45. Because Chester needed the money and was not sure he could make it to town in bad weather and poor health, he sold them on the spot, reluctantly agreeing to buy the customer a beer to bind the sale.

The man gave the chairs to his son and daughter-in-law. The latter did not like the two-in-one rocker, she told me, because the front rockers in the middle caught her heels when she rocked and the tops of the center posts in front got in the way of her legs. Both father and daughter puzzled over the large number of pegs on the rockers (fig. 88), the reason for which neither could divine; they concluded the pegs were "just for decoration."

"That two-in-one is a beautiful chair," commented Chester. "It's got quar rockers on hit down here. The rockers has got big pegs plumb all the way through 'em. On the top side of 'em. I think they're spaced about two inches apart. They look like big beads or buttons or some'un."

86 Chester's fourth two-in-one rocker, made of black walnut in late 1963 or early 1964, sold for $30.

87 A sewing rocker (hence no arms) that Chester made as a companion piece to the two-in-one rocker *opposite* and sold to the same buyer for $15.

88 Detail of chair in figure 86, showing pegs used to disguise mistake in drilling holes for the posts.

"Why did you make it that way?" I asked him.

"I don't know, I just thought I'd . . . ," he began to say, and probably would have attributed this feature to his propensity to experiment with design elements. But he stopped in midsentence, for there was another reason. "Well, one reason I made 'em was I made a mistake borin' the hole. And, uh, I decided, now, I can make a peg to fit that with a big round head on it. I went all through that on all four of them rockers with them things fixed like that. Boy, it made it a beauty. An' ever' round in it all the way around is pegged just like that big bookcase rocker you got. Ever' round is pegged with them big ole pegs."

Other customers, too, complained that the two-in-one chairs are not very comfortable because of the extra legs and rockers in the center front of the chair. The space between the center rockers is not large enough for most people to put both feet there. The sitter must carefully place his or her heels between whichever set of rockers makes this least awkward (imagine trying to back your feet into a pair of stirrups). The octagon-shaped seat is too deep for some people; their legs hang over the edge, and the tops of the front posts of the middle rockers press into the tendon behind the knee. And always the sitter must carefully place the feet so that a rocker will not jab the achilles tendon or ankle on the downswing.

If rocking in this kind of chair demands skill, think of the skill required to build it. Chester had to imagine a satisfactory way to bottom an octagon-shaped seat. He needed patience and skill to place the several legs properly on rockers, evident in the fact that he miscalculated on this chair and drilled the holes in the wrong place. Perhaps most difficult was figuring out the correct angles for the many stretchers.

The slats for an ordinary rocking chair are quarter bent, according to Chester; those for his two-in-one chairs are half bent, requiring additional time and effort. Blocks are inserted behind half-bent slats in the slat press to curve them properly. The effect of these half-bent slats in a chair is, however, "just like somebody huggin' you."

"It's regular difficult to get one 'em right," complained Chester, after he summarized the problems arising in the manufacture of a two-in-one chair.

Why make such chairs at all, given the criticisms by users and the many difficulties in production?

"I couldn't sell the cheap chair," he said, "so I just thought up that kinda chair."

The "cheap chair" was the five-slat rocker priced at about $25, or the settin' chair selling for about $12. Neither boasted much ornamentation, but both were durable, comfortable, and pleasing in appearance. Although Chester managed to sell the odd and fancy chairs to wealthier customers, the price was no more commensurate with the work required than the income from the cheap chairs had been. Besides, he continued to make cheap chairs on occasion.

Chester always had mixed feelings about his two-in-one rocking chairs, too. Sometimes he viewed them as attractive and appealing; at other times he said he did not like them, or they were too fancy for him. He may indeed have constructed the odd chairs to attract attention to himself and to sell more chairs at higher prices, but he was also experimenting with designs, manipulating form for its own sake, making conceptual statements about the design and use of chairs, and perhaps coping with situations that admitted no easy solutions. The half-bent slats were "like somebody hugging you"—just what Chester needed when his world opened onto the busy highway.

ODDITIES

In 1953, when Chester began making chairs exclusively with a drawing knife instead of turning them on a lathe, he created his first eight-legged side chair and then a seven-legged armchair (figs. 28 and 29). He had been experimenting with the chair parts and discovered that, because each piece he made had eight facets, each facet would accommodate a stretcher. As he pondered the concept of eight-sidedness, he realized he could make an octagon-shaped seat if he used eight posts; this would produce an interesting design—the octagonal seat repeating the octagonal shape of each post and stretcher. The next step, of course, was to add rockers and more slats to make a rocking chair, but he did not do this until his wife left him for the second time, a decade later.

89 One of Chester's few
upholstered chairs (about 1953).

He built a total of ten eight-legged chairs and five seven-legged armchairs in 1953 and 1954, and one seven-legged upholstered armchair in 1953 (fig. 89) that the owner later painted black. As far as I know, all of these chairs, except the upholstered one, were made of black walnut, a fact worth noting in itself; few craftsmen worked with this expensive, fragile wood that had become an index of social and economic status for the customer and that held special meaning when used by a craftsman for a chair of his own.

Chester was sitting by the roadside with the first of what would be ten eight-legged chairs. Dave Harley, the owner of a hardware store, happened by. "He seen me with that chair an' he talked me out of it—wanted to buy it." He paid Chester $2 or $3 for it. He also bought a seven-legged chair. "And the reason he bought it, now, he really didn't need 'em I don't guess," Chester told me in 1967. "He just bought 'em 'cause they was odd. I don't guess the man really needed 'em. He just bought 'em cause they was different. That's the first'un I ever made. Bet a feller couldn't buy that off'n him for $60, I bet."

Another chairmaker, Hascal, whom I met two years later and to whom I showed photos of many chairs, said that while the eight-legged chair was the most unusual settin' chair he had seen, he did not like it. "That back'll bump things when you turn the chair around." He added, "The design is all right. It's pretty. But that's a useless thing [the two legs in back] to have on a chair; it could be dangerous." Beechum, who worked in the chair shop with Hascal, said, "That I don't like. It should have only four posts. It'd be all right just to set back an' look at," but not to use. He echoed Hascal's criticism about the dangerousness of the back legs. To him, this was one of the ugliest chairs in all of the photographs I showed him.

Harley claimed credit for the seven-legged chair that Chester made later.

"I told him about what I'd like to have. 'Instead of getting your legs in so close,' I said, 'don't bunch 'em up so much.' I drew him out a little sketch on a piece of paper, you know. I guess that's the first one he ever put arms on. I guess I was the first man to ever get him started sandin' 'em."

Chester seldom sanded a chair. It took too much time, he did not enjoy the work, and most of his chairs were so carefully and precisely shaped with a drawing knife that he and many others felt that sanding was unnecessary. Harley varnished the chairs himself, which again Chester rarely did, so he could "leave 'em out in all types of weather."

Harley's comments evinced amazement at Chester's skill with a "few crude tools." He puzzled over Chester's "secret of chair-making" (i.e., the absence of glue and nails in most of his chairs). He concluded our conversation with the remark, "Chester doesn't have a worry in the world; he raises a garden in the summer and just loves to make chairs in the winter."

A chair that suggests that Chester did indeed enjoy the cre-

90 One of Chester's favorite chairs, a dining chair built for his daughter, Brenda, but later sold to buy her a pair of shoes.

ative task and use it as a form of expression is a black walnut dining chair that he constructed about 1961 (fig. 90), a year or so before Ruth left him. The chair is special in several respects. First, black walnut is rarely used in a chair that the craftsman intends for his own home. Second, it is the only true dining chair—as Chester conceptualized this category—of all the chairs to which Chester assigned this designation. It has a high seat, five slats, and overwhelming ornamentation, all of which preclude its being used to just sit and tip back in or lean against the wall. Although they were decorated and had relatively high seats, other dining chairs that Chester made from 1965 through 1967 had three slats like a settin' chair. Third, Chester hand-rubbed the chair with oil and then finished it with varnish, refinements he infrequently bestowed upon any chair, regardless of the price offered.

I asked Chester what his favorite chair was, excluding rockers.

"You mean the one I like best? The favorite chair in a settin' chair," he said, "I sold it to Miss [Naples], works at the employment office—black walnut."

At the time of its manufacture, this fancy walnut chair was in fact a settin' chair, despite its present dining-chair qualities. It did not have the hearts and some other ornamentation when it was first built. In addition, when he made this chair, Chester had not yet clearly differentiated between settin' chairs and dining chairs; he did not make such a distinction until five or six years later, about the time I met him, when he was trying to appeal to the values of wealthier clients.

Chester admitted that it is an "espensive" chair. "But if I ever make a complete dining room outfit for myself," which he never did, "I'm gonna make it on that design only with a wooden seat in it. "I like the backs the way they is made; they's real close together and the back rest is good in 'em." Chester had made the chair with a solid wood seat, but he replaced it with a bottom of white oak splints before he sold the chair.

"My brother said he wouldn't give me fifteen cents for that chair, but I like it," said the woman who bought it. "I was going to have Chester make me a table and chairs till I got this other table" (a factory-made piece).

One unusual feature of the chair is that Chester carved a heart in the center of each slat. And why not? He had made the chair specifically for his daughter Brenda, vowing never to sell it. About five years after its manufacture, Brenda told me it was her favorite of all the chairs her father had built, but of course she no longer had it. Chester sold it to Miss Naples because winter was setting in and young Brenda needed shoes.

Sometimes Chester created chairs and then sought buyers. On other occasions he made chairs on order and according to customer specifications. In the case of the chair in figure 91, he did both. Chester had made a chair somewhat similar to this one that he had sold to a local barber. The man requested another. He

91 Chester sold this ten-slat sassafras rocker about 1961 for $40.

wanted ten slats in the back rather than the usual five or seven, Chester said, and he wanted them deeply curved to give him greater back support. The barber offered Chester $50 for the chair plus extra for the additional slats.

Made in 1963, the chair is sassafras with black walnut pegs. The front posts are flared at the top. The back posts flare out and back a third of the way down from the top at about the seventh slat. A couple of years later, Chester bent the back posts at about seat level for greater stability and balance on chairs of such height (about six feet, sometimes more). There are stiles on the back posts above the armrests. Each of the ten slats is held in place with double pegs at both ends. The relatively thin armrests also are pegged from the top into the front post, and then that peg is pegged below the armrest to prevent its pulling out. It would have been simpler to have made the armrests thicker, which Chester did on chairs made a couple of years later.

For some reason the barber reneged. Hefting the chair onto his back, Chester trudged the streets of town in search of a buyer. Finally, a man named Johnson who worked at a parts store bought it for $40. His wife did not know who made the chair. But she really liked it, she said (her brother-in-law envied it, she told me, and wanted one like it). She kept the chair indoors; indeed, it was in the living room near the front door—the first object one saw upon entering the house. She added a thin cushion for greater comfort.

On many other chairs after this one, Chester added ornamentation (this one has no notching). He said he was trying to attract wealthier customers.

About 1965 Chester had begun to bend the top stretcher—the seat round—in the same curvature as the slats for appearance, comfort, and, he said, to attract interest in his chairs.

"Hit makes it comf'tabler an' also makes hit look better, an' people got kinda tired of the reg'lar-lookin' things an' I hada change it around a little bit to get more sales," he explained.

"Did it help?"

"Hit didn't improve much. Hit didn't improve wouldn't say but a little bit. Specially on the rockin' chair. I guess hit'd be 'bout, uh, 'bout twelve rockin' chairs that I done like this. An' a mighty few settin' chairs."

The earliest chair I saw with a rounded seat in the back is the settin' chair that Chester made in August 1965 (fig. 37). The chair had a special seat and double pegs of contrasting color because it was to go to a museum. I am aware of only one rocking chair with a rounded seat (fig. 24) and two dining chairs with rounded seats that Chester made just before working on the rocking chair (fig. 41, on right; also fig. 23).

I watched Chester weave the seat of the museum settin' chair (fig. 22). Lacking nails, he drove screws into the top seat round about every three quarters of an inch. The screws were to keep the bark splints from slipping as he bottomed the chair, he said. But the screws did not stay in place. Finally he abandoned the idea, pulling the screws out before he had finished weaving the seat. I wondered at the time whether the problems were caused only by the lack of nails or whether Chester was really not accustomed to the technique.

The idea for bending the seat stretcher may have been stimulated by Chester's manufacture of two-in-one chairs with octagonal seats. Perhaps he included some of them in his count of a dozen chairs, but he was not specific about the source of this design element.

"I just thought that up myself," he said. "Not many people notices that. No there ain't, there shore ain't. Ain't many people notices that that buy a chair—a rockin' chair or a settin' chair, either one. I've had two or three to notice hit," which may well include Chester, my wife, and me. "'Bout two or three is all."

Such a remark makes one doubt that changing the appearance of a chair for the sake of increased sales is the principal or only motive. Yet that was the reason he gave for making two-in-one rocking chairs, beginning in late 1961 or early 1962.

"If you make a simple thing you gotta sell at a simple price," Hascal said, "and Chester's tryin' to make a livin' at it." The corollary would be that you must make a complex thing to sell it at a higher price.

"These are just a marvel to look at as art," said Hascal in regard to Chester's two-in-one rocking chairs. "I respect any man that's got the patience. He oughta get five thousand dollars for that chair," meaning the mayor's rocking chair, for which Chester received $100. "Musta taken a month and a half of solid work to make that."

The first two-in-one rocking chair that Chester created in late 1961 consists of white walnut with black walnut double pegs (fig. 35). It is one of the earliest examples of Chester's using two pegs at the end of each slat in a rocking chair. The chair also has extensive notchings, which was unusual in late 1961 when this chair was made. Chester said several times that the rocker required 356 hours to make, and he asked $300 for it, but no one wanted it at any price, regardless of how many hours of work he had put into it.

Ed Nunn did not want the chair either, but Chester stopped by his shop and his home so many times trying to sell it to him that he finally paid Chester $50 for it and spent another $50 to have it sanded and varnished.

Chester built his second two-in-one rocker a few months later, in 1962 (fig. 92). This redbud chair, purchased by Phil Banks, who owned an automobile franchise in town, is one of the few with spokes under the arms similar to those in Chester's early square-post, panel-back chair (fig. 93; compare with chair in fig. 64). The chair measures 47 inches in height. The eight deeply curving slats are about 1⅛ inches apart where they join the posts; they almost touch each other toward the center. The posts measure 1¾ inches in diameter. The back posts are 23½ inches apart at the top, narrowing to 19¼ inches at the seat. The seat is 21¾ inches deep. The rockers are 30 inches long; those in the center are 6 inches apart, and the outside rockers have about 3¼ inches of space between them and the center rockers. The curvilinear armrests are 1½ inches thick; they measure slightly under 25 inches from their top surface to the bottom of the outside rocker, suggesting that the seat is relatively low (about a foot from the floor). The spindles beneath the armrests are 12½ inches long, with about 2 inches of space between them. The pegs holding the armrests in place are 1¼ inches in diameter; those on the stiles of the back posts and on the finials are about ⅝ inch.

This second two-in-one rocking chair is the first to have elongated finials; 3½ inches long, they measure 1½ inches across at their widest point and 1¼ inches thick. Chester's first chair like this, and the next four, have mushroom-shaped finials. He used elongated finials again on his seventh two-in-one rocking chair, the Bookcase Masterpiece (and on a chair similar to the Dolph rocker ordered in 1966).

This was his first chair with so many pegs—eighty or ninety— all of which have been carved with a pocketknife in a pattern of alternating ridges and grooves. Chester did not know where he got the idea for the peg heads, but the motif is common and may be seen on the glass or plastic pieces used to hold mirrors on the walls in service station rest rooms in the area, although Chester may have conceived of the design independently. He used decorated pegs on only two other chairs, the Bookcase Masterpiece and the rocking chair that he revised for himself in 1967.

92 Chester's second two-in-one rocker (early 1962) is about fifty inches tall and has eighty or ninety hand-carved pegs with grooved heads.   **93** Detail shows spokes under the arms of the rocker, which Chester said he had not used since the 1930s.

"I don't like that there design on a rockin' chair for myself a-tall," said Chester. "Lot a people does." He claimed that the decorated pegs especially are "too fancy for me," but that was before he had made them for himself.

The second two-in-one rocker and the Dolph rocker were manufactured only for "rich people wantin' somethin' differ'nt," Chester contended. "That chair's too fancy for a poor man," he said in reference to Banks's rocker (fig. 91). "Takes a rich man to buy stuff like that. Hit's really beautiful, hit really looks handmade, but it's too espensive for me. If I was wantin' one fer myself I'd like that one Smith has" (fig. 33).

Banks paid Chester $75 for the chair, which Chester said took him about three months to make. Coated with paste wax for protection, the rocker sits in the corner of Banks's office.

"Chester's quite a character, isn't he?" said Banks, trying to make small talk as I examined the chair. "He doesn't have a worry in the world; he loves to sit out there and make chairs." Banks was sitting at his desk piled high with bills, receipts, and invoices; with a far-off look in his eyes, he seemed to be contemplating Chester's life for a moment. "He doesn't have a thing to worry about. Or at least if he has, he doesn't worry about it. I wish I were as lucky. What do you think of that old man? Yes, sir, he's quite a character," repeated Banks, shaking his head and shuffling the papers on his desk.

The mayor's chair (fig. 42), differing from its predecessors in being made mostly of woven hickory bark panels, was the third two-in-one that Chester was to build. He said, "If that bark was laid together it'd run plumb acrost the United States," which is why he made only one other chair of this type (his eighth two-in-one rocker), in the winter of 1966 at the special request of a woman in the area who then moved to the Midwest. The duplicate is taller but narrower; it has slender, elongated finials instead of mushroom-shaped ones.

In 1965 Chester told me that the mayor's chair was the prettiest chair he had made because it required the most work, he received the best price for it, and it attracted the greatest amount of attention.

"A hunnert people saw that chair when the mayor first bought it," said Alvin Hampton, who owns the swamp willow chair that

Chester made earlier (fig. 69) and who thinks Chester is "the best chairmaker I've ever known. He's always been a chair-maker. He takes the time an' he's got the patience." Some people, he said, thought $100 was too much money for the mayor's chair, "but there's a lot a work in it."

Everywhere I asked about Chester's chairs, people enthusi-astically directed me to the mayor's chair or Dolph's chair, or the Dolph rocker. It was on the basement level of the mayor's depart-ment store, so probably most people in town saw it. After the mayor bought the chair (I think in early 1963), an illustrated article appeared in the local newspaper calling attention to the chair, to the mayor, and to Chester (this was the first public notice of Chester of which I am aware).

Chester's fourth two-in-one rocker (made in late 1963 or early 1964) is the one mentioned at the beginning of this chapter (figs. 85 and 87). Unlike the first two and several subsequent chairs of this type, the fourth one does not have notching on the posts and rounds. Chester did, however, put a notch at the end of each slat where it joins the posts. And, of course, there are many pegs, including double pegs on the stiles and the rockers (the latter to disguise a mistake in drilling holes for the posts).

The fifth two-in-one rocker that Chester made (fig. 94) was constructed during the winter of 1964-65 of black walnut; the hickory pegs contrast with the darker walnut. It has seven slats. Earlier two-in-one rockers have eight slats, except the very first one, which has six slats. The chair measures 53 inches in height—6 inches taller than Banks's chair. The slats are notched at the ends where they join the posts. The top slat is 3¼ inches wide; the others diminish slightly in width down to the last and narrowest one.

The rockers measure 31½ inches long; the center rockers are 7 inches apart, and the outside rockers are about 5 inches away from the center ones. The rockers are only about 1¼ inches square; they were not cooked and put in a press but were dressed from a bolt of wood of this shape. Chester explained to me that he did not have as much raw material from which to work as he wanted; hence, the smallness of the rockers. He sold the chair to a man in Knoxville, who returned in 1966 to have him replace the rockers with larger ones. Chester never did this

94 Chester's fifth two-in-one rocker, of black walnut with hickory pegs, was made in the winter of 1964-65. This is one of the earliest examples of Chester's use of contrasting pegs.

because by then he was too busy trying to keep up with the orders he had begun to receive.

In November 1965, Chester began work on another two-in-one rocking chair—the Bookcase Masterpiece. Like the earlier ones, it was not ordered by anyone. Unlike its predecessors, it was not constructed from wet wood but built with boards purchased from a lumber company. Because of the number of orders he was receiving, Chester would make more chairs after this from kiln-dried, sawed boards than he would from trees that he cut in the hills or logs from a sawmill.

The eighth and ninth two-in-one rocking chairs were made according to customer demand and specifications. The eighth chair was built on order for a local woman who wanted one like the Dolph rocker. I never saw the chair, but Chester's description

95 Chester had to build this sassafras two-in-one rocker (late spring, 1967) to pay for ambulance service for his crippled son.

of it suggested that he simplified the construction to make it more quickly than he had its forerunner. Chester made the ninth two-in-one rocking chair (fig. 95) out of sassafras during the late spring of 1967 for Melvin Begley, who owned a funeral home across from Phil Banks's car franchise. "They varnished it," Chester told me, "and said hit's the prettiest thing ever was," though Chester did not seem particularly attracted to the chair.

Begley provided the ambulance service to transport Chester's son to the hospital after Lester slipped on the ice and broke his hip. Begley asked Chester to repay him with a chair exactly like the one owned by Banks.

"That am'blance is chargin' me $45 to take Lester down there an' back. First three trips I made 'im a rockin' chair to pay for the trips. He allowed me three—b'lieve it was three trips—or was it four? Had to pay 'im $25. An' I still owe 'im $25. That's the way hit was; he allowed me four trips."

Begley placed the chair in the reception room of the funeral home, but later he moved it to small living quarters on the second floor. The chair differs in several ways from Banks's.

Because many people had complained about the front rockers of the two-in-one chair "bitin' their heels," Chester varied the angle of the rounds so that the two center posts in front would not project so far forward; "that's the reason on the last chair I drawed them posts in a lot," said Chester.

While somewhat more comfortable than earlier two-in-one rockers, Begley's chair lacks the complexity of design found in Banks's rocker. Chester had no intention of duplicating the earlier rocker. The chair that he ultimately sold to Banks was a tour de force. It required months to construct, and as apparent in the careful attention to detail and the meticulous rendering and synthesizing of complex elements, it was an act of total involvement on Chester's part. The chair was made not to someone else's specifications, but in accordance with Chester's own predilections at the time.

In contrast, Begley's chair was made by a man who simply did not want to make the chair at that time and who felt imposed upon because of Lester's accident. When Chester initially told me about having had to make the rocker for Begley, his tone was bitter. No doubt it was a disconcerting interruption at a time when Chester had pressing commitments to other people for many chairs and when the value of the ambulance service was equal to what Chester was then getting for an ordinary seven-slat rocking chair of black walnut. Chester made the rocking chair rather grudgingly and with little interest, as is evident in the absence of notching, the presence of six rather than seven slats, the use of very wide bark in the seat (which can be woven rather quickly), and the simplicity of design.

SHORTCUTS AND SIMPLIFICATIONS

Another example of simplification in construction and design is a series of chairs Chester made in late 1965 and early 1966, right after he built the Bookcase Masterpiece (for example, figs. 96 and

96 Under pressure to meet demands for chairs precipitated by an article in a national newspaper, Chester started buying boards from a lumberyard, which he did not cook or bend (photo by Chester).

97). The form derived directly from the Abner chair of a few months earlier, but resulted more from the desire to speed up production than from Chester's wanting to make chairs with an old-timey quality.

Chester discovered when making the Abner chair that it took much less time to mortise the holes completely through the posts, and then insert the slats and saw them off to the right length, than it did to *not* mortise the holes too deeply and to measure the slats precisely to fit. He had done this on the Abner chair because the log he used had only enough wood for posts 1⅛ inches in diameter after dressing—too thin to secure the joints the way he was accustomed to doing. He knew he could build a chair even more quickly if he did not have to cook and

97 One of four rocking chairs made quickly to fulfill orders. The slats and stretchers extend through the posts (photo by Chester).

bend the slats and posts, or dress the posts and rounds eight-sided with his drawing knife. Not having to locate logs, get them to his house, and hew them would further reduce the time needed to construct a chair. Having developed this design partly by accident, partly by necessity, and partly by identification with the characters and furniture in the Li'l Abner comic strip, Chester then relied upon it to meet the sudden flood of orders for his chairs.

Chester seemed to be seeking a wealthier clientele. That was the reason given for creating the odd chairs, he said. A local article about the Dolph rocker in 1963 led to another essay in the *Hazard Herald* in the spring of 1965, and then an article in the *Louisville Courier-Journal* in June. Chester got his break a few months later when David Hacker, a staff writer for the *National Observer,* published an article about him.

"Lettres Went to comin in froum East South North West Wantin to no if they Culd Buy a Laddre Back Rockker and they said they Engoid Redin About me in the natin advzer new Papre," Chester wrote to us at the end of December 1965. "I try to ancer Ever Lettre and tell thim that I dinton have iney." I do not know how many people wrote to him for information. But during the next six months he filled orders for a settin' chair for a person in Plainfield, Illinois; a child's rocker for someone in Pittsburgh; and at least six rocking chairs for people in New York, Illinois, North Carolina, Oregon, Colorado, and Michigan. He also tried to sell his masterpiece to Loughhead, and he revised a counter stool (brought to him for repair) by substituting double pegs for single ones so he could photograph them for prospective customers.

At least four rocking chairs, including the two illustrated here, were made very early in 1966. Under extreme pressure, Chester took shortcuts. He purchased red oak boards from a lumber company for all the pieces of the chair. Because he could not cook and bend the posts, since they were sawed both across and with the grain and would have broken, he set them at a slight angle for greater comfort in the chair and also tipped the front posts outward slightly. The chairs are more compact because the boards he purchased for slats were all 19 inches in length; he lost upwards of 3 inches of this length when he extended the slats through the posts.

He had the armrests and rockers milled (at a cost of $4.50 per hour). He also paid the lumber company to saw the wavy slats with a jigsaw (reminiscent of the McIntosh chair in fig. 30 but, of course, not bent). Although he had been using double pegs, he put only one large peg at the end of each slat in these chairs.

Later he admitted to me, in regard to the wavy slats, "I jest don't like the looks of hit, the design of hit." He said he preferred slats that were straight along the bottom edge and rounded on the top.

Chester had been deluged with queries and orders. People who read the article in the *National Observer* and ordered chairs expected to get fancy, pegged, handmade chairs such as those described. The price given was $79. But Chester really wanted $89 to $100 plus the cost of making a crate (which took a day or two) and shipping (sometimes he did not include the cost of a taxi to take the crated chair to the freight office in Hazard).

Chester sent us Polaroid photos of the chairs in early 1966, but without comment. When I asked him about them in August 1966, he was evasive. Later, when pressed, he admitted quickly (and then let the subject pass) that he had made four rocking chairs and two dining chairs under considerable pressure. Apparently he was displeased with and embarrassed by the chairs.

The principal model for the rocking chairs that Chester used shortcuts on was the Abner chair. He had built it on his own, not on order. A year and a half to two years before, sometime in 1963, he had constructed another rocking chair of his own volition. He conceived of it as old fashioned, too, referring to it as the Old-Timer. The person he ostensibly created it for did not live long enough to see it. She had not ordered a chair, nor did she know Chester was building one for her.

In late 1963 or early 1964 Chester sold the chair he had made for Hattie Tuggle to an unidentified tourist from Lexington, receiving half the $127 he was asking for it. Before he sold the chair, Chester took two photographs of it with a box camera (fig. 98). The chair has nine wide slats that nearly touch each other, with double pegs at each end of the slats. The thick posts are capped with mushroom-shaped finials. Chester bent the posts backward and outward near the top rather than at seat level (which he would do later on chairs of such height). The seat is about two feet from the floor, which is extraordinarily high for a rocking chair. There is a woven basket beneath the seat into which a footrest slides when not in use, much like the Dolph rocker built a few months to a year before.

"That was the most beautiest chair, I mean for a reg'lar rockin' chair, I ever made," Chester told me in June 1967.

A few months before he made the Old-Timer, Chester had built half a dozen black walnut high chairs for the arthritic Mrs. Tuggle, for which he received $10 each. These chairs have roomy seats that are lower—therefore closer to the floor—than is usual

98 Chester's only Old-Timer
(early 1963; photo by Chester).
The seat is high, 24 inches from
the floor, so that an arthritic
woman could more easily sit
down.

in high chairs or counter stools. He did this so that Mrs. Tuggle
would not have to climb in and out of them, which might pain
her joints, but could ease into them without bending much.
Chester "took a notion" to make the Old-Timer for her, too,
which is why its seat is so much higher than is usual in a rocking
chair; ordinarily the distance from seat to floor is twelve to
fourteen inches, about the same as in a settin' chair.

"You got to make a chair to rest in comfortable, you got to
make 'em pretty low," he said, but he made the seat in this
rocking chair pretty high.

In November 1965, Chester and I discussed the Old-Timer.
"How many big chairs have you made?" I asked him.

"Well, last winter I made the two-in-one, and, uh, winter
before that I made an 'Old-Timer'—I call it that. It's, uh, a big
chair with a real high back and a real high seat an' it had a footrest
that would fold up in front, and when you set down you could

reach that footrest an' it made you set away up high like a king or some'un."

At that point Chester laughed nervously. It was the same peculiar jittery laugh that followed his remark that the half-bent slats are "like somebody huggin' you" as well as other comments that were not funny or intended to be joking statements.

"I called it an 'Old-Timer,'" he repeated. "I sold it to a man down in Lexington, Kentucky. I don't remember his name. I just only made one of 'em. If they wasn't so much work an' so much expense—I couldn't get more'n half of what I asked for it an' so I never did try no more of 'em—like the mayor's bookcase rocker, I never did try no more of 'em" (although he did make a bookcase rocker the following year on special demand, which he sold for $169).

On numerous occasions Chester justified his having built odd chairs as an attempt to increase sales by appealing to those looking for something different. Or he said he was seeking a wealthier clientele. Or he implied that he was trying to increase the base price of all his chairs. Or he said he could not sell the cheap chairs to anyone so he thought up the complex chairs in order to have any sales at all.

Sometimes these justifications seemed to be reinforced. Dave Harley bought an eight-legged side chair for $2 or $3 because it was odd, he said, and he encouraged Chester to build a seven-legged chair. Ed Nunn purchased Chester's first two-in-one rocking chair for $50 because of its uniqueness. The mayor gave Chester a $100 bill for his woven-bark bookcase rocker; it was the kind of chair he could donate to the White House because of its unusualness. Several articles about Chester's chairs in a variety of publications led to invitations to participate in regional craft shows and eventually to show in Washington, D.C. Perhaps Chester was correct in his justifications.

He sold the odd chairs that he made in the mid-1950s for the same amount, and up to about twice as much, as he received for ordinary chairs (i.e., $3 to $5 for eight-legged chairs as opposed to $2 to $3 for the normal settin' chairs). In the early 1960s he sold his first four two-in-one rocking chairs, most of which he claimed had taken 350 to 500 hours to build, for $50, $75, $100, and $30, respectively, as opposed to the $18 he normally received for an ordinary five-slat rocking chair. To sell the rocking chairs at all, he had to pack them on his back and tramp through town, knocking on the doors of shopkeepers and home owners until he found someone who would bargain with him, paying him the lowest price he would consider. "I guess if a man gets to where he needs the money real bad, he has to give in to 'em," said Chester. In other words, the odd chairs did not bring him more money when one considers the greater time and effort to build them and find buyers for them.

Chester certainly needed money. In 1965 he had a wife and five children to feed and clothe. His rent was $22 per month; his electric bill was about $10 every other month. He received $50 a month from the government for his service-related disability. In the summer, he sold a few dollars' worth of field corn, sweet potatoes, and gourds from his garden. And he made chairs. He kept a ledger during 1965, but what he recorded was *income*, not income and expense (fig. 99).

About this time Gurney Norman or someone else who had taken an interest in Chester noticed that the family was not on welfare. The amount of food stamps a family was eligible for depended on income. Perhaps this is why Chester began keeping a record of sales of gourds and chairs. At any rate, not long after this, Wendell Berry published an article in *The Nation* called "The Tyranny of Welfare"; in describing the inequities and injustices of the system, he used Chester as an example of how a family in dire straits had their eligibility for food stamps appreciably reduced every time the craftsman worked, selling a chair for whatever he could get.

Most of Chester's sales (quantity, not income) were for dipper gourds—dried squashes in which he had cut a hole. In September, 1965, for example, he sold more than fifty gourds at 50 cents each. He also received income from repairing chairs. According to the articles in the *Hazard Herald* and the *Louisville Courier-Journal*, he had sold two chairs that winter. His ledger for January reads: "One Rocker 2 in 1 Regler P [price] $269.00 Sold for $30.00" (that would have been his fifth two-in-one chair—the one that the customer returned the next year because the rockers

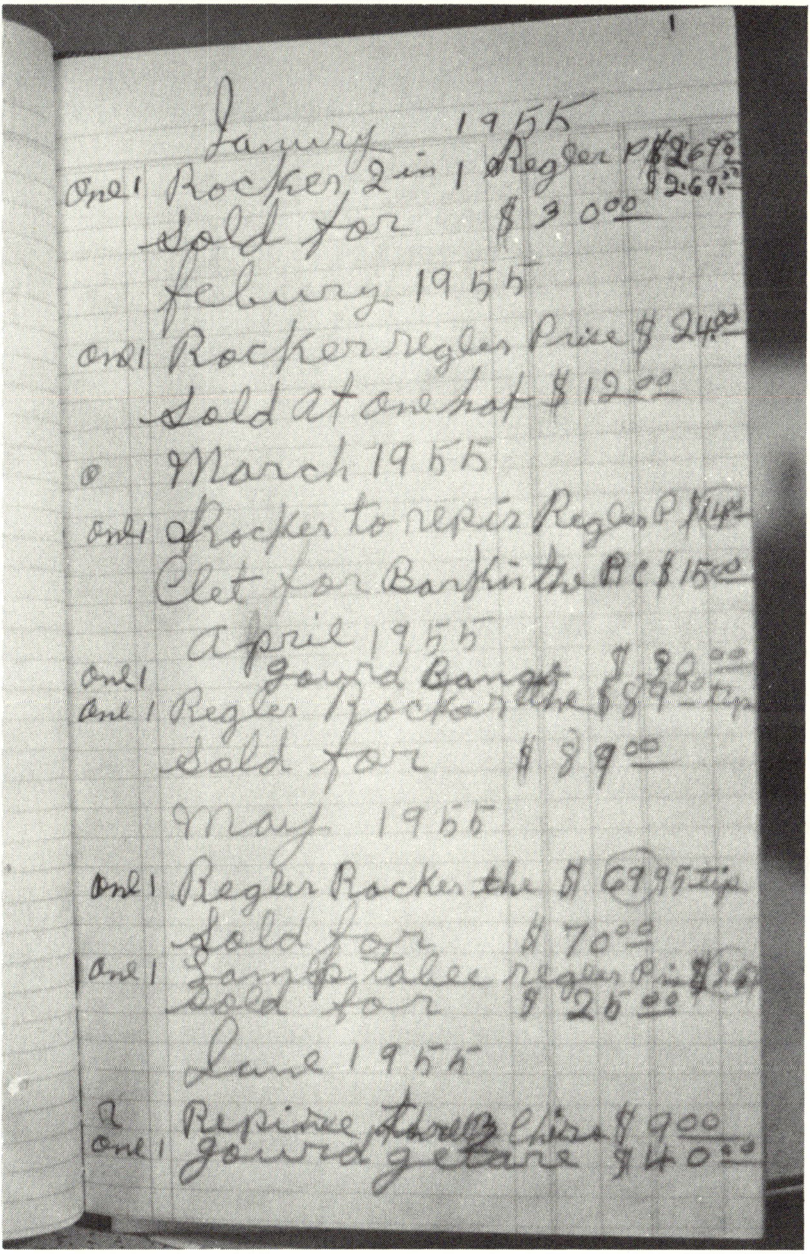

January 1955
One 1 Rocker 2 in 1 Regler P $26⁹⁵
Sold for $30.00

Febuary 1955
One 1 Rocker Regler Price $24.00
Sold at one half $12.00

March 1955
One 1 Rocker to repir Regler P $14
Clet for Barkin the B C $15.00

April 1955
One 1
One 1 Regler Rocker the $89.00
Sold for $89.00

May 1955
One 1 Regler Rocker the $69.95
Sold for $70.00
One 1 Lamp table regler P $26
Sold for $25.00

June 1955
One 1 Repire Chis $9.00
One 1 get one $40.00

99 One page from a ledger that Chester kept in 1965 and 1966
(erroneously dated 1955).

were too small). For February there is also only one entry: "Rocker regler Prise $24.00 Sold at one haf $12.00."

Chester noted in April that he had sold a gourd banjo for $30 and a regular rocker for $89. In May he sold a regular rocker for $70 and a lamp table for $25. He repaired a chair for $9 and sold a gourd guitar for $40 in June. In July he sold a rocker for $69.95, the Abner chair for $70, a book rack for $8, and a gun rack for $8; he earned $10 and then another $3 for repairing chairs. The chairs that he sold for $70, he indicates, were priced at $69.95; he refers to the difference as a "tip."

Business was better in August. To the $554 he had grossed the first seven months of the year was added $50 for a gourd banjo (for which he had asked $75), $70 for a regular rocker, $18 for a child's rocker (he had requested $35), $12 for another child's rocker, $15 for a settin' chair, $35 for yet another child's rocker, $16 for a footstool, and $17 for another settin' chair.

During September he sold only dipper gourds, grossing about $25, and six ears of corn and a few sweet potatoes for $2.25; he also repaired a chair for $5.50.

In October he sold more gourds and a few sweet potatoes for about $53, two settin' chairs for $33.90, and a rocker for $90. He also received $20 for "interetame Ment," having taken part in a local fair.

The next month he sold a peck of potatoes for $1.50, some dipper gourds for $12.75, an ax handle for $2.50, one rocker for $90, and two "dinin table chires" for $60.

There are two entries for December, one in the amount of $100 for a rocking chair and the other for $20 for "one diner Chire."

His income in 1965 from his efforts was slightly over $1,300; he also received $600 in disability benefits, so the total income was about $1,900. His wife's son-in-law, with no children or health problems, drew $5,000 a year through employment with a mining company. Families on welfare exclusively were receiving up to $1,920 in food stamps and other benefits.

It had been a good year for Chester. He had finally sold several chairs at the prices he wanted. By the end of 1965 he no longer had to accept, say, $30 for a two-in-one rocking chair or $12 for a regular rocking chair.

He kept records for 1966, in case he netted more than $2,000 and would have to pay income tax. His ledgers for 1966 indicate that he ceased to sell vegetables and dipper gourds; that in no instance did he have to negotiate price, accepting less for his chairs; and that for every sale he recorded not only income but also expense. (Because he had begun to purchase materials and even services from a lumber company, he had out-of-pocket costs.)

He had no income in January 1966. In February, March, April, and early May he sold five rocking chairs for $89 each that had cost a total of $75 in lumber and milling charges. He sold a chair modeled after the Dolph rocker for $169 (costing $22 in materials) and a dining chair for $40 (that cost $11). By midyear he had grossed $654 and spent $108 for materials and services.

In August he sold two gourd banjos for $190 that had cost $69 for materials and the Bookcase Masterpiece for $200 that had cost $89. The next month he sold a song stand for $14 and a stool for $40 that had cost him $4 and $20, respectively. In October he received $25 for one day's work at a fair, which he entered in his ledger as "inertament." He sold a child's rocker for $79 in November; it had cost him $18. The same month he sold a table lamp for $25, a lamp table for $25, and a rocking chair for $125 at no cost for materials (he made them from a walnut log I had bought for him in August from a sawmill and hauled to his house). He sold another walnut rocker in December for $150 (at a cost of $40), along with a red oak rocker at $125 (that cost $25).

Chester wrote in his ledger following the entries for December:

totle in all	$1398.00
Caust in all to make	635.00
net Profit in all	865.00

According to my calculations from his records, however, Chester grossed $1,627 from his chairs and $25 for demonstrating his craft at a fair. The materials and charges for labor came to $400. Thus he netted $1,279 (excluding the $600 pension and whatever he might have obtained, if anything, through the food stamp program).

It does not really matter which set of calculations is correct; the implications are the same. Chester's income was low, even in the best of years. In addition, he made many more chairs in 1966 than he did in 1965, selling them at substantially higher prices than he had before; although his income in 1965 and 1966 was many times greater than it had been in earlier years, and the highest in 1966, he actually netted less that year under pressure to meet an ever-increasing demand for his chairs.

Moreover, Chester did not indicate in his ledgers the costs incurred in 1966 for Ruth's pregnancy and the birth of their daughter in the spring. Nor did he note the expenses resulting from Lester's breaking his hip the day before Christmas and having to be transported by ambulance to Lexington, where he was hospitalized for several weeks.

Chester had financial worries. Perhaps he did indeed make odd chairs to attract attention to himself, creating strange chairs when he could not sell the ordinary rockers (but also making "cheap chairs" when he received little for the expensive chairs). Financial problems lay beneath marital ones; in the late 1940s and early 1950s he tried other kinds of work at Ruth's insistence, and she left him in the mid-1950s and again in the early 1960s because of their poverty and isolation. If Ruth expressed her concerns through her actions, then presumably Chester did also.

THE OLD-TIMER AND THE MASTERPIECE

Sometimes there were inconsistencies in what Chester did, or contradictions between words and deeds. The Old-Timer is a case in point. He said he made it for a specific customer, but she never ordered a chair. He created a rocking chair with a high seat allegedly for this arthritic person to get in and out of easily (comparable to some counter stools she had ordered from him earlier). He also designed a footrest for her comfort; however, it would have required her to straighten her legs once she was seated and bend them again to get out. She would also have had to bend forward and use wrist motion to remove the legrest, to extend it, and then to withdraw it. She was an elderly woman, and not particularly tall, but this rocker with nine wide slats was the tallest Chester had built.

"Why did you make the Old-Timer?" I asked Chester in November 1965.

"Well, there was an old lady in Hazard, I don't recall her name [he did a few days later], but she's passed along now—she was gettin' well up in the years an' she couldn't hardly set down or get up—an' she got me to make her six big high-back armchairs that she could set down in. An' I took a notion to make this rockin' chair an' make it in that design an' ever'thing so she could set down in hit an' get up easy. Made a footrest that folds up here in front for her to rest her feet in so her feet wouldn't have to be on the floor. Make a chair real high like that so she could set—that's really what caused me to make a chair like that. She passed on b'fore I got the chair done. I b'lieve I could a sold it to her if I could a got it done."

"How tall was the chair?"

"I don't recall how tall the chair was, but the seat was 'bout twenty-four inches from the floor up to the seat," so the chair must have been between six and seven feet tall.

"Is that the usual height?"

"I usually make a chair, from the floor up to the seat, 'bout fourteen or fifteen inches to rest in. Now to make a chair to rest in you got to make 'em pretty low. Like a davenneck chair—these here upholstered chairs?—they're mighty low chairs to set down in. If you wanna rest comf'tably in a chair you gotta make it so you kin stretch your legs out an' rest. If you make any kinda chair an' you're gonna set in it, you gotta make it kinda low to rest in. Like these dinin' room chairs like I made for you—they're made with extry high seats, you see."

The Old-Timer is certainly not the kind of chair one could rest in (perhaps not even an elderly arthritic woman), for "if you wanna rest comf'table in a chair, you gotta make it so you can stretch your legs out an' rest." Chester was too small a man—only about 5 feet 6 inches or perhaps 5 feet 8 inches tall—to rest in this chair. For what other purpose would one use a rocking chair, then, if not to rest in?

When describing the Old-Timer, as he called it, Chester had said that the high seat in this chair "made you set away up high like a king or some'un."

The contradiction between making a rocking chair to rest in

and then not being able to rest in it because the seat is too high, and Chester's having drawn an analogy between the chair and a throne suggest that the chair might have been symbolic.

The first and third bookcase rockers were "masterpieces." But the Old-Timer "was the most beautiest chair, I mean for a reg'lar rockin' chair, I ever made," Chester told me in June 1967.

The Old-Timer and the Masterpiece have in common an association with the past, the first chair through the name Chester gave it, and the second through the inscription "Old, Kentucky." Both chairs are impressive structures. The Old-Timer is imposing because of the height of its seat and the height of its back; the nine very wide slats that nearly touch each other seem to climb higher and higher until they finally stop, looking like an armor breastplate. Of heavy, impenetrable walls, the Bookcase Masterpiece surrounds the sitter.

It is easy to imagine these two chairs, and some others that Chester made, generating a feeling of power and control as well as a sense of protective seclusion. The two factors are closely related—one has power and control in the world that he himself creates. It would be in character for such qualities to express Chester's desire to isolate himself from others and to control what went on around him. As Jung suggests, "A lonely island where only what is permitted to move moves, becomes the ideal." These chairs could offer Chester control and protection, security and power, because they are very large, they elevate the sitter above others, and they surround the person using them.

But Chester also at times had a marked nostalgia for the past, which he romanticized. He would like to have lived in the past, or lived *as in* the past. Pine Mountain was his ideal of a "lonely island" where he was in control of events. Perhaps that is why he conceived of the masterpiece chair.

Although Chester never overtly likened his masterpiece to a throne, most other people who have seen it have called it that—probably because of its gothic qualities, including the spires. "At first I liked it real good, uh, but I'm kinda like other people, I—it don't look right some way," said Chester, who then laughed nervously.

"You don't think it looks right?"

"No, it don't. It don't look like it b'longs here." Again the nervous laugh.

"It doesn't look like what?"

"I said, I believe, uh, it don't look like it b'longs here yet. I b'lieve it come here too early, or some'un or other, or too late, one."

After a moment he said, "Uh, it's so odd that, uh, bet it come too late or too quick, one; I don't know which." He laughed again.

Perhaps Chester considered these chairs antiques and old-timers not because he associated their designs, traits, or construction techniques with his own chairmaking tradition, but because they resemble thrones. If so, then maybe they did come too early or too late. Either way, they could have symbolized to Chester the power, control, and rulership he had sought in his own life and affairs but perhaps had not always achieved, although he had proven by the kinds of chairmaking problems he set for himself and solved that he was a king among chairmakers.

Chester certainly was a master craftsman. Nearly every chair of his that I saw seemed to challenge what others had taken for granted, inquiring into the fundamental nature of chairs and setting forth new concepts regarding materials, manufacture, use, structure, durability, comfort, or appearance. He conceived of himself as a chairmaker, having sometimes tried other kinds of work but always returning to the making of chairs. Each strange chair may have begun with doubts—about how to create it, and perhaps about whether or not he was capable. When completed, such a chair probably served as a testament to and reaffirmation of his identity as master chairmaker and as a source of strength for the man and the artist.

Journalists who published regional and national articles about Chester portrayed him as a superior artist without equal, and many people wrote the same sentiments to Chester in letters or suggested them in conversation. In one article, for example, the author wrote that Chester "is possessed of an inborn knack and inventiveness that in another time and setting might have made him an official cabinetmaker to a king." What better way to

inform the world that one is without equal, or that one's furniture is fit for royalty, than to build a throne and carve one's
name and address on it?

Chester often complained about the traffic roaring past his
house next to the highway, the people who would stop just to
take a picture, how "nervous" he became around strangers, and
the seemingly endless interruptions to his work. Each time that
Ruth forced him to move from an isolated hollow to the highway
Chester grew a beard and seemed to bury himself even more
deeply in his work, rhythmically shaping by hand again and
again the eight-sided pieces needed first for the eight-legged
chairs and later the two-in-one rocking chairs.

Shortly after he began work on a special chair for my wife and
me, Chester suddenly received nationwide attention and was
inundated with letters: "then Letters Went to Comin in froum
East South North West Wantin to no if they Culd Buy a Laddre
Back Rockker and they said they Engoid Redid Abut me in the
natin advzer news papre." But Chester had "never herd of this
news papre." To him, "Ever thing is so strang," just as he
described the chair on which he was working during this unexpected incursion into his privacy. Did this chair, then, offer him
protection—with its massive barriers—against the onslaught of
strangers who had suddenly invaded his world?

The feeling of enclosure was most pronounced in his eight-
legged chairs of the early 1950s and in the six eight-legged
rocking chairs made between 1961 and 1965. Even the "ordinary" seven-slat rocking chairs during this time were tall and
had many wide slats. These characteristics were particularly
apparent at the time of Chester's emotional and economic problems, of his moving to the highway, of his change in body image
to that of the stereotypical hillbilly, and of the composition of his
song about his old Kentucky mountain home.

Whether slat-back, bark-back, or wood back, all the two-in-
one chairs "hug" the occupant. One might make something of
the generic name for these chairs: "two-in-one." Not two chairs
in one, perhaps, but two people? Someone whose arms are
wrapped protectively and comfortingly around the other individual? Or one person within another, i.e., a womb?

Or did the Masterpiece stand for a coffin? As noted earlier, Chester's song, which he composed a few months before the Masterpiece was built, gives no indication of the particular war referred to by the narrator. Perhaps from his point of view, Chester had had many battles to fight. He was unable to return to his old Kentucky mountain home—Pine Mountain—which is what the narrator in Chester's song longs to do and assumes he will do once the war is over. If Chester never tasted victory but always suffered defeat, then maybe the solution to his battles in life was death.

Chester told me something interesting about the Bookcase Masterpiece. After he said that the chair "don't look like it b'longs here," I asked him, "Is there anything in particular you don't like about it?"

"Well, uh, the particular thing I don't like about it is, uh, fella have to have, uh, footrest to go with it, stool to lay your legs upon to make it more comfy and, uh, it'd have to have, uh, to make it look just right, it'd have to have a genuine leather upholstery cushions for the back, seat an' arms, and, uh, I found out what'd cost to get the leather to make the cushions," at which point in this atypical rush of words he laughed nervously.

"Quite a bit, is it?"

"Oh, boy! It'd cost two-three hunnert to get enough leather to make cushion upholstery. Outa genuine leather. I didn't know who else to see about it but the shoe shop over there. He said genuine leather, enough to cover that'd cost two-three hunnert dollars." To be "more comfy" the chair needed a legrest (like the Old-Timer?) and "genuine leather upholstery cushions."

About eighty years ago in Chenango County, New York, one Henry Caulkin, a skilled craftsman specializing in wagons and furniture, reportedly made his own coffin in his spare time. He built for himself "a roomy, high-backed chair, complete with arm and foot rests. It was well-padded and covered with the traditional funereal cloth. Now to complete this strange coffin he built a box in the shape of the chair, but without a back and deep enough so that it could be placed over the chair and its occupant and fastened tightly to it. This, too, was lined with tufted cloth, and the upper part of it was glass."

It is an intriguing coincidence: Chester's Bookcase Masterpiece is remarkably like Caulkin's chair-coffin. Interesting, too, in this respect, is the Old-Timer, with its high back and its footrest, which Chester made for an old crippled woman without her knowledge who "passed on b'fore I got the chair done." Would the Old-Timer have been a throne for the aged woman who Chester knew was ill, a chair in which she could "set away up high like a king or some'un," or would it have been her coffin (or Chester's)?

For several years I considered Chester's "two-in-one, bookcase rocker, masterpiece of furniture" just as out of place as he did. Nothing like it followed, so it was not one in a series of closely related works in an evolving career. He did make many other chairs before and after the Masterpiece, of course, some of which were tall and highly ornamented pieces; between them were squeezed small, unimposing works to be sold cheaply, and there were some chairs of clean, swiftly flowing lines. If the chair meant life or rebirth, it came too late, I reasoned, because Chester's world, or at least the world of men, collapsed within the next three or four years; no wish to return to the womb and try life once more would have helped him. If the chair was intended as an earthly throne, it still was not of this place and time, I thought, because Chester never seemed to master the outer world, and even as a king of chairmakers he ruled few subjects and had no heirs apparent.

COPING AND ADJUSTMENT

Nevertheless, one has the feeling that these themes are related in some way, and that in them we have identified several strands in the tangled skein of Chester's behavior, the beliefs he expressed, and the experiences he described. There are the female and male elements: the womb and the tomb = enclosure = security, plus the source of creativity; and the throne, Pine Mountain, and the huge chairs of powerful form = virility and self-assurance as a man and a master craftsman. Together in the Bookcase Masterpiece they produce and reveal the whole man.

"Such a consciousness would see the becoming and the passing of things beside their momentary existence, and not only that, but at the same time it would also see the Other, which was before their becoming and will be after their passing hence," writes Jung about individuals such as Chester. Perhaps this unusual craftsman, with his strange visions and his unique subjective perceptions, could indeed see the becoming and the passing of things.

Of one thing I am certain—the process of grieving over a loss, resulting in the idealization of the past and the withdrawal from others expressed in Chester's chairs by old-timey traits and a sense of enclosure, is related to the creative process as well. And in this relationship lies the significance of the two-in-one, book-case rocker, masterpiece of furniture for understanding certain aspects of human behavior generally, and the chair's meaning to Chester as a masterpiece.

Without doubt, bereavement affects the works of individuals already making and doing things expressive of themselves, as we have seen in the nostalgia and the withdrawal apparent in Chester's chairs. Among the many personal experiences expressed in artists' works, grief is an especially poignant one. More interesting is the way in which it can precipitate expression, resulting in the production of a few objects, stories, or songs during a brief period, or more rarely, recurrent expressive activity from that moment on.

"Many times out of sickness, disappointment or sorrow, there will be some good come out of it," wrote an elderly farmer in Kansas to me. He had composed a "sacred song" some years before while recuperating from a serious accident. "Had those mules not run away with me I would never have written these inspiring words." Seldom does intense involvement in production and performance endure after the initial expression of grief, though occasionally it does.

The wellspring of creativity is not buried in a stratum of grief. Chester's rocker is a masterpiece because of his skill, not because it expresses his feelings or emotional needs. But many individuals who only rarely produce songs, stories, or special objects do so while grieving over a loss. And the character of some objects or activities made or done by those who regularly create these forms may also express their suffering.

Public expression relieves one of feelings of guilt for having possibly caused the loss, generates sympathy for one's plight, and projects the problems outward, away from oneself, where they can be dealt with more easily. For some people, a song or a story expresses the anxiety or frustration of personal failure; the expression perhaps exonerates the individual who finds the cause of his or her problems in the machinations of others, but also helps the person find and express order and meaning. Incapacitation, incarceration, or the loss of a friend, a relative, or one's own health fosters introspection, which in turn may promote the production of a song, a story, or other work. Such expressive activity helps the individual readjust to life and its vicissitudes. Those who have suffered loss are charged with nervous energy, sensitive to the human condition, and most aware of themselves and their own frailty.

Part of the grieving process for any individual, metaphorically speaking, is one's death and rebirth as a different individual. Grieving and creativity have much in common: the search for structure and order, and the reaffirmation of self. In grief there is loss, followed by a feeling that the world is empty and poor. Expressive structures and objects that one creates fill the void caused by the loss—first comes a state of doubt, then order and belief, then wholeness once more. Intense mourning and introspection discharge the emotions of loss, hostility, and guilt, and ultimately lead to reintegration of the self. "Now the war is over," sang Chester hopefully but perhaps prematurely in 1965, "so I thank God in heaven that I'm on my way back to my ole Kentucky mount'n home." His "ole Kentucky mount'n home" was less a place than a state of mind—a state of mind at peace, attainable only through creative activities such as chairmaking.

When his self-assurance as a man and as a craftsman faltered on the threshold of the outside world, when the severity of his problems increased, and when he lost the security and strength allowed him within his hollow in the mountains, Chester attempted to adjust to his losses and reaffirm his identity by building chairs that gave him protection. In the process he was reborn and his strength was renewed; once again he could stand proud as a man and an artist, and he could produce any kind of chair.

Dreaming of a return to Pine Mountain was escape and perhaps death, but building chairs was adjustment and regeneration. Chairs like the Old-Timer and the Bookcase Masterpiece are testaments to both creativity and grieving. When constructing these chairs, Chester began with doubt but ended with certainty. The human problems were real enough; the artistic ones, precipitated by the others, were self-generated as a test of strength and identity, and because they were successfully solved, served to rebuild the man.

"I don't see how the ole man done it," remarked Beechum in regard to Chester's second California rocker. "He just must a took a lot a time with it."

"He's that way with ever'thing he does," Ruth told me. "He wants to be sure it's perfect before he puts it together. He figgers it all out in his mind b'fore he makes a chair, I know he does." Two days earlier, when angry at Chester for not helping her care for the children, Ruth had used this same trait of absorption in chairmaking against him. "I swear, I could do as much in half an hour as he does all day!"

If the essence of Chester's style was that of extending the limits of chairmaking accepted by his predecessors and his contemporaries, then many chairs that he built of his own volition represent in some way a working out of one or more concepts concerning the very *nature* of chairs. Each "strange" chair, every "odd" piece—the mention of which was accompanied by a nervous laugh—was an extreme example of Chester's propensity to immerse himself in the conceptual aspects of chairmaking.

In the California rocker (fig. 74) Chester integrated the idea of a caned seat with the technique of weaving a hickory splint bottom. The Abner chair (similar to fig. 96) was a slat-back rocking chair made with very thin posts—too thin to mortise in the usual way. The New Design chair, made of salvaged scraps of light and dark wood, was a six-slat rocking chair transformed into a seven-slat rocking chair (figs. 46-48). Earlier adventures in chairmaking for Chester were conceptualizing dining chairs (e.g., fig. 30), a category that did not exist in Chester's tradition; making a settin' chair with a panel seat rather than a woven one (fig. 41); combining square posts with turned posts (fig. 66); and so on.

The strange and odd chairs were conceptual statements, too.

The first eight-legged side chair originated in Chester's experimentation with the eight-sided posts that he had been making
by hand for several years. Eight-legged rocking chairs extended
the concept of the eight-legged side chair. The Dolph rocker saw
a change from slats to woven bark panels, and the Bookcase
Masterpiece added shelves and spires.

But unlike other chairs, the strange and odd ones were no
longer really "chairs" making conceptual statements. Rather,
they puzzled and befuddled the viewer. Chester had become
fixated with one feature or another. He worked on it over and
over and over and over. He spent 356 hours, 500 hours, ...

This was not chairmaking but ritual. No longer was he exploring concepts; he was repeating motions again and again, lost in
thought about other matters. He decorated ninety pegs on the
Banks rocker. Day after day at his drawing horse Chester shaped
not only eight slats for the rockers, but also eight posts with eight
facets each, two dozen stretchers with eight sides each, many
yards of eight-sided doweling from which to cut pegs, and eight-
sided spindles to be mounted below the armrests. He pulled the
drawing knife toward him, removing a tissue-thin strip of wood
from the piece. Again and again and again. Then he altered the
position of the piece one eighth of a turn, and pulled the knife
toward him . . . over and over and over again.

The ritual process that Chester engaged in is analogous to
other people's cleaning the house, washing the dishes, mowing
the yard, or polishing the car while musing over some vexing
problem. Chester became preoccupied with some aspect of
chairmaking, ritualizing the manufacture, when his personal
problems were greatest. He was not building chairs but creating
symbols.

This was why he wrote about the Masterpiece that "They are
somtin strange about this Rocking chire   I dont Reley no what
hapin   I just startied workin on hit   Seems to Be sometin
Kidin me   so strang."

More than any other chair, the two-in-one, bookcase rocker,
masterpiece of furniture epitomized the processes of creativity
and grieving, demonstrated Chester's enormous skill, and af-
forded Chester the opportunity to reconstruct himself, his life,

and his world. He built it ritualistically, his mind on many things, which was why "somtin new about Ever day has got to Be Adied." He may have been as surprised as everyone else at its nature when the chair was completed. One thing was certain: This was not just a chair.

Not everyone who makes things does so with the skill of Chester or with his commitment to the creative act. But other craftsmen are worthy of study, if for no other reason than they heighten our appreciation of Chester and his works. As we will see in chapter 6, other craftsmen often say much about themselves, and sometimes something about life, through their chair-making.

SIX

It Takes Half a Fool
to Make Chairs

"I always liked repair work," said Verge, who since 1915 had sometimes made chairs. "I'd rather repair 'em than make 'em new. You can make good money 'cause the owner thinks it's a good chair, and there's not too much work in it."

A farmer and an occasional chairmaker, Verge had also been a musician but, according to his son Hascal, he put down his banjo when he took up fundamentalism. Tight-lipped and stern, he was not a man to joke about either religion or chairmaking, but Hascal, another man named Beechum, and the craftsman Aaron, all of whom worked in the same shop as Verge and whose chairs exhibit many qualities in common, enjoyed repeating one of Verge's favorite sayings: "It takes half a fool to make chairs and a whole fool to make baskets."

Most men in this section of southeastern Kentucky seemed to feel the same way, which partly explains why there were few chairmakers and fewer basket makers. Even Verge, who "makes 'em for the money" and not for the "sake of makin' a good chair," as one of his relatives charged, preferred to repair chairs rather than build them because of the greater financial rewards.

Many times when I asked if there were any chairmakers around I was told that none remained: "You should have been here a decade ago in the 1950s; there were a dozen of them then." In point of fact, however, in the mid-1960s I met or learned about more than a dozen chairmakers. Few of them engaged in craftwork with much enthusiasm or superior skill, but there is no reason to suppose the situation in the past was radically different. The basic techniques of construction are rather easily learned by men who need to fashion make-dos for their homes, or by those who must find an immediate source of income to help them through financial crises, or by those who simply want to keep busy during the winter and decide to make a few chairs. All are called chairmakers by someone else, even though these men did not "do it for a livin' " and are not "old-time chairmakers."

As a lifetime occupation, chairmaking was bound to attract few individuals, because, like any process of making things, it required considerable interest in and commitment to the creative act.

"Do you think it takes a special talent to be a chairmaker?" I asked Chester.

"I don't b'lieve so," he said.

"You think anybody could be a chairmaker?"

"No, I don't b'lieve just anybody could—too hard a work."

"Does it take some special skill?"

"Yes sir, it does. It takes a skill specially for, uh, you got to learn how to use that drawin' knife—use it just right to take off hick'ry bark with or whatever you're making," though other chairmakers used a drawing knife much less frequently and for fewer tasks than Chester did.

"Can anyone learn how to use a drawing knife?"

"I'd say so, exceptin', uh, you got to learn to get interested in anything to learn it—you have to learn to get interested in a thing like that before you could learn it. And anyway, I b'lieve anyone could learn how to use a drawin' knife and do that work."

"Anybody could learn how to be a chairmaker, then?"

"Well, yes, they could, but they'd have to learn to be interested in that first."

"Do you think you have a special talent for making chairs? Something you're born with, an ability to work with wood?"

"No, I don't think so. I think, uh, what you grow up with is one reason that you do that."

THE CHAIR SHOP

We have already considered what Chester did and why he did it, but what about other men who grew up with chairmaking? What happened to them? How much interest did they have and what

100 Armchair with bark back and seat made by
Verge in 1934 (photographed in June 1967).

did they learn? Who were the dozen chairmakers in the 1960s,
why and how did they make chairs, and what happened to
them? Let us begin with Verge and the individuals who were
influenced by him.

I did not spend as much time with other craftsmen and their
customers as I did with Chester and his. My intent was to
compare generally the craftsmen's tools and techniques, designs, commitment to chairmaking, and attitudes toward tradition. My information is sufficient in scope to make some
generalizations in the final chapter.

When Verge found religion, he apparently lost all interest in

101 Bench and rockers made by Verge about 1935-40.

fancy things. His chair style is so plain it would probably make a devout Shaker think he had backslidden (figs. 100 and 101). "For myself, I like a *decent*, plain-made chair," declared Verge, who objected to turnings and other ornamentation used by his son Hascal and by Chester and Aaron.

A decent chair, as Verge's works indicate, would be made of material better known for its structural soundness than for its appearance, such as ash: "now it makes a good chair—solid and heavy." Verge also sampled hard and soft maple because "that makes a good chair"; white poplar; walnut, which is "pretty but not too strong" and therefore unsuitable; oak; sassafras, which is "easy timber worked, and light, but awful easy burst"; and white "linn" which is "pretty soft and easy worked but not too stout." He finally settled on plain ash.

"I don't like the nubs on the posts," Verge said, referring to all chairs made with finials. For him, the most offensive chairs were many of Chester's works. "Some of them rockers are the ugliest chairs I've ever seen." After viewing each photograph of a chair made by Chester or by Aaron he repeated, "I don't like all them rings and nubs." He was also displeased by the height of their rocking and dining chairs. "I don't like a low seat with a real high back. I always made my own front posts 19 inches and the back posts 41½ inches."

Verge claimed not to have altered those dimensions in half a century. I did not try to track down his earlier chairs or measure all that I saw. The chairs I did find, however, in his home and in the homes of customers in the immediate area, suggested that Verge increasingly simplified his designs.

Born in 1895, Verge began helping his father at the age of eleven, learning first to turn the chair spokes or stretchers on a foot-powered lathe and then to make the posts. Finally he learned the most difficult task of all, bottoming or weaving the seat in a chair.

In later years he continued to be critical of other men who did not know how to make chairs but who offered to bottom them. "Most don't know how to do it. They don't weave the bark underneath—just let it hang—so the seat sags." His father, said Verge, "would brag on my work, of course, if I got it right."

And Verge seemed to be pretty certain his way was right. His earliest chairs, he said, had flat, wide arms, but eventually he tapered them so they would be "good lookin'." A chair without tapered arms, he told me, is "ugly." The taper of arms varies considerably on his chairs, but one feature is constant: the absence of turnings. His brother Everett, who flirted with the useless, chiseled two circles into the back posts of his chairs; Verge could not quite accept that much ornamentation.

In his own defense, Verge contended that most of the "people around here say I make the best chair of any one fella that's made 'em around here. They don't say I make the *best-lookin'* chair—just the best one."

A vociferous minority, however, refuted Verge, claiming that he was more interested in making money than in "makin' a good chair." He implied as much in his remarks about preferring repair work. In addition, his notion of an ideal business was that of quantity production with modern machinery on a contract basis, "so you know you have a sale for a certain design." He said, "The better the machinery, the more you can make," meaning both chairs and money.

Like many men, Verge was especially keen on achieving rapid production of huge quantities of chairs, even suggesting that there was a diminished number of chairmakers because of the absence of adequate remuneration. "Not many chairmakers around now 'cause they can't make chairs fast enough to make any money," he said. Yet when I asked Verge for his definition of a "good chairmaker," he said, "He'd have to work slow enough to do perfect work."

Verge claimed that he always boiled the slats of a chair and pressed them, unless, of course, he was rushed and had to put the slats in the chair green, which seems to have been often, according to Hascal and Aaron. Verge also said he seldom marked the back posts but mortised them by sight so that he could make chairs faster. When Verge stopped helping his father and started his own chair shop at the age of thirty, squeezing in chairmaking between farming and delivering mail, he sold most of his settin' chairs on contract for sixty cents each to Hindman Settlement School, which in turn resold them. He also peddled a few for fifty cents apiece to local people, usually coal miners, " 'cause that's about the only money there was in this part of the country then." By the mid-1930s a settin' chair sold for a dollar and a rocker for three; thirty years later the price was five times as much.

Verge was vague about the sources of his designs, but he did mention that some came from mail-order catalogs and some from his father and brother. Others "we'd just figger up ourself to see which different designs would sell better." After all, the "more designs a chairmaker'd know to do, the more sales he could get." But apparently Verge's designs were not numerous. A chair of white ash and hickory bark splints, which he made in 1934 and still owned in 1967, is typical of his work (fig. 100).

Most of Verge's armchairs, rocking chairs, and benches have bark backs rather than slat backs or panel backs. The design was not unique to him, but he used it the most. Aaron said that the bark-back chair is "fairly comfortable, but not as pretty as ladder-back chairs. And it takes too much bark to make." Aaron objected to the design because he hated to skin bark, prepare it for weaving, and bottom the chairs. When Verge, Hascal, and Aaron worked together, it was Verge who bottomed all the chairs, a task that, like repair work, he seemed to enjoy. On each arm of the chair shown there is a flat surface at the end, underneath, to which a small projection of the post is affixed with a nail. Whether the arm was to be flat on top (as Aaron made them), flat underneath like this one, or entirely round depended on the customer's request, although Verge preferred the particular design he used. Chairs that Verge made in the early 1960s have no flat surfaces on the arms at all. These chairs look somewhat more squarish, and the bark panels in the backs are narrower.

The times of Verge's greatest productivity, he said, were the early 1930s and the 1960s. This was when he worked in a chair shop at a local school founded by a woman from the East. Ascetic to an extreme, she shared the fundamentalist values of Verge and other "creek people" in his area. "She didn't want no finish work," said Verge; "she just wanted what you done with the chisel," which suited him. Although bark ¾ inch wide looks the best in chair bottoms, "she wanted inch-and-a-half bark 'cause she said the wider bark lasts longer." In essence, "she didn't care for the looks. The same way with buildings. Put 'em rough 'cause that was the cheapest. She said she'd rather have more rough buildings for more scholars to get an education instead of just a few pretty buildings for just a few scholars." Verge's chairs and his remarks evince much the same attitude that this woman had. He spoke of her with reverence.

The years of least productivity for Verge's son Hascal, however, appeared to be the mid-1960s in the same shop. During my eight visits to the shop, only Beechum was working, not Hascal. Hascal managed to explain away his inactivity by saying that he could get into more trouble with the school by doing the wrong kind of work than by not working at all. He also contended that the administrators would like him to work all the time, though slowly, but they wanted so many chairs that if he worked, he would have to work rapidly. If he had his own shop at home, he said, he could take his time and make chairs slowly and properly. But then he said he was too nervous and wanted to finish a job as soon as possible after starting it, although in the chair shop it was Beechum and other men before him who finished the projects suggested by Hascal.

Hascal claimed he did not like to work in the shop because he had to produce to order and could not experiment, yet if he had his own business he would prefer mass production of standard items to ensure large sales. He said that during slack times, as in the summer of 1967 when I was in the shop, the school in fact permitted him to make sample items following his own design. He was not doing so because, he said, he was not supposed to set up the equipment to make certain kinds of chairs as it might be the wrong setup for what the administrators wanted next.

Hascal wanted to make chairs, he said, but he was really not able to because he needed electrical equipment to render the task easier. I noticed, however, that the shop was well equipped with drill presses, jigsaws, and an expensive lathe—more and better machinery than other chairmakers had—which Beechum used but Hascal never touched. Finally, he said that he was supposed to train others to make chairs, not produce them himself.

Hascal, who was thirty-two years old when I met him, was the only one of Verge's three sons to identify himself as a chairmaker. Asked why he made chairs, Hascal replied, "I saw everyone else was doin' it an' it looked like good money," but then he complained about his low income. The job was a form of relief work for which the men were paid $40 a week plus food stamps in exchange for making chairs to be used at the school or to be given as gifts to outsiders who provided donations supporting the institution.

Hascal had considered a job offer from a furniture factory in

102 Maple armchair made by Hascal (1963 or 1964) at the request of a woman who never picked it up.

Berea at three times his wage, he said, but turned it down because it was not as much money as he needed or thought he was worth. Although he had tried several jobs—"I get tired of doing the same thing after four or five years and change"—he said he would never stop making chairs. In August 1967, he quit the chair shop and assumed janitorial duties at another school because, he said, "there isn't much work to it" and "I wanna work as little as possible."

Chairmaking, however, was the only job he had tried which did not make him nervous, he said, spilling tobacco on the floor as he attempted to roll a cigarette. He had a "sick stomach" so he could not eat greasy foods but had to drink "sweet milk" and cream. Chairmaking, though, did not "bother" him.

Because Hascal was not making chairs at the time (and

according to Aaron, who worked in the same shop earlier, Hascal never made many chairs), it was impossible to note in detail his work procedures. But he posed for pictures and summarized his production techniques, which were common among other chairmakers. As he hopped from one piece of equipment to another, it was apparent that when and if Hascal ever made chairs, he did so rapidly, not steaming and pressing slats, but putting them in green and refusing to bend walnut posts or slats at all because of the patience required to do the job properly. Aaron's brother said that Hascal "was so nervous he nearly cut himself with the chisel while mortisin' chair backs; his hands really shook."

Hascal claimed to have originated many chair designs himself, but he was embarrassed when we looked around the shop and could not find any. He said that a person could not make anything good in the shop, that the administrators who did not even know what a "round" was tried to tell him how to make a chair, and that he would prefer working at home where he was free to innovate and where "if I wanted to spend two weeks on one thing I was really interested in working on, I could." Later he asked me for some photographs of chairs so he could "get some ideas" for designs if he ever started his own shop.

Hascal said he was the designer of, among other chairs in the shop which I photographed, an unfinished maple rocker made about 1963 or 1964 (fig. 103), which looks rather like an early chair of Aaron's. This and other works also exhibit similarities to Verge's chairs, such as the tendency toward simplicity of design and execution and the tapering of the arm at the end that enters the back post. A nonchairmaker in the area who looked at the photo of the maple rocker said he did not like it because it was too simple and without turnings at all (in fact, it does have turnings on the posts beneath the seat).

"The seat's too little in it and the rounds are too close to the bottom," said Chester, assuming it was an armchair and not suspecting that it was an unfinished rocking chair. "Look a whole lot better if the rounds was at least six inches or better from the bottom. Hit wouldn't make it no solider but you take a chair now, in a few years hit'll wear plumb off to the rounds.

103 This unfinished rocking chair (June 1967), allegedly made by Hascal in 1963 or 1964, is remarkably similar to Aaron's early chairs.

"Looks like hit's got a comf'table back on it," continued Chester. "The only fault I see with that chair is the bottom of hit, the way it's fixed. Hit's too 'dubby' I call it. If you wanted to get a rubber gasket to put on it to keep from damagin' the 'noleum rug, you couldn't find one to fit."

Chester made the same criticism about another of Hascal's works, a maple barstool made about 1964 (fig. 104). Hascal said he had designed it himself and that it was one of more than a hundred he had made. Chester proclaimed it "a very nice-lookin' stool, but they fixed the points on the bottom so peaked you can't put any rubber things on it." He said he would have added another round so the stool could be used as a stepladder. Chester also said he would have carved out the seat "to make it comf'tabler."

Another of Hascal's productions I photographed is a maple

104 Barstool made by Verge's son, Hascal, about 1964.

footstool dating from about 1965 (fig. 105). In Chester's opinion, "Hit's too open. It'd look a lot better if the rounds hadn't been so close to the floor. An' if it wasn't square it'd looked a lot better. It's interestin' to know that some people don't try to change their patterns none."

Yet that is precisely what Hascal said he was doing. How was it possible that this man could claim originality of vision in a mode of production in which he seldom engaged and in products that seemed rather conventional? He had learned the techniques of chairmaking from his grandfather, his uncle, and especially his father, so why could or would he not build chairs; what was he doing in a chair shop?

Most of the time Hascal talked, expounding to everyone his religious views, his drinking excesses, and his extramarital sexual exploits. Although he was born and reared in this small

105 Maple stool made by Hascal (about 1965).

community, and his father and his kin were still there, Hascal considered himself an outsider who did not share the fundamentalist religious beliefs, the asceticism, and the puritanical attitudes of the "creek people," including his father, just as he challenged (in his mind, anyway) the conventional chairs made by his father and by other men.

To his own regret, Hascal never finished high school; guided by correspondence with a Seventh-Day Adventist preacher, however, he studied the Bible thirty minutes a day for a couple of years. "It didn't cost me anything as long as I got a C in the course," said Hascal. "That was the only thing I ever got free from church." He also taught Sunday school for a year and a half, complaining later that he never got paid for it although he "managed to get a suit out of it." He claimed to be religious, but of course in an unconventional way. He summed up his attitude with the following anecdote: "A man told me he might get me a job as pastor of a church and another guy standin' there interrupted an' said he thought pastors ought to be religious or at least believe in God. And the first man said, 'To hell with God, this man needs the damned money!' "

Hascal had no compunction about expressing his attitudes toward sex as well as religion, and sometimes combined them. For example, there was a story he told twice with great relish to the other men assembled in the chair shop, repeating the punch line several times, concerning a preacher with "a fourteen-inch tool" who had "ruined" several women—"killed one or two by rupturing their wombs"—and who wanted to seduce a married woman in church. Hascal also reminisced about his own alleged extramarital sexual activities. Several men in the chair shop told me later that some of the exploits were probably true.

Hascal appeared to relish the attention of others. Perhaps because of this, he once worked as a disc jockey on a local radio station and also performed with a band. Nothing seemed to please him more than an audience at rapt attention to his unceasing flow of words. What Hascal had to talk about in the chair shop, however, was of interest because it titillated. He appeared to hold attention by degrading himself and others, an act that tended to deny him acceptance by many people in the local community. At the same time, he achieved notoriety, which brought many men to his shop to listen to his "wicked" ideas and hear about his activities. By denouncing local customs and beliefs, he may have proved the originality of his ideas and attempted to endear himself to outsiders, to whom he claimed to feel spiritually akin in some of his values and with whom he sought friendship. In making his sins public and in reveling in them before an audience of local people, however, Hascal seemed also to be punishing himself by exposing his excesses to the very people who would indeed be most shocked and most inclined to censure him.

Hascal was an intelligent man with some skill as a musician and as a woodworker. His critiques of chairs were usually articulate, to the point, and defensible. He had the potential for contributing significantly to several traditions. He seemed sincerely to want to develop his unique insights and discoveries. But he appeared to be paralyzed.

In the chair shop he did not work but merely talked about what he would do or allegedly had done. His ideas for new chair designs were never executed. He wanted to work slowly but lacked the patience. He hoped to make chairs, as his father did, but could not. Always when he started a job, there was enthusiasm initially, but tasks were left unfinished and aspirations went unfulfilled. His hands shook and his tongue rattled.

Hascal's "nervousness" was like the classic example of an experienced singer who suddenly cannot reach the high notes because of an inhibition verging on hysteria. Hascal no longer knew what he wanted, or he wanted impossible things, and he could do nothing at all. His bravado in the chair shop belied the existence of problems he was unable to solve at the time. Perhaps that is why he quit the shop altogether.

Aaron, who also worked in the chair shop in the early 1960s, appeared by contrast to be a quiet, even-tempered, retiring man who did not say much to anyone about anything but devoted most of his attention to shaping, sanding, and shellacking chairs with a finesse not characteristic of other craftsmen in the area. Aaron was careful—no, meticulous—and patient. He was also of good humor and generally satisfied with himself, his work, and the things he made.

Scrutinizing a rocking chair he had just constructed, Aaron said, "The way it is now looks balanced to me. Now I don't know how the general public would feel about it." He cared about the feelings of others, and he was responsive to consumer demands if they were reasonable. Sometimes they were not. The "ugliest" chair Aaron ever saw was one he himself had made on demand for an arthritic woman who wanted it built with a high seat, a tall back with four slats, and one armrest so she could crawl in and out of it more easily. (This was probably Hattie Tuggle, the woman for whom Chester made the Old-Timer.) He also had been asked to make chairs with posts "as thin as a broomstick," but he felt that the legs as he typically made them "don't look so chubby" and posts smaller in diameter would make the chair "too frail lookin'."

Despite his general satisfaction with the things he made, Aaron was not pleased with all his works. Earlier rockers had too many "spools" that were not well made, he said. While later chairs were "kinda pretty," they "don't set too good, 'specially the dining chairs." He and his brother Myron joked that a dining

106 Aaron oils a post or leg as it spins in place on the lathe.
107 Aaron, always the perfectionist, uses a square to align stretcher holes in post.

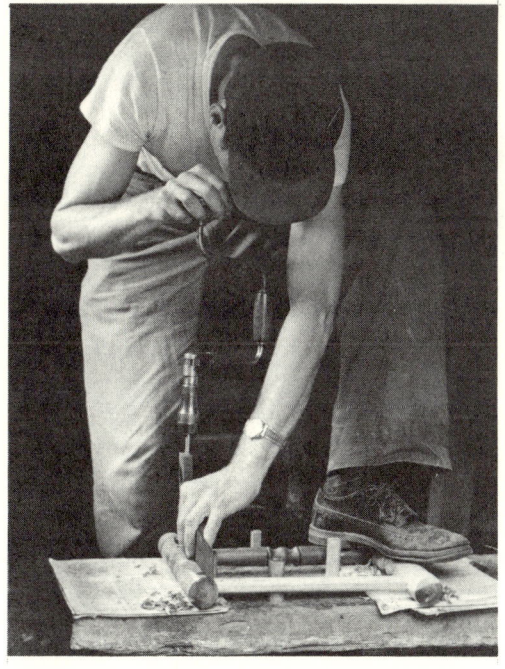

108 Aaron's slat press and tub for cooking slats; posts were not usually cooked or bent.

chair should not be too comfortable anyway, as a person might sit at the table too long and eat too much. To increase the comfort of the dining chair, Aaron made the back posts half an inch shorter than the front legs. Nevertheless, "nothing 'cept upholstered chairs set as good as settin' chairs."

But Aaron did not make many settin' chairs, first, because this kind of chair must be made of a strong wood like ash or hickory but he preferred to work with walnut, which "makes a pretty chair but it's easy broke"; second, because the five or six dollars he usually got for a settin' chair made the effort scarcely worthwhile; third, because the design is too simple to appeal to him; and, fourth, because he simply did not like to make settin' chairs and had had little practice.

He started making chairs in 1962 by patterning a settin' chair after one made by a neighboring chairmaker who was no longer alive. Aaron measured Harry's work exactly and duplicated as closely as he could the chair's features and dimensions. On the basis of a smattering of knowledge gained from his father and other men, he built his own settin' chair of maple and ash (figs. 109 and 110).

The two chairs are not quite the same. Harry put a large peg in each end of the top slat, whereas Aaron used small pins of wood that blended with the chair. The posts of Harry's chair flared backward in a fashion that would never appeal to Aaron. The distance between the top of the back posts and the bottom of the legs was more nearly equal in Aaron's chair, again suggesting greater containment in expressive quality. All these elements indicate that every handmade chair, even a copy by a neophyte, is in fact a unique product, exhibiting characteristics peculiar to the individual who made it.

From settin' chairs Aaron graduated to rockers, stools, and dining chairs, but he did not remember how many of each he had made. "Never thought I'd make enough to fool with keepin' track of 'em," he said.

Why fool with making chairs now? "I swore I'd get a job two years ago, then last winter, but I never did," he told me in the summer of 1967. In fact, Aaron held several jobs before he began to make chairs. Born in 1926 and never married, he lived at home with his father, an unmarried brother, and a married brother and his family. After Aaron returned from service in the Pacific at the end of World War II, he attended the local academy where a decade and a half later he would make chairs for a couple of years. He taught in elementary schools in the area for three years but despised the work so much, he said, that he allowed his certificate to lapse to force himself to find some other kind of employment. Then, for several years, he wandered from one northern city to another, working at various semiskilled jobs such as operating a drill press and making television cabinets and stands. Disillusioned and unhappy, he finally headed back to the hills of Kentucky, where he started doing what many southern mountaineers are infamous for, drinking.

One day in mid-1962, he said, while recovering from a week-

109 Maple settin' chair (painted green) made about 1960 by Harry, a neighbor of Aaron's.   **110** Aaron's first copy (1962) of Harry's chair.

long bout with the bottle, he heard that the school would soon reactivate the chair shop and needed craftsmen. Several men had already signed up to work under Verge's supervision, and one of the teachers who had befriended Aaron encouraged him to accept the job, which he did. It was a halfhearted response, because the shop reminded Aaron of the factories where he had given up his freedom to work under someone else's direction. Verge and Hascal were amazed at Aaron's skill and knowledge when he joined them, and they remarked to me about his diligence and his talent as a craftsman—when he worked.

Often he drank, they said, taking a nip on the job in defiance of the academy rule forbidding faculty and staff to smoke or drink at all. It was not the first time Aaron had broken the rules, for when he was a student at the school in the late 1940s, he was the only one who lived at home rather than in a dormitory and the only one who had a car and roamed about at will. But Aaron the chairmaker went a little bit too far when he ventured onto the post office lawn one day, lay down, and drank his bourbon lunch.

In early 1964 he again was without a job. He began to make chairs at home, at first to support his drinking habit, but later to help overcome it. By the time I met him, he was firmly on the wagon, with a tight rein on his problems, and the empty half-pints lining the walk to his house were like ruts in a road, covered with more than a year's accumulation of dust.

It also took awhile for Aaron to shake himself loose from the influence of Verge and Hascal. The form of a black walnut rocker made about 1962 and owned by Aaron (fig. 111) is typical of works produced at the inception of his career. It is a panel-back or vertical-back chair with indistinct turnings. The back posts have stiles because the post on the right had a structural fault, which Aaron cut out with a drawing knife, and because Aaron happened to like stiles at that time.

Another black walnut rocking chair, made in 1963 or 1964 (fig. 112), has more distinctly developed turnings and a more sharply defined form, suggesting greater self-certainty in its maker. The rockers are still rounded on the top edge, a design element that Hascal claimed to have developed. The academy dean who

111 An early black walnut
rocker made by Aaron in 1962.
The notch in the top slat became
Aaron's trademark.

"wanted something a bit different" suggested the idea; Hascal
said he "figgered out the best way to make 'em was to hew 'em
out and take the corners off" on the drawing horse, but "this
type scoots worser than others on a rug or where you've waxed."

Both these chairs resemble those I found in the chair shop
made by Hascal or his father, but they differ somewhat in that the
posts are less tapered. Also, they are made of a more fragile,
expensive, and "pretty" wood—walnut. They reveal a definite
interest in ornamentation. And they exhibit the unusual trait of a
hole in the top slat, which Aaron admitted was his trademark.

Some customers would like all the slats in a chair to have a
notch in the center, said Aaron, but the notch weakens the slat or
panel and should not be there at all, he told me. Why make the

112 Black walnut panel-back rocker made by Aaron (1963 or 1964). The separate elements are more distinctly formed than in his earlier chairs.

notch then? He said he made some chairs with it and others without; potential customers always chose the chairs with the notch. Therefore, he began making all chairs with a notch in the center of the top edge of the slat. But he was also seeking to develop his own distinctive kind of chair.

"I like that chair," remarked Verge about Aaron's earlier work reminiscent of chairs produced in the shop under Verge's super-vision. "But for myself I wouldn't have them rings and nubs. But you gotta make it how the customers want" he said, not realizing that Aaron was making the chair as he finally wanted. "I like the round arms," concluded Verge. The rounded arm was the only major element of Verge's and Hascal's chairs that Aaron main-tained in his later works, though he wanted to depart from it.

Chester was more explicit than Verge in his assessment of Aaron's early chairs. Of the rocker shown in figure 111, he said, "That's a good lookin' chair if they was a few improvements in it." He listed eight.

- He would have bent the crest [the top slat] "to fit the head better."
- "The top slat oughta been wider where it goes into the postees."
- "You need the panels nar'er than that to make it comf'tabler."
- "I'd a put more rounds in it, put in at least two rounds b'low the seat."
- "Hit shoulda had more designs [turnings] b'low the arms, kinda like the decoratin' b'low the seat."
- "I never did like this type of arm," by which he meant the barrel design, the only element in the chair of which Verge approved because it was similar to his; Chester, however, usually made flat arms, although he had used barrel arms on quite a few chairs.
- "Now that decoratin'," Chester noted, "hit's unusual an' a little bit differ'nt. I've never seen decoratin' like that b'fore. That's what people are lookin' for." Chester agreed that "the number of panels is right for the chair. But if he'd made a real crook in the backs like I made 'em he'd a had to a made the panels nar'er an' he'd have to have more of 'em."
- "The chair needs patchin'—you need to patch the gaps in 'twixt the bark."

The gaps in the seat were formed when the splints drew away from each other as they dried. To my knowledge only Chester used winter bark (skinned in early fall) taken directly from the tree. Aaron and other men in his area used summer bark, which has more sap and consequently shrivels up more when it seasons. In addition, Aaron and others stripped off and discarded the top half of the inner bark; thus the splints were only half as thick as Chester's and the edges turned down as they dried, leaving gaps which Chester found objectionable.

Chester was more impressed with Aaron's recent works, as was Aaron. "That's a new design on me," Chester said about a chair made in 1967 (fig. 113). "I've never seen that decoratin'

113 Black walnut slat-back rocker made by Aaron in June 1967. Aaron switched to the slat-back design because he thought his earlier chairs looked too much like factory-made rockers.

before on a chair. Whoever made this chair's interested in makin' somethin' differ'nt." Chester had never met Aaron or seen his chairs; rather, he selected these works for special comment from a stack of photographs of chairs I had given him.

"The wood in them backs has been sawed," he continued; "it's not been riven out 'cause the grain in each slat's differ'nt. Can't tell 'bout the postees. I'd a put that bottom round closer to the seat—that big hole don't look good. Hit's a well-built chair like the other'n; there's nothin' out a line. That's the reason I'm sure he's an old-time chairmaker."

That remark would have pleased Aaron, who was generally content with his recent works, which he thought were "kinda pretty" in form and design. Aaron's brother said that the dining and rocking chairs were pretty because "they got all them knobs on 'em." Referring to a black walnut rocker he made in late July 1967, however, Aaron muttered to himself that "it ain't the prettiest one I ever made." He said that it showed knots and white wood and that the grain was not straight on all the pieces. To Aaron—the perfectionist—the component elements should have matched in all respects.

For the most part, however, Aaron felt that his chairs were attractive in their harmony of design and form. The spools were of the proper shape, number, and location on the chair. The wood was inherently pretty. The chairs were of good proportions with design elements unified. By the time I met Aaron in 1967 he was making rocking chairs on which the turnings had become quite clearly delineated, the rockers and slats were sharply defined, the form—slat back rather than panel back—no longer resembled factory-made chairs, which looked "cheap" to Aaron, and the back posts had been made smaller in diameter, increasing the elegance of the chair. In other words, Aaron was executing works that were distinctly his own with only a nod of recognition to his predecessors—chairs in which, from his point of view, all the elements were perfectly integrated.

If that was so, then why did he make a dining chair in August 1967 with flat arms that obviously were not in harmony with the rest of the chair (fig. 114)? The barrel arms still disturbed Aaron because they were like Verge's; he had wanted to employ some other design but had no idea what. In mid-July I had shown him photographs of some of Chester's works, a few of which he examined closely, but he remarked only on the arms of two of the chairs (figs. 50, 73), saying, "Both of 'em's pretty. That armrest's pretty and it'd be easy to make."

I did not realize at the time why he had singled out the armrests for comment. In late August a niece of Aaron's asked him to make some "end tables" (fig. 115) and eight dining chairs, one of which was to have arms, although Aaron usually made such chairs without arms. His niece thought that the surface area of the arms should be larger than that of the barrel arms; Aaron agreed, so he tried to make them like the armrests on Chester's

114 Black walnut dining chair with arms, made by Aaron in August 1967 for a customer who did not want the typical barrel arms.

chairs. The results disappointed and embarrassed Aaron, who became apologetic. Although his niece seemed satisfied, Aaron said the arms were too thin, the small ends of the arms which fitted into the posts were not small enough, and the inside of the curve was too deep. In essence, the chair "can be improved on."

Aaron felt the design had possibilities and might be attractively realized, but it was a problem he would have to work on in the future. That he had the patience for such a task was obvious. As I watched him make chairs, he measured each post with a handmade micrometer to get every two exactly alike. "Get 'em all alike and you don't have to worry about whether they'll set right or not," he said. Aaron sanded each piece while it was on the turning lathe, using fine sandpaper and emery cloth, despite his contention that "I dislike this job worse'n any job of chairmaking—too dusty." Meticulously he measured the angle of every hole he drilled in the posts; carefully he tested the smoothness of each slat he sawed to shape and sanded; and conscientiously he turned the rounds twice a day as they seasoned

115 An unnamed piece of furniture Aaron made in August 1967 for a customer who wanted an end table; Aaron made chairs and stools only, not tables, but he was loath to call this table a stool.

above the wood-burning stove in the kitchen. "If you don't turn 'em like an ole hen turns her eggs," he warned, "they get a crook in 'em."

"He's experienced as a chairmaker," said Chester as he examined photos of Aaron's chairs. "He must be a slow worker an' a sure worker." Aaron, in fact, seemed to be second only to Chester in his willingness to "fool" with chairmaking, that is, to take is seriously.

CHESTER'S RELATIVES AND OTHER CRAFTSMEN

Many other men were making chairs in the 1960s, but not necessarily with pronounced skill or real interest. Two men who

116 Baby rocker made by Chester's grandfather
Cal about 1907 was rebottomed by Chester's uncle
Linden in 1966.

helped Verge build chairs in the early 1960s switched to tuning
cars at a service station. Beechum, who was born in 1940, worked
in the chair shop with Hascal for a few months because "they
was about to close me out" of carpentry work. In July 1967, he
said he would not make chairs if he could find other work
because "the money's too slow. I just can't make much money at
it." A month later he quit the shop and headed north in search of
work in order to support his wife and three children whom he
had left behind in a mountain hollow. He tried four different jobs
in a week; that was the last I heard of him.

What about Chester's relatives? His sons, of course, could not
learn chairmaking from him. Two cousins and a nephew who

117 Rocking chair made by
Chester's brother Kenton about
1955 was in use on the front
porch of his house in a hollow
near Cumberland in 1966.

helped Chester make chairs in the early 1940s never became chairmakers because the financial rewards were inadequate and the work was uninspiring. Chester's uncle Linden, who lived near Cumberland, spent more time repairing seats than making chairs, both Chester and his uncle told me. Linden was once known for the speed with which he produced chairs, turning them on a foot-powered lathe. He never made octagon-shaped chair parts, as Chester did, although he admired his nephew's work. "Never had enough patience to shape 'em out," he told me. "Man, they're pretty the way he makes 'em." Chester said his uncle "was a fast worker, but I've had people tell me they [Linden's chairs] weren't no account. He put 'em together too green or somethin'." Linden was not putting them together at all by the time I met him because, he said, "I'm too nervous." He was an alcoholic, Chester said.

Chester's brother Kenton could never make chairs properly either, and he, too, spent most of his time drinking according to Linden, Chester, and Ruth. "I think he makes one ever' now an' then, but he's not able to do much work," said Chester, rather charitably. On another occasion Chester told me that his brother "couldn't put 'em together, no sir; he put 'em together lopsided and every which way," as apparent in a chair on the front porch of Kenton's home in a hollow near Cumberland (fig. 117). The posts were turned on a makeshift lathe Kenton kept in a shed behind the house, but the rounds were roughly hewed with an ax. The arms are ill fitting, the panels in the back were chopped from boards, and the chair as a whole is poorly constructed.

Kenton told me that he had not made chairs for several years because he could find no customers to buy them. That seemed not to have troubled his wife, Emmafair, who, according to other members of the family, "doped" Kenton into marrying her, that is, "charmed" him with affection and with her skills as a house-wife. Deformed from birth, she was a jealous wife who used to follow Kenton wherever he went for fear he would desert her. A few years before I met her, when Kenton was getting bark in the woods to bottom a chair, she fell and broke her hip; after that, she could not walk at all. "Lord have mercy, ain't that awful?" exclaimed Linden. "Poor ole Kent. Boy, I wouldn't have that on my hands, would you? Lordy!"

Living near Cumberland were three other men who, I was informed, made chairs. Courtney identified himself as a farmer, however, not a chairmaker. He had made two rocking chairs during the winter of 1964-65, turning them on a neighbor's lathe (fig. 118). Chester thought the chair in the photo I showed him looked like a factory-made chair. Hascal remarked, "I just don't like them kinda chairs; they're just an ordinary chair built on rockers." Aaron concurred: "I don't like it. It's nothin' but a settin' chair on rockers."

To pass the time, Courtney also whittled a few chairs with a pocketknife, like the small cedar chair in figure 119. Courtney claimed that a man from Harlan wanted him to make eight settin' chairs at $8 each, but he had not done it by the time I left in 1967, and there is no reason to think he ever did.

118 Rocking chair made by
Courtney in the winter of
1964-65.   119 Cedar settin' chair
made by Courtney in 1964; he
whittled it with a pocketknife.

120 Stool made by Hugh in 1966; he copied it from a magazine illustration.

Hugh, a coal miner living near Viper who wanted to work with wood when he retired, was not a specialist either (see fig. 120). Said a neighbor, "He ain't no chairmaker; he jest pranks around with it."

One might reach the same conclusion about Morris, a farmer at Hoskinston. In his early thirties at the time, he had made a bed frame, a table, a dulcimer, some baskets, a picture frame, two banjos, and a couple of chairs. But he did not want to be a full-time craftsman because "I can't make no money at it. I'd always be a poor man." Morris could not tolerate poverty, one infers, for then he would have been unable to maintain his home and grounds, which were the neatest and cleanest in the hollow, a point made by a neighbor from whom I asked directions to Morris's home. Morris seemed to be a fastidious man; he refused to be photographed with his chairs because he feared the soil on his work clothes might show.

In use in Morris's home were two chairs with square posts that he made about 1958 (figs. 121 and 122). The electric lathe he then owned was of no use to him because he had no electricity. He had a drawing knife, too, but no drawing horse, so he hewed out the pieces with an ax and tried to smooth them on a bench using a hand plane. He hewed the slats, too, and did not cook or press them. The bark for the seats was thin, poorly cut, and full of knots and weak places, but Morris seemed not to notice. One chair originally had arms but he cut them off because anyone larger than himself (he was about 5 feet, 5 inches tall, and weighed 120 pounds) could not sit in it.

"Morris can make chairs so good you couldn't tell 'em from those you buy in the store," one woman told me. Not everyone agreed with her. Another person said that the chairs were too simple, heavy, and plain, and "the rockers are tapered too thin in back and won't hold up." Hascal remarked simply, "I don't like all that flatness." Chester, too, disapproved of Morris's work, commenting on the rocker: "Hit's not true; it's a little bit 'sygoglin,' I calls it. I'd say it's got the 'rickets': everything was made green. Hit's not a good-lookin' chair a-tall. Looks too much like a factory-made chair. Hit's got too low a back. A body couldn't rest in that chair, less'n he was gonna use the banister for a footrest—the seat's too high.

"That rockin' chair's made for an old lady—real high up 'un," he continued. "Hit's handmade—ever'bit of it," though that was a fact, not praise. "They ain't 'nough rounds in 'em—they'd oughta had another round in back like I make 'em. Don't see why them postees is square and the rounds is round. Hit don't look right thataway.

"Whoever made that chair's not a chairmaker. He don't do it for a livin'," concluded Chester. "Looks like he made it for his own use."

Morris would have liked to have picked up a few dollars making baskets or musical instruments. A heavy, awkward banjo, he felt, was worth a lot of money because his father, who once was a pretty good banjo picker, told him that "it rings like a five-

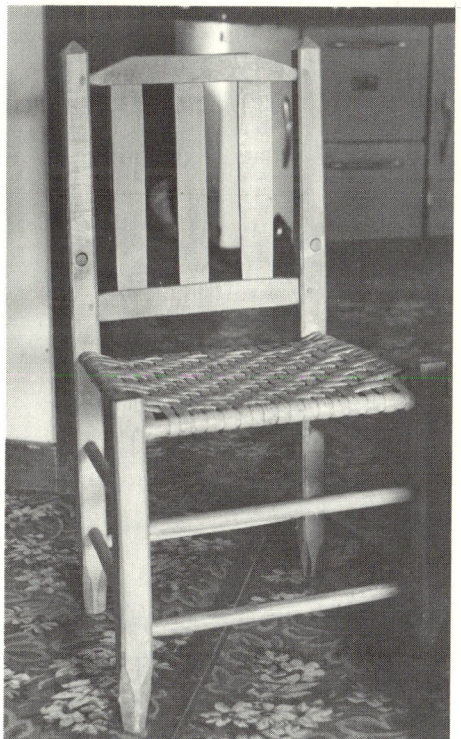

121 Morris, a farmer living near Hoskinston, made this rocking chair with an ax about 1958.
122 Morris also made this chair using only an ax; it was supposed to have been an armchair, but nobody except Morris could get in and out of it, so he had to cut off the arms.

hundred-dollar banjer." Morris's baskets, however, seemed to be much better designed and made.

Two other men should be mentioned. Coy, who was born in 1894 in North Carolina, lived in a mountain hollow near Wooton for more than forty years. He claimed to have been called to the area by the founders of the Frontier Nursing Service at Wendover to make chairs, a craft he learned from his stepmother who showed him pictures of chairs. In the 1960s he still occasionally made chairs, which he said he sent to an outlet in Massachusetts, but the only customers I know about were tourists who stopped in front of the Hyden town courthouse where Coy was peddling his stools.

"Them look jest like factory-made chairs. He's copied them off a factory-made chair shore 'nough," said Chester in regard to Coy's chairs (fig. 123). Hascal even suggested that one of the chairs was not handmade at all but rather was a factory-made chair that Coy was falsely claiming as his own. Coy was elderly and in poor health when I met him in 1967. His sons refused to make chairs, he said, or to help him make chairs (one is a farmer, the other a coal miner). Coy was then producing only a few stools and rolling pins.

The other man was O.P. Jackson. Born in 1891, he had had, he proudly repeated several times, only five months of formal schooling. His son, who lived close by, made beds, chests and tables in cherry and black walnut in direct emulation of the imitation Early American high-style furniture produced in the furniture factories in Berea. "I never liked to make chairs and still don't; you can't make no money at it," said O.P.'s son, who claimed to have taught his father how to use a lathe and how to make chairs. Until 1930 O.P. whittled chairs with a pocketknife; together father and son "packed 'em" five miles to Wayland to sell, receiving $1 for a settin' chair and $5 for a rocking chair. "Boy a dollar them days looked big as a bedspread," said the son; "we thought that was a lotta money." Thirty years later they had increased the price of a rocking chair ninefold, but hoped to get still more.

O.P. contended that the box-bottom chairs (fig. 124) and stools he once made were based on his own ideas. "I don't have no

123 Two settin' chairs allegedly made by Coy, of Wooton, Kentucky, in 1937 (*left*) and in the early 1950s. The later one may not be handmade at all.

education, never been to school more'n five months in my life, but you know there's gotta be new designs once in a while. You can't keep goin' with only one design. I just started makin' chairs with box bottoms an' everyone like 'em so I kept makin' 'em." Coy, who also claimed to have originated the double-bottom or box-bottom chair, said that somebody in the Wayland area got the idea from him about 1960, and that is indeed the time O.P. said he began to make that kind of chair. O.P.'s works seem eclectic (figs. 124-126). It would not be surprising, therefore, to discover that he had in fact borrowed the box-bottom design from Coy, although I do not know when or from whom Coy got the idea. Box-bottom chairs are also found in western Kentucky, although Coy may have developed the idea independently.

124 Photograph (by the author) of a photograph by O.P. of two box-bottom chairs he made about 1960.

By the mid-1960s O.P. was no longer using bark for the bottoms of chairs or stools because he could not skin it himself in the hills, he said, or pay anyone else enough money to do it for him. Instead, he used "reeds" (white oak splints) bought from a furniture store in Jackson. He did not cook or press the slats or posts, and for the preceding six or eight years he had not made slat-back chairs but plaited-back ones. By the time I met him he was making no chairs at all, only stools. Like Coy, O.P. was too old to spend much time working in his shop. Nor could he find anyone to assist him in producing chairs, although he complained that a young man nearby had borrowed the idea of the box-bottom chair from him and was competing with him by charging only half as much for dining and rocking chairs of this design.

125 Plaited-back rocker made by O.P. about 1940.   **126** Dining chair by O.P., who used a stencil for the slats.

THE FUTURE OF CHAIRMAKING

What is the future of the tradition of making chairs? In 1965 Chester believed that "in a few years chairmakin', it's gonna fade plumb away."

Anyone who asks whether or not there are any chairmakers around today will probably be told that none remains, that he should have been in southeastern Kentucky a decade or two ago when there were a dozen of them. Some of the men who made chairs in the 1960s have died. A few lacked the interest to develop their skills further. Others may have been crippled with arthritis or debilitated by alcoholism. Beechum and several others just "pranked around" with making chairs until they found more lucrative employment. Hascal seemed to be paralyzed emotionally, although he may have solved some of his problems later. Chester moved to Indiana and then to Cincinnati; he made his last chair in 1977, and died in 1981. His sons were too "nervous" to learn chairmaking. His nephews and cousins who knew how to make chairs preferred singing and storytelling as modes of expressive behavior and loading coal and pumping gas as vocations. Ironically, of the dozen men mentioned in these pages, only Aaron was actively engaged in chairmaking in the 1970s—Aaron, who never learned the craft in his youth, who did not grow up with chairmaking, and who backed into the occupation at forty years of age while trying to keep other problems at bay. But anyone can learn the craft and someone else probably will, as Aaron's career reveals.

Later Chester corrected himself, saying, "People'll always have to set, an' my opinion, there'll be a need for chairs as long as time lasts."

There will be people who need to make chairs, pots, quilts, or other objects for the associations engendered, to express themselves and deal with personal problems by making things, and to satisfy a creative urge by producing something that is pleasing to look at and use. A few people might become specialists in these activities. More often the needs will be sporadic and the activities occasional, without participants necessarily conceiving of the process as an occupation or the product as art.

SEVEN

The Beauty Part
and the Lasting Part

"Buddy, when he threw one together, hit was together," said Chester's uncle Linden about his father.

Chester agreed, noting that the chairs made by Cal and other kin "weren't comfortable, but one thing about it, my grandfather's chairs—if you could see one today—it'd be good an' stout. They didn't make for the beauty part, they made for the lastin' part, he did."

Chester said about himself that he made "an awful good easy chair, restin' chair an' ever'thing, but I still say, I'm not as good as my grandfather in makin' a chair that'll last." Cal's chairs, he said, "don't set good but they last good."

Chester also contended that Cal and Linden as well as his paternal grandfather Pike and Pike's brother Hiram did not have as wide a variety of designs for feet or finials as he, nor did they use as many different patterns and splint sizes for the seats. But imagination in chair designing is not the only criterion for identifying a "good" chairmaker, or perhaps even the principal one. Possessing and utilizing a range of designs might increase sales, however.

The chair seats or bottoms made by Chester's kin were of one width of hickory bark—about an inch—whereas Chester used several widths. The choice depended on what Chester thought was in keeping with the chair's design, on what he inferred customers wanted and on how much he hoped to charge for the chair. To get the narrow splints, Chester had to cut and strip hickory poles only two or three inches in diameter. His kin, he said, "would never fool with makin' a little bitty nar' chair [meaning the strips of bark in a chair bottom]. The wider you make it, the longer it'll last is the way I look at it. 'Course, the nar' looks better and sets more comf'table. But I doubt it'll last as long as that big, wide, ugly stuff would.

"If I had two chairs settin' out there, one of 'em with wide weave an' t'other with the nar'," said Chester in regard to customer preference, "they'll pick the nar' ever'time. So they pick for the looks, not the lastin' part."

Chester had differentiated between craftsmen who made chairs emphasizing appearance and those who made them with durability uppermost in mind. Both visual appeal and structural soundness are aspects of useful design. One or the other concern might be given priority by a particular craftsman or in a specific object. Sometimes the two were valued equally, and achieved in one work.

Other people separated chairmakers who "make 'em to sell" from those who "jest prank around with it." Some distinguished between those who "make 'em for the money" and those who "make 'em for the sake of makin' a good chair." If the polarization of the beauty part and the lasting part points to the fundamental nature of chairmaking as useful design, then the other typologies speak to chairmakers' motivations and aspirations, values, technical skills, and degree of professionalism and dedication. These ideas are essential to understanding why objects have been made a particular way or why they exhibit certain traits. All three typologies have implications for the study of traditional craft work.

In this chapter I summarize some findings of my study of craftsmen of the Cumberlands. My comments are guided by ways in which craftsmen and their customers perceived the making of chairs as I documented these through observation, interviewing, and the compiling of life history information. I also discuss methods in research on folk art, suggesting how the field of folklore studies relates to and yet differs from several other disciplines in which traditional forms and processes have been examined.

TRADITION IN CHAIRMAKING

My understanding of chairmaking evolved as I carried out my field study. My initial concern was the kinds of chairs craftsmen made and how. I measured and photographed different workers' tools and chairs. I kept detailed logs of what Chester and Aaron did throughout the day and evening. I recorded remarks of many chairmakers about the woods used—their attractiveness, strength, and ease of handling. In this way I was able to establish similarities and differences, constructing an overview of the tradition as a first step in my research and a basis for exploring other issues.

One realm of tradition in chairmaking is that of *the overall forms of chairs*. The ladder-back or slat-back chair has been identified as a distinct type, for example, different from, say, the New England Windsor chair whose back consists of vertical spindles held in place between an arch and the wooden seat. Both forms have been repeated often enough that they are immediately recognizable, even to a nonspecialist.

Among ladder-back chairs is the "square-post slat-back with tapered rear posts, a folk type found widely in Europe since the Middle Ages, rarely in New England, commonly in Quebec and eastern Ontario, and occasionally in eastern Virginia," writes Henry Glassie in *Patterns in the Material Folk Culture of the Eastern United States* (see C, fig. 127). A related form in Glassie's typology is the mule-ear (or rabbit-ear) chair, common in the South since the second quarter of the nineteenth century. Its back posts taper downward; they also curve backward rather than stand straight (D, E, and F).

"From the early nineteenth century to the present," writes Glassie, "the southern mule-ear chair has undergone continual modification so that, while the same chairs can be found throughout the South, the South's subregions also present distinctive subtypes." In eastern Virginia, he observes, the chair typically is bent backward rather dramatically and has two slats—the top one twice as wide as the lower one. Through much of the Deep South the posts curve little. "The mountain mule-ear has moderately bent rear posts and, typically, three slats of about equal size and shape." The mountain-style settin' chair dominates in southeastern Kentucky.

Other types or subtypes include ladder-back rocking chairs (with or without ornamentation), dining chairs, panel-back

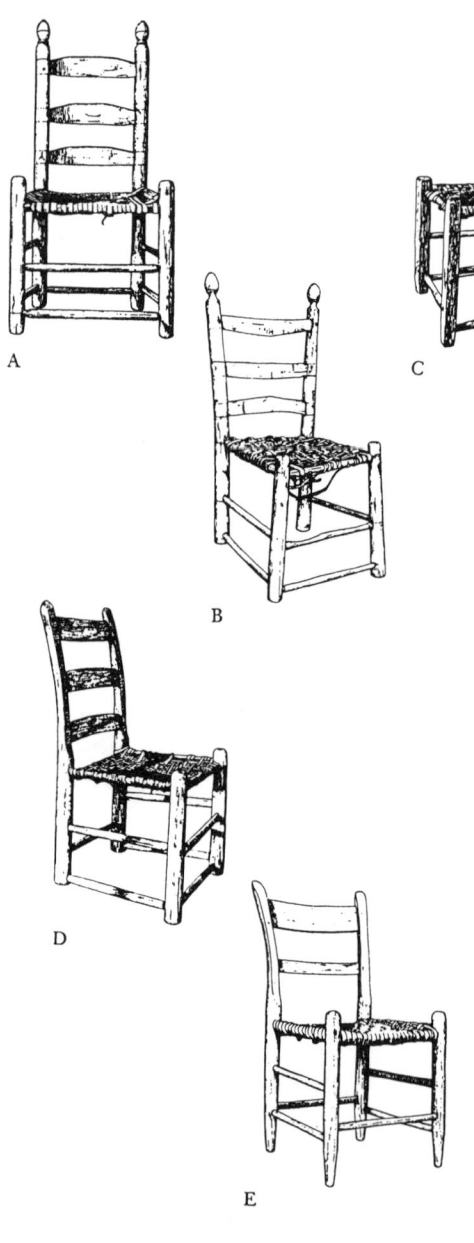

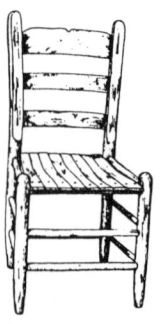

127 Types and subtypes of slat-back chairs: A. Slat-back chair from Middletown, Massachusetts. B. Slat-back chair, south of Orchid, Louisa County, Virginia, C. Square-post slat-back chair, southeast of Gum Spring, Louisa County, Virginia. D. Mule-ear slat-back chair, north of Alpharetta, Fulton County, Georgia. E. Mule-ear slat-back chair from near Louisa, Louisa County, Virginia. F. Mule-ear slat-back chair in Paxville, Clarendon County, South Carolina. Henry Glassic, *Patterns in Material Folk Culture of the Eastern United States*, pp. 230-31.

chairs (both rockers and settin' chairs), and bark-back chairs. Some chairs have woven seats, others are panel-bottom. Types and subtypes are traditional (not just the researcher's analytical constructs) when reflecting "native cognitive categories" and serving as models for craftsmen, thereby exhibiting, or testifying to the existence of, continuities and consistencies in human thought and behavior.

Aaron's first settin' chair, for example, was closely patterned after a mule-eared chair made by a neighbor; Aaron conceived of it as typifying handmade rather than factory-made chairs, and therefore as traditional in form, material, and manufacture. Chester's two-in-one chairs constitute a distinct category of chairs. Although the overall form was unprecedented in other men's works and not emulated by contemporaries or successors, it extended or transformed concepts of traditional form and design (e.g., handmade, ladder-back, mule-eared).

Some craftsmen repeated or reproduced certain *design elements* within a general form, which therefore are traditional. A rocking chair by Chester's uncle eighty years ago has finials, barrel arms and turnings (fig. 63); so does a rocker that Chester made fifty years ago (fig. 66). Rockers constructed by Verge, Hascal, and Aaron in the mid-1960s also have barrel arms; on some of the chairs by the latter two the arms have flattened surfaces on top, so there are no turnings on the arms (e.g., figs. 102 and 114).

Some *symbols* are traditional, and some traditions or transformations of them are symbolic. The heart motif on Chester's chair for his daughter represents love. Chairs of walnut and extensive ornamentation are seen as expensive, special, and suggestive of social and economic status. Plainness and simplicity of design might be associated with austerity, lack of ostentation, and nonmaterial values. To Aaron, the slat-back form and evidence of personalization of design stood for traditional values and ways of doing things in the region with which he identified strongly. Factory-made chairs suggested to some a lack of personal pride in making chairs and connectedness with people. The deeply curved slats on some of Chester's chairs were like "somebody huggin' you," protective and providing security.

Apprenticeship is another area of traditionalism in chairmaking. Chester began making things by hand as a small child, later operating the turning lathe while his grandfather Cal made chairs and aiding his uncle Linden as he wove seats. Aaron's training came when he joined Verge and Hascal at the chair shop. Hascal had helped his father Verge and uncle Everett with minor tasks. O.P.'s son taught him to use a turning lathe and other equipment. Coy's stepmother gave him rudimentary instruction and showed him illustrations of chairs as models. The tradition is that of learning through doing under another's supervision rather than that of formal classroom education or reliance on instruction manuals. The process entails establishing a work rhythm, modeling behavior, and immediate feedback (as well as narrating, ritualizing, and other expressive behavior characteristic of firsthand interaction) that communicate and reinforce ideas about the best ways to do things and the appropriate forms to make.

Tools, techniques of construction and choices of materials constitute yet another dimension of tradition in chairmaking. A person can construct a chair from pieces whittled with a pocketknife or shaped with an ax. Those who made chairs for their own use often did this rather than going to the expense of obtaining a turning lathe and the trouble of learning how to use it. They knew, however, that those who made chairs as a livelihood employed more elaborate equipment, including lathe, workbench, slat and post presses, drawing horse, and so on. Working wet wood typified traditional chairmaking. The absence of glue, screws, and nails in chairs surprised people unaware of the arcane method of making chairs using a combination of green lumber, partially seasoned wood, and fully dried pieces. This was the mystery or secret of chairmaking, known by those who learned the craft directly from others.

Tradition was entailed in the most frequent choices of materials and the conventional wisdom regarding wood characteristics. Chairmakers cited the same attributes of each wood, perhaps having made similar discoveries but sometimes seeming to repeat what they had heard from others. Remarks about walnut virtually took the form of a litany: "It's a pretty wood but awful easy burst," said all chairmakers, some of whom had never actually used it. While craftsmen typically chose a common hardwood for settin' chairs, which was the "right" choice, given the chair's heavy use and the value of durability, walnut traditionally was used, if at all, for fancy and expensive chairs, serving as an index of wealth and status or a vehicle of special meanings.

Some people thought of the *activity of chairmaking* as traditional because they associated it with an older way of life. A nephew and two cousins of Chester who had helped him make chairs in their youth, the farmer Morris who made some chairs for his own use, and Chester's wife viewed chairmaking as a typical subsistence endeavor from the past that was out of place in a contemporary cash economy. On the other hand, Chester and Aaron esteemed old-time chairmaking forms and construction techniques for what they expressed or symbolized about craftsmanship, aesthetics, and a way of life with which they identified.

Finally, some *individuals* were conceived of as traditional—as types who embody a complex of behaviors, values, and ways of doing things continuing from the past. When examining photographs of chairs by Aaron (about whom he knew nothing), Chester praised Aaron as an "ole-time chairmaker" because of the form and design of the chairs and the construction techniques and skills that were apparent. To Beechum and Hascal, Chester epitomized the traditional (and master) chairmaker. Some townspeople spoke of Chester as a "character" because of his old-fashioned appearance and ways.

Why did some chairmakers emulate the construction techniques, the forms, or the designs of other craftsmen? Why did some of them sometimes transform the traditional, producing innovations? Why were some people drawn to the tradition of chairmaking as an occupation or a preoccupation while others were repulsed?

Aaron reproduced his neighbor Henry's chair to learn how to make chairs. In the chair shop he emulated Verge and Hascal because he was learning but also because he was of subordinate status. Having learned not simply forms and designs but an interrelated complex of construction techniques, material selection, and conventional wisdom, he continued to reproduce the chair forms. Gradually, he transformed the techniques and designs to distinguish his works from those of the chair shop and himself from the other chairmakers. He opted for the ladderback style with multiple turnings or decorative ornaments because to him this was traditional, making his chairs stand out from mass-produced, factory-made chairs. Because they were traditional, he thought his chairs more attractive. They were also more uniquely his, of concern to him perhaps because of his unpleasant memories of life in northern cities where he was just another anonymous worker in a factory. In traditional chairmaking he seemed to find himself. The craft allowed him to live at home in the mountains, gave him a degree of independence, and provided him the means of doing something well with which he could be pleased.

Chester responded to customer stipulation and selection. He built odd chairs to attract buyers and to attract attention to himself, enlarging his consumer base. Having become known for strange chairs and new designs, there was the expectation of more from him and the promise of publicity. He increased the number and prominence of pegs in chairs in the belief that this distinguished him from other chairmakers, bringing him customers. He experimented with materials, construction techniques, and designs because of his skill, capabilities, and dedication to chairmaking. Rather than simply reproduce a chair, he would focus attention on an aspect of it, exploring how to make rocking or "settin'" a more pleasurable experience, how to build a chair out of readily available but otherwise wasted materials, or how to develop a single design element into a complex pattern. Sometimes he ritualized the making of chairs, losing himself in thought and immersing himself in chairmaking as a way of coping with emotional problems. The solidity, large size, and sense of enclosure unique to some of his chairs symbolically expressed his need for seclusion and protection. His preoccupation with tradition, and his claims to traditionalism even in the face of techniques and designs that were transformations or innovations, identified him with a period prior to the times of stress. He was a chairmaker because he grew up with the craft, because he found in it a source of identity as well as livelihood, and because he was driven to it periodically as escape; it was a means of coping, a way of adjusting, and a solution to personal problems.

Some people who knew how to make chairs refused to do so. It reminded them of subsistence living and the deprivations associated with it; chairmaking would not provide them with an adequate income, they were not particularly talented, or they derived little satisfaction from making things by hand or for a living.

For Verge and Hascal, making chairs sometimes was a way of making money. Verge turned out chairs of one size, using a simple design and wide bark for the seat because standardization maximized productivity and because plainness in form was a moral virtue. Hascal often claimed to innovate or to want to innovate, but his chairs were strikingly similar to his father's whose values he challenged, not through chair designs, but by describing licentious behavior in which he allegedly engaged. If and when he made chairs, Hascal repeated or reproduced traditional designs because of the dominance of his father, his own fixation on the idea of breaking free, and the paralysis that ensued.

Coy made the kinds of chairs his stepmother urged him to produce and that the Frontier Nursing Service purchased from him in large quantities. To Chester, Aaron, and Hascal, Coy's chairs were uninspired and uninspiring, too closely resembling factory-made chairs. Morris and Courtney were farmers who made chairs only for their own use; lacking equipment, knowledge, and customers, they turned to models that were most easily emulated. O.P. bottomed chairs in later years with rushes that he bought from a store; he was too old to locate and strip hickory bark in the woods as he had once done and as other chairmakers did, and his son refused to help him. Some of O.P.'s chairs had box bottoms; a principal motive for using the design, he implied, was economic. "I don't have no education, never been to school more'n five months in my life," he said, "but you know, there's gotta be new designs once in a while." He complained that someone else in the area had recently taken up chairmaking using this design, competing with him for customers.

The chairmaker repeats or reproduces designs to learn his craft. Once he becomes proficient, he finds he has acquired a set of behaviors so numerous and so integrated that it requires great dedication, desire, and ability to disentangle the behaviors, or to transform or abandon one of them. Construction techniques or designs are used or rejected owing to persons or ideas associated with them, their relationship to the maker's identity, or customer selection or stipulation. Innovation may be the product of experimentation or seemingly idle play with materials, as well as the outcome of others' suggestions or expectations and of emotional states and psychological processes. Of special importance in understanding why forms are repeated and activities are emulated is the fact that, first, they have proven effective and, second, they define the situation, providing models for what to do and how to do it. While novelty is exciting, familiarity is comfortable. The two forces compel much of human behavior.

I encountered a curious situation in the 1960s. A museum director had declined the opportunity to purchase some of Aaron's chairs for the museum's collection; they seemed too refined. He thought Chester's unsanded and unvarnished chairs epitomized folk things. In contrast, the owner of a bookstore and gallery chose not to purchase Chester's chairs. The sophisticated design and utility of his work assailed her notion of what folk craft objects ought to be.

Which craftsmen and whose chairs were most traditional? Chairs by Courtney, Coy, Verge, and Hascal evince the greatest continuities and consistencies in form and design. Except for Coy perhaps, none of these men identified himself exclusively or even principally as a chairmaker; indeed, several even denied they were chairmakers. None was very good at chairmaking, nor did any of them further the craft by developing ways to exploit the materials, enhance the comfort and appearance, or improve the construction of chairs.

When we consider not only design elements, but also apprenticeship, tools and procedures, and especially involvement in and dedication to chairmaking, Chester and Aaron stand out as traditional craftsmen. Indeed, they made traditional chairmaking central to their lives, deriving their essential identity from it. On the other hand, they were the most innovative. By taking tradition to heart, Chester and Aaron developed the skills and will to utilize, as well as transform, others' knowledge, procedures, and designs. They needed the comfort of tradition and the stimulation of novelty, which together yielded a sense of self and self-esteem.

CONCEPTUALIZATION AND IMPLEMENTATION

Some people construct chairs for their own use. Perhaps they cannot afford to purchase one, or they want to learn new skills, respond to a challenge, or seek diversion. Each step in the process may be a learning experience, and the product may be a chair that "could be improved upon." Others build chairs for a living. If they work in a factory, they probably do not know, or rarely interact with, the consumer. The product and its manufacture are likely to be standardized; designs may be predetermined and construction largely mechanical. A few craftsmen make chairs not only as a livelihood but also as custom production. They fulfill specific requests and are sensitive to customer selection. Objects may be personalized and expressive. The processes of conceptualization and implementation discussed here characterize the manufacture of handmade or homemade chairs intended for sale by a maker who has direct experience with some customers.

A chairmaker must decide what, exactly, *is to be constructed.* Of what materials? Using what techniques and tools? If a chair of a certain design and material has been ordered, then the craftsman's choices are narrowed. When the chairmaker builds unsolicited works for which he then seeks customers, the constraints on forms, materials, and construction techniques are more ambiguous. He can construct chairs according to his own sense of beauty and goodness. He may repeat what has proved successful in the past, either appealing to the lowest common denominator of taste or to a narrow range of interests and values. He might try something new. While the choice is his alone, bearing on it are concerns about income, willingness to cater to the whims of others, and personal preferences and predilections, as well as exigencies of the moment (such as whether construction is routine work or fulfills expressive needs).

Before he can build it, the craftsman must visualize the chair. It is likely to fall into an existing category, its overall design a familiar one. This is because in learning to make forms he has learned typical forms themselves. Moreover, he is creating an object that serves a practical purpose, whether for settin' or for rocking. Those forms produced widely over time and space must have something to recommend them, and many consumers and prospective customers want no other. Utility and expectation precipitate the image of a particular form, be it a settin' chair or a sewing rocker, a slat-back chair or a bark-back one, or "a chair just like the one made for _____."

The craftsman may have a feeling, a desire to do something different: to use an atypical material, to turn a different kind of spool on the leg or stretcher, to make the chair special somehow. The chair's image is vague, or only part of the form is sharply focused. Trying to clarify it brings to mind images of other chairs, or aspects of them, and perhaps of tools or construction techniques. To achieve what he feels he wants, the chairmaker may have to experiment, discarding what doesn't work.

If he is repeating a design, then the craftsman is likely to emulate existing techniques of construction. When selecting an unfamiliar wood, however, or one that is difficult to work, he must ascertain its characteristics and imagine how he will shape it to achieve the chair he wants to make. If he is transforming a familiar design and bringing into existence something novel, he will probably recall prior experiences with various materials and procedures, choosing some as precedents, while developing other, unprecedented solutions through trial and error..

Conceptualization and problem-solving do not end when the *implementation process* begins. Decisions, choices, visualization, experimentation, and other processes continue as the craftsman manipulates materials and constructs the chair. And while building one chair, he may imagine another. Unanticipated difficulties could provoke a change in procedure. The grain or color of a wood may have an unexpected effect. Correcting a mistake might alter what was originally envisioned. The rhythm of work and sensations in working can influence the outcome. As one aspect of the chair takes shape, perhaps the earlier desire, vaguely felt, suddenly crystallizes into an image.

During the building of the chair, and certainly after it is completed, there is a process of *feedback and response*. The craftsman has perceptual evidence by which to judge his capabilities, the defensibility of his initial vision, the skills required to master techniques. The form is perfect, all things considered, or it is not. The chair is just what the customer hoped for or it is disappointing. It is practical but not very attractive, visually appealing but not too useful, satisfying in both form and function or a complete failure. Whether others wax enthusiastic, complain, or make suggestions for changes, the craftsman infers much from their reactions. Some of these attitudes, values, and expectations may influence what he makes, how he makes it, and of what material.

Like their customers, chairmakers have criteria of beauty and utility often expressed as preferences and as standards of excellence. Chester preferred the light color of freshly peeled bark in a seat, for example, and splints of narrow width. He used the entire thickness of bark for strength, whereas Aaron and others split the bark, discarding the top half with its diamond pattern and coarser grain as unattractive. Aaron made small pins to hold the slats in place and hid the pins in the back of the chair; over the years Chester gave increasing prominence to pegs, turning them into decorative features. All chairmakers seemed to find pleasing the juxtaposition of different colors and textures. To produce cheap chairs quickly, some craftsmen inserted slats of green rather than seasoned wood; later these loosened, rattling when the chair was used. All knew the "right" way to make chairs, but they did not always take the time or have the patience to season the various pieces properly.

Some criteria were stated as rules of design and construction. "I don't like a low seat with a real high back," said Verge. "I

always made my own front posts 19 inches and the back posts
41½ inches," he insisted. Also, he was appalled at ornamentation. "For myself, I like a *decent*, plain-made chair." Verge refused
to make chairs with square posts or to bend the back posts
backward or outward. According to Chester, if a chair was made
from square posts rather than turned ones, then horizontal slats
would not look right; such a chair required a crosspiece at the top
and another above the seat with a wide vertical panel in the
center flanked by two narrow panels (fig. 63). Chairs with eight-
sided pieces demanded slats, not panels. "That's the only thing
about it," he said, "you got to kind of make your back go in with
the postees." He also contended that he *always* bent the back
posts above the seat, or carved them to thrust backward.

Craftsmen sometimes do not verbalize preferences or articulate standards but let the chairs speak for themselves. Or they
imply their biases when remarking on the works of other chairmakers rather than explaining their standards during the construction of their own chairs. However their opinions find
expression, the craftsmen's values and attitudes regarding
useful design affect what they create and how.

INTERACTION IN FOLK ART

As late as the 1960s (and perhaps in some quarters today),
scholars tended to assume that by definition folk art lacks originality, that craftwork is overwhelmingly utilitarian without aesthetic concern or expressive qualities, that "country" furniture
imitates high-style fashions, and that, once established, tradition dictates form. A study of chairmaking in southeastern Kentucky challenges these assumptions and uncovers a situation of
greater complexity than had been thought to exist, particularly
in regard to why the chairs exhibit the characteristics they do.

Given the fact that in the craft of chairmaking someone constructs something for sale to another person, an object's character owes much to the tools, materials, and techniques of
construction, as well as to the customer and the craftsman. Many
chairmakers found walnut difficult to work, for example; if they
used it, then they tended to bend the slats and posts little, if at

all, in contrast to the way they shaped chairs of other woods. A turning lathe produces an entirely different surface from a drawing knife or an ax. When Chester used a router on his new drill press, he produced rough notching in contrast to the sharply incised ornamentation he had made with a pocketknife.

Customers influence the nature of the product through stipulation of design elements, materials, and construction. The ugliest chair he ever made, said Aaron, was a one-armed high chair requested by an arthritic woman in Hazard. On another chair, he substituted flat arms, modeled after those on Chester's recent chairs, for the barrel arms he usually made because that was what the customer requested. Craftsmen also infer customers' expectations through what they have selected in the past, the comments they have made, and the ways in which they have treated chairs. Given a choice between a chair whose seat is of wide bark and one bottomed with narrow strips, insisted Chester, the customer will select the latter. Aware that some customers let their chairs weather, he also made seats with wide bark, which is more durable, he said.

Ultimately, however, control over form rests with the individual who uses the tools to manipulate the materials creating the object to be purchased. Is the craftsman an ole-time chairmaker or does he just prank around with it? Does he make chairs for the sake of the money or for the sake of makin' a good chair? Does he emphasize the beauty part or the lasting part? In addition to motivation for making chairs and the degree of professionalism and dedication, an individual's values, criteria of beauty and utility, skill, and style affect the things he makes.

Chairs are supposed to be useful. Finials that break if the chair is tipped against the wall or turnings that weaken the chair are not acceptable on settin' chairs; a sewing rocker should not have arms. While constraining a craftsman, utility also offers opportunities to explore. How do you prevent a rocking chair from tipping over backward? How do you increase accessibility in a high chair? How do you prevent the feet of a settin' chair from damaging linoleum floors? In the chairs he built, Chester addressed these issues, and more.

Many chairs made by hand are communicative, expressive, or

even symbolic. People attribute meanings to chairs and consider their ownership (or lack of it) a reflection on their aesthetics, values, or station in life. To one woman it was "sort of an honor, I guess" to own a handmade chair in a world of mass-produced furniture. Although he liked many of the chairs he made, Chester contended that some were "too fancy for a poor man like me." The brother of the woman who purchased the chair with hearts that Chester had made for his daughter said he "wouldn't give fifteen cents" for it. Chairs are the objects of associations. They may stand for something as a symbol. Some of Chester's chairs and tools reinforced a museum director's ideas for an exhibit of "vanishing industries" from a "bygone era."

If the objects are symbolic to people after they are constructed, then they and the process of making them are likely to be meaningful to the craftsmen who build them. Because of the materials, design elements, or other features, chairs may be special and intended to make a statement about the relationship between the craftsman and the person for whom the chair is made. A chair that is difficult to construct might stand for the craftsman's mastery. Features associated with the past and prized for this association could become symbolic, a visible sign of invisible ideas and qualities. The identity of chairmaker might evoke a cluster of unpleasant associations or build self-esteem.

Tradition plays a part, not as a force but as a source of ideas about how to do things. Traditional forms and processes may serve as models, having proved effective in the past or being taken as a definition of people and their ways. All the chairmakers made certain types or subtypes of chairs associated with the area. Aaron, in fact, balked at the idea of a Windsor chair, which I described to him; he considered it inappropriate to himself and to southeastern Kentucky. In addition, both Aaron and Chester cultivated traditional forms and processes as a way of defining themselves.

The chairs have the features they do because of the immediate circumstances in which they were made. This situational context encompasses every feature and circumstance mentioned before. Folklore studies in particular, among the several fields in which traditions sometimes are examined, direct attention to the actual situation of manufacture and use of objects (or the performance context, in the case of storytelling, singing, and so on). After all, folklorists look for, document, and analyze traditions. These they elicit from individuals or observe in people's interactions, noting when and under what circumstances traditions were learned or manifested.

To answer the question of why products of traditional manufacture exhibit particular characteristics, those engaged in folklore research concentrate on circumstances in which these things are conceptualized and brought into existence. This requires attention to at least the following four matters:

- *Technology:* The tools, techniques of construction, and materials, as well as the uses to which the object is to be put and the means of utilizing the object.
- *Producer:* the craftsman's self-concept, motivations, and aspirations, knowledge of and skill at this endeavor, values and intentions, and criteria of formal excellence, in addition to preferences and predilections, on the basis of which a characteristic mode of execution, construction, and presentation develops.
- *Consumer:* Customer stipulation of form, materials, and design elements, as well as customer selection of, treatment of, and comments about such object from which the craftsman is likely to infer values, attitudes, preferences, and associations that inform the customer's expectations, satisfaction, and object use.
- *Product/Producer Interface:* Models and precedents for a work, the requirements of useful design (e.g., appearance, access, strength, durability), the process of conceptualization as it affects and is affected by implementation, and the craft identity, activity, or product as a vehicle of expression or locus of symbols.

As I discovered in my research, every chair had its story. The craftsman remarked on some circumstance under which it was built, purchased, or used. He dated it, identified its materials, described the procedures or problems in manufacture, commented on some of its features and sources, and sometimes assessed its quality, attractiveness, and utility. A customer referred to the date, price, and circumstances of purchase, commented on the chair's construction, design, or use, and expressed opinions, attitudes, and values through treatment of the chair as well as statements about the object or its maker.

ART, AESTHETICS, CREATIVITY, AND STYLE

In my study of traditional chairmaking I heard the word "art" only once. "These are just a marvel to look at as art," said Hascal in regard to some of Chester's chairs. "Beautiful," "pretty," "nice," and "looks good" cropped up occasionally. So did "fits your back perfectly," "sets good," and "lasts good."

When I asked what they thought art is, a few individuals alluded to arrangements of flowers or leaves and cones, and the like, or knickknacks having only a decorative purpose. Such things were not labeled art but were referred to as "a pretty" or as "pretties." I heard some young children use the terms "a pretty" and "pretties" in reference to a broken toy, or a chewing gum wrapper, and other objects that appealed to them, but seemed to have no useful purpose. Beechum's miniature corn sleds provoked similar responses (fig. 128); they were the sort of thing that should be put on a fireplace mantel and admired, said several people who saw the sleds or photos of them. Despite contending that he made chairs "for the beauty part," Chester identified himself as a chairmaker only, not an artist, an artisan, or a craftsman. Searching for an example at my urging, Chester hazarded a guess that the wooden jewelry a visitor had made and proudly shown us might be "art."

In response to my question about what art is, Aaron told me about a man who could have been a "real artist," for he made excellent drawings. One was a pencil sketch of a boy beside a lake fishing, his pole stuck into the bank with the line adrift and the boy asleep, a straw hat tipped forward on his head and a can of worms beside him. Aaron's sister-in-law and friends suggested as examples of art paintings by a local woman.

I pressed Aaron, asking him if he thought chairs and chairmaking are art. He reflected on the issue while closely inspecting a completed chair, sanding a bit here and filing a little over

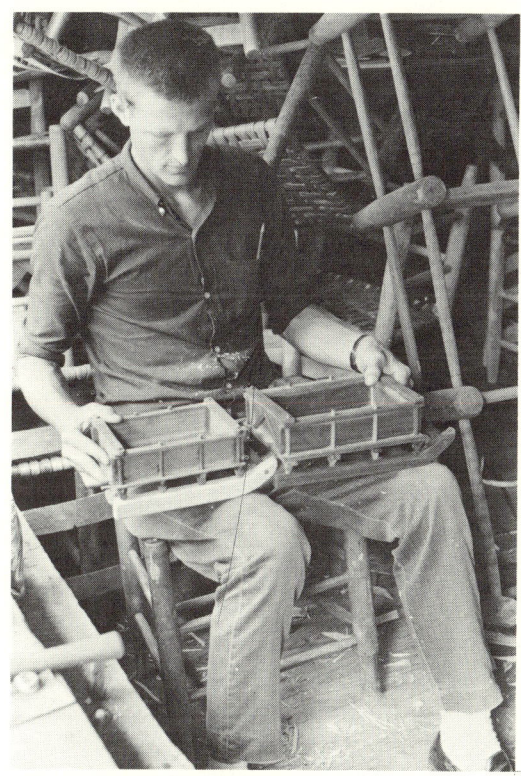

128 Beechum with his miniature corn sleds.

there where the surface seemed to his delicate touch to be slightly less than perfect. "No," he said, looking up from his work, "chairmaking's not art." He explained that he had had an art appreciation course in the local junior college. He learned that art is easel painting and sculpture produced by a few highly gifted individuals and intended for contemplation rather than use. Reluctantly he allowed as how his work might be craft because it was useful, but still, neither he nor what he made was special.

Inculcated with centuries-old beliefs that distinguish art from utility and the genteel arts from mechanical pursuits, many people in our society apply the term *art* to a particular class of objects or examples of them, or restrict it to certain endeavors. They often cite painting and sculpture first. They may follow with other fine arts such as ballet, theater, and so on, perhaps ending with various decorative arts, including jewelry, tapestries, and ceramics. Being useless, but not necessarily without purpose or value, these objects and activities are justified by their beauty alone.

It does not follow, however, that practical objects are imperfect, made without skill, or incapable of stimulating admiration and reverie. Some chairs made by craftsmen in southeastern Kentucky—both unadorned and ornamented, simple and complex—were said to be "beautiful," "pretty," and "nice." This was because of the skill, mastery of technique, and perfection of form evident in their construction.

Highly decorated chairs evincing masterful workmanship commanded attention, provoked respect, and precipitated a state of reflectiveness. The decoration was useless, of course, not serving the immediate objective of sitting or rocking. Matching the color and grain of wood contributed nothing to a chair's strength or durability. In the transformation of an ordinary chair into a two-in-one chair, the object became something to look at rather than simply to use. Chester strove for comfort, the sine qua non of chairs, but like Aaron, he could not suppress the urge to develop the parts of a chair into fields of decoration or the chair itself into a display of virtuosity.

Skill also enhanced the usefulness of utilitarian objects and was appreciated for this fact. Recall Smitty Smith's rocker that won't tip over, nor has it been weakened by turnings. Moreover, "it fits your back perfectly." The chair is small enough to be used in the narrow confines of the front porch; its components are thick enough and durable enough to withstand weathering. Constructed of pieces hewed with an ax, exhibiting a skill and economy of motion few craftsmen could match, the chair was, for many, a model of appropriate form in these circumstances of use and treatment.

One way to further the concept of art is to realize that the aesthetic impulse exists beyond the established categories of genteel and inutile endeavors. As Franz Boas wrote in *Primitive Art* (1927), virtually all human activities "may assume forms that give them esthetic values" (p. 9). Owing to the skill and mastery of technique in producing them, particular examples of motions, utterances, or objects appeal to the senses and intellect for their excellence. Tools that are well designed and well made, for example, are admired for their workmanship and appreciated for their contribution to efficiency. Hence, the term *art* can contribute to an understanding of human behavior if it is made more encompassing; the broader view can uncover examples of the desire to perfect form and the appreciation of formal excellence in various human endeavors, including unpretentious, traditional chairmaking. Those engaging in an enterprise might not label their activities or products art, but do they remark on ways to master techniques? Recognize the attainment of skill? Find particular forms satisfying?

The word *aesthete* is from the Greek *aisthētē*, one who perceives form. Aesthetics became a philosophy and set of verbalized principles regarding formal elegance corresponding to the notion of art as something decorative and fine. As summarized, but not necessarily approved, by Alan P. Merriam in *The Anthropology of Music* (1964), factors in the Western elite concept of the aesthetic include psychic distance (i.e., responding to form per se, distancing oneself from associations and other considerations, including the context of manufacture and use), the intent to create something aesthetic, the manipulation of form for its own sake, the ascription of emotion-producing qualities to form, the attribution of beauty to the product or activity, and the verbalization of a philosophy and of principles regarding form. Judgments should be disciplined; mere likes and dislikes must play no part in criticism.

These factors prescribe norms for behavior. They are not principles of behavior derived from observation of how people actually create, perceive, or respond to form. In regard to traditional chairmaking, the matter of perceiving form encompasses principles of form, criteria for evaluating objects, and associations engendered by the forms. Perception of form may trigger a strongly felt positive or negative reaction. A unique configuration of intellectual state and physiological condition, this aesthetic response is expressed in gesture and demeanor, rudimentary vocalizations, and sometimes verbalized principles.

All skillfully made chairs exhibit such formal principles as symmetry, balance, harmony, rhythm, repetition, variation, and centrality. Craftsmen differ in how they achieve these, however. Chairs possess or lack ornamentation, have smooth or rough surfaces, and have an applied finish or no finish; some are simple forms, others complex. A few chairmakers state rules of composition and construction, which vary among them and which they sometimes break.

In addition to being seen, chairs in use are experienced kinesthetically and tactilely. They can be heard, too. Seats that quickly numb one's posterior, ornamentation that jabs the body, chairs that thrust the sitter forward, rocking chairs that move unevenly or threaten to tip over backward, and slats that rattle or loose joints that squeak offend the senses.

Evaluations include associations. Verge's assessment of chairs depended heavily on the ethics of simplicity, while his son Hascal's preference for ornamentation arose out of his rejection of creek people like his father and their fundamentalist values. Chester and his daughter Brenda, for whom the chair was originally constructed, were enamored of the extensively ornamented walnut chair with the heart motif. "I wouldn't give fifteen cents for that chair," said the brother of the chair's later owner, expressing his revulsion at the elaborate decoration and the hearts carved in the slats.

At times, chairs are taken for granted; they evoke no strong feelings. When they are the objects of either admiration or revulsion, however, things that people make and do precipitate out of the human experience a unique state of being, both intellectually and physiologically. A pleasing aesthetic experience typically includes muscular tension and release as well as a heightened awareness of form, the subordination in importance of other stimuli, and the suspension of time. The outcome is a feeling of well-being, sometimes even a sense of oneness or unity of self with the object, the maker, or some aspect of the circumstances of manufacture and use (or the performer and performance context). Not only is a pleasant aesthetic experience enjoyed when it occurs, but also the conditions giving rise to it are often cultivated to trigger the response again. Finally, the memory of the experience may be savored, and elements of it may be later recalled and relived.

Perhaps the quintessential positive aesthetic response is Chester's reaction to and memory of Robert Fields's singing "Man of Constant Sorrow" when Chester lived on top of Pine Mountain. "You couldn't hardly keep from chokin' up to hear him sing it," said Chester, when he recalled hearing the plaintive melody and evocative phrasing rising from the valley below on a crystal-clear morning. This was the "most touchin' song" he knew, its tune and some phrasing the basis of his own composition, "My Old Kentucky Mountain Home."

Reactions to sounds, motions, or objects also might be intensely negative. In an unpleasant experience, one in which the perception of form is distressing, tension goes unrelieved. The intellectual state welcomes, indeed cries out for, other stimuli to distract attention; time seems drawn out rather than suspended. The result is not a feeling of well-being at all, but of doubt, loathing, or even disgust. Verge couldn't flip through them fast enough when I showed him photos of Chester's chairs, many of which were large, decorated, and to some people, "pretty." His face held a look of disdain. These were among the "ugliest" chairs he had ever seen, he said, adding, "For myself, I like a *decent*, plain-made chair."

The aesthetic response is usually expressed in gesture and demeanor: a smile or frown, an expansive opening up to the object or an apparent cringing from it, and so on. Sometimes the expression occurs through rudimentary vocalizations such as "uuuuummmmm" or "aaaahhhhhhhh" or "ugh!" Although simple, such expressions are neither trivial nor trivializing; often they bespeak sudden surprise or shock, and sometimes a reaction to forms that is too complex to put into words. Rarely do respondents verbalize principles in explanation of why they react the way they do. An exception is Chester's eight specific criticisms of one of Aaron's chairs, touching on the chair's comfort, appearance, and strength.

In sum, aesthetics concerns the perception of and reaction to form, the expression of responses, and the effect of likes and dislikes (or taste) on attitudes toward and evaluations of particular forms that are perceived. The notion of the aesthetic as a philosophy of formal perfection and a system of articulated principles might be relevant when art exists as a separate cognitive category delimiting a certain class of objects, but it does not apply to traditional chairmaking. More broadly conceived, however, aesthetics can inform inquiry into a variety and range of behaviors heretofore neglected or ignored.

In its basic denotative meaning, *creativity* refers to bringing something into being or causing something to exist. Anything produced is thus created. Usually the term connotes doing something well (with skill and mastery of technique). Sometimes, especially when associated with art conceived of as major monuments, creativity is equated with innovation. Problems arise when tradition and innovation, or tradition and creativity, are thought of as opposites.

Tradition testifies to the existence of continuities and consistencies in human thought and behavior; this does not mean, however, that traditional craftsmen lack the capacity to make things well. Nor does subscription to tradition preclude innovation; those chairmakers consciously identifying with tradition were the most innovative. Tradition is a mental construct, not a force existing in its own right or a set of norms for behavior somehow mysteriously enforced by a craftsman's community. One ramification of the study of traditional chairmaking, then, is that assumptions about creativity may require reassessment, particularly when creativity is equated with innovation and juxtaposed to tradition.

To some, a *style* of art defies definition or description, its form without fixed limits and its essence untranslatable. To others, style is constant or a fixed form; not only can it be described and named, but also as a unit of development or analysis it can be used to differentiate periods in an artist's career, as well as to identify works whose authorship or cultural origin otherwise would be unknown. Judging from the evidence of traditional chairmaking, a useful concept of style lies between these extremes.

An appropriate concept of style would recognize that, at least outside the narrow realm of the fine arts, there may be discontinuities and inconsistencies in the character of products. Craft work is participatory, involving both the craftsman and the consumer. Customers differ in their values, preferences, and expectations, a fact that many craftsmen attempt to accommodate by producing varied forms or yielding to stipulations in form, designs, and materials. In repairing objects, craftsmen also may update them. The notion of periods, then, might or might not be defensible. Certainly, the customer must be considered when explaining the character of an object. Craftsmen's preferences and predilections are apparent in their works—in proportions, shapes, and lines; in arrangements of masses and interrelationships; in the treatment of surfaces; and in the conception and rendition of details. The maker may also be seen in a characteristic mode or manner of construction, execution, or presentation, but propensity does not imply constancy or fixity.

The constructs art, aesthetics, creativity, and style were developed in reference to works largely in the privileged rather than the public realm. They can be made more accessible and enlightening, however, through the ethnography of unpretentious forms produced by unassuming individuals. Once enlarged, these terms can be applied to a variety of situations in which people manifest concern over skill and mastery of technique leading to the production of objects that conform to both preferences and standards of excellence, evoking pleasant associations and experiences. The likely result will be evidence that the perception of form and of response to it, the impulse to perfect form, and the ability to make and do things skillfully and uniquely are pervasive among members of the species regardless of their education or social standing and the forms produced.

THE STUDY OF TRADITION

Anthropologists, sociologists, psychologists, and art historians or museum curators—to name representatives of only a few fields—have described and interpreted traditional processes and forms. What differentiates these studies is the one or more distinguishing concepts around which all the assumptions, questions, and hypotheses cluster. There is overlap, of course, or cross-fertilization of ideas. Nevertheless, the work of an individual in one discipline will differ from the research done by a person in another field.

In folkloristics or folklore studies, the dominant construct is that of folklore or tradition rather than, say, culture, society, psyche, or art. The word *folk* is from the Anglo-Saxon *folc*, meaning a group of kindred people. *Lore* derives from the Anglo-Saxon *lār*, that which is taught (hence, wisdom or counsel). *Tradition* comes through Old French from the Latin *tradere*, to give up, to transmit.

William Thoms coined the Anglo-Saxon compound *folk-lore* in 1846 to replace the term *popular antiquities*, which had long been in vogue. Other English language designations include *oral traditions* (appearing at least as early as 1777), *traditionary lore*, and *popular traditions*. Among the terms in other languages are the French *traditions populaires*, the German *Volkskunde* and *Volksleben* (literally, the "goods of the folk" and "the life of the folk," respectively, used regularly after 1806), and the Swedish *folkliv* ("folklife," employed as early as 1847, but in 1909 combined with "research" to yield the name of a field of study—*folklivsforsning*, or folklife research). The term *folkloristics*, popular since the mid-1960s, refers to the study of folklore rather than to the subject matter that is documented and interpreted.

Although definitions vary, most suggest that folklore consists of (1) symbolic forms and processes, (2) learned or manifested largely in firsthand interaction, and (3) exhibiting continuities or consistencies in human thought and behavior over time and space.

What is folk art? It is traditions on the one hand and the aesthetic impulse on the other. Folk art, then, is (1) products, processes, or performances, (2) learned or manifested largely in people's interactions, (3) exhibiting a striving to perfect form, and (4) testifying to the existence of continuities or consistencies in human thought and behavior.

Some forms and processes studied as folk art in recent years are chain carving, decorating the interior of the Appalachian house, creating and exchanging homemade gifts, canning and arranging jars of fruits and vegetables, making walking canes, painting window screens, remodeling houses, decorating automobiles, and creating objects for one's own use from materials in the work place. The landscaping of yards in suburbia or the preparation and serving of ethnic or family foods in the home results in sculptural forms that, when they appeal to the senses, are repeated and reproduced, emulated and imitated or transformed. Exhibits at a county fair, religious processions, and the carving of pumpkins at Halloween are usually both traditional and aesthetic phenomena. These objects and activities are similar to the paintings of nineteenth-century itinerant portraitists and twentieth-century visionaries, and the quilts, duck decoys, and other forms usually said to be "folk art" in displaying continuities or consistencies in behavior and thought, as well as strivings toward perfect form.

Questions that folklorists ask vary with researchers' training and interests. Many investigators attempt to establish what the traditions are, characterize and define genres, establish types or subtypes, and ascertain motifs, themes, and styles. They may analyze the structure and the rules that seem to underlie the forms, or specific examples of them. Researchers usually inquire about how and why the forms and processes, or aspects or examples of them, were generated, perpetuated, modified, or extinguished. They also seek to uncover meanings, symbolism, uses, and functions.

Because many traditions are expressive and hence aesthetic phenomena, folklorists usually consider artistry and style of product or performance. Because lore is literally wisdom or counsel (in this sense, the distinctive ways of doing things and perhaps the values of, or that which is valued by, a people), some folklorists inquire about how folklore relates to culture. Since folklore is learned and manifested by individuals in interaction with others, folklorists often ask questions that are similar to those addressed by psychologists and sociologists. Always the focus is on traditions, however, rather than on some other centrally informing construct.

Several perspectives have been popular in the study of people's traditions; one considers folklore an index of historical processes. Some researchers, for instance, have used folklore to reconstruct the past or to examine historical events and movements. Others have treated examples as diffusible entities that have spread and changed through time and space; after establishing an approximation of the original form, the task has been to trace the development or devolution of a tale, ballad, proverb, or building technique to confirm laws of continuity and change or to isolate specific factors accounting for these processes.

A second perspective views folk art as an aesthetic phenomenon. Researchers discern authorship and ascertain style, describe stylistic development, explain iconography, prepare case studies of objects or texts, write biographies of producers or performers, and research community and genre traditions. They may analyze the morphology of objects or the structure of texts, the rules of composition or construction and the laws of form; sometimes these are considered against a backdrop of history, culture, or psyche, but not always.

Treating folk art as an element of culture and therefore an index of sociocultural processes is a third perspective. Researchers might examine how art reflects world view, maintains cultural equilibrium, reinforces social stratification, or serves purposes of adaptation and survival during cultural and social change.

A fourth approach concentrates on folklore as a behavioral phenomenon. Investigators explore traditional, expressive forms as an index of psychological states and processes. Or they examine cognitive and interactional processes such as learning, communication, and social dynamics.

Characterizing folklore studies as a field of inquiry in its own right, regardless of perspectives within it, is its concentration on a particular phenomenon—that of tradition manifested in people's interactions—as well as its questions, assumptions, and hypotheses. Solutions to problems about the nature, generation, and functions of specific traditions provide understanding of the pervasiveness and role of tradition generally in people's lives. They contribute to an appreciation of what people are capable of and what they accomplish. They direct attention to a sphere of interaction often taken for granted or relegated to secondary importance but significant in its own right—that of how we do things and express ourselves on a day-to-day basis.

Through the study of the aesthetic impulse in everyday life, one discovers that all people develop skills and master techniques in varied endeavors. They produce forms that satisfy because of their perfection, the meanings conveyed and associations they engender, or their utility. Moreover, all people seek pleasant sensory experiences and avoid negative ones. By studying the aesthetic impulse we gain insights into ways that people interact, communicate, express deeply felt emotions, cope with problems, and strive to improve the quality of life.

Research indicates that no one is bound by tradition—nor can anyone survive without traditions. By communicating perceptions and perpetuating values, traditions help individuals or peoples maintain their identity and integrity, cope in present, and survive in future. Traditions can bring new beginnings connected to the past.

What appeals to folklorists is the study of traditions—something in which all people of every time and place engage. The enduring contribution of folklore research is its discoveries about traditions—how they are generated, why they exist, and what they reveal about our humanity—historically, aesthetically, culturally, socially, and behaviorally.

Bibliographical Notes

1 THE CHAIRMAKING BUSINESS

Ronald L. Baker provides a list of course offerings and folklore programs in "Folklore and Folklife Studies in American and Canadian Colleges and Universities," *Journal of American Folklore* 99 (1986):50-74. Fourteen instructors describe folklore courses and discuss pedagogical techniques and concerns in *Teaching Folklore*, ed. Bruce Jackson (Buffalo: Documentary Research, 1984).

For books and articles about folklore fieldwork, see William A. Wilson, "Documenting Folklore," in *Folk Groups and Folklore Genres*, ed. Elliott Oring (Logan: Utah State University Press, 1986), 225-54; two chapters called "Being a Folklorist" and "Folklore Research" in Barre Toelken, *The Dynamics of Folklore* (Boston: Houghton Mifflin Co., 1979), 263-329; Kenneth S. Goldstein, *A Guide for Field Workers in Folklore* (Hatboro, Penn.: Folklore Associates, 1964); Bruce Jackson, *Fieldwork* (Urbana and Chicago: University of Illinois Press, 1987); Edward D. Ives, *The Tape-Recorded Interview: A Manual for Field Workers in Folklore and Oral History* (Knoxville: University of Tennessee Press, 1974); and Robert A. Georges and Michael O. Jones, *People Studying People: The Human Element in Fieldwork* (Berkeley and Los Angeles: University of California Press, 1980). See also articles in Parts II and IV ("Methods of Research" and "Presentation of Research") of *Handbook of American Folklore*, ed. Richard M. Dorson (Bloomington: Indiana University Press, 1983), 359-539.

John D. Alexander, Jr., provides an excellent discussion of the principles and techniques of working with wet wood in *Make a Chair from a Tree: An Introduction to Working Green Wood* (Newtown, Conn.: Taunton Press, 1978).

For comparative historical and geographic information about chairs and chairmaking, see John Cummings, "Slat-Back Chairs," *Antiques*, 72, no. 1 (July 1957):60-63; Irvin Phillips Lyon, "Square-Post Slat-Back Chairs: A Seventeenth Century Type Found in New England," *Antiques* 20 (1931):210-16; L.J. Mayes, *The History of Chairmaking in High*

Wycombe (London: Routledge & Kegan Paul, 1960); and Robert F. Trent, *Hearts and Crowns: Folk Chairs of the Connecticut Coast 1720-1840 as Viewed in the Light of Henri Focillon's Introduction to Arte Populaire* (New Haven: New Haven Colony Historical Society, 1977).

Other examples of traditional chairs and chairmaking can be found in Henry Glassie, *Patterns in the Material Folk Culture of the Eastern United States* (Philadelphia: University of Pennsylvania Press, 1968), 228-34; John Robert Vincent, "A Study of Two Ozark Woodworking Industries" (M.A. thesis, University of Missouri, 1962); the anonymous articles, "An Old Chair Maker Shows How," *Foxfire* 3 (1969):11-16, 53-55, and "Cash Crop in North Carolina," *Mountain Life and Work* 44 (1968):14-17; Jonathan Williams, "The Southern Appalachians," *Craft Horizons* 26 (1966):35-67; Allen H. Eaton, *Handicrafts of the Southern Highlands* (1937 reprint; New York: Dover Publications, 1973); the short article on a West Virginia craftsman entitled simply "Authentic," *Mountain Life and Work* 40 (1964):45-48; Warren Roberts, "Turpin Chairs and the Turpin Family: Chairmaking in Southern Indiana," *Midwestern Journal of Language and Folklore* 7 (1981):57-106; Charles E. Martin, "'Make 'Em Fast and Shed 'Em Quick': The Appalachian Craftsman Revisited," *Appalachian Journal* 9 (1981):4-19; Gerald Milnes, "West Virginia Split Bottom: The Seat of Choice," *Goldenseal* 12, no. 3 (Fall 1986):9-15; and an article called "Jimmy Carter, Craftsman," *Popular Mechanics* 161, no. 8 (August 1984):73-75, 113.

Called "Hand Carved," a ninety-minute film documents Chester Cornett in the late 1970s (who was living in an apartment in Cincinnati at the time) constructing chairs. Produced by Herbie Smith and Elizabeth Barret, the film is distributed by Appalshop, Whitesburg, Kentucky.

One of the most extensive treatments of technology in a traditional craft, its historical origins and present-day manifestations, is Charles G. Zug, III, *Turners and Burners: The Folk Potters of North Carolina* (Chapel Hill: University of North Carolina Press, 1986). Two other works of interest are Carlos C. Drake, "The Traditional Elements in the Cooperage Industry," *Keystone Folklore Quarterly* 14 (1969):81-96; and Darrell D. Henning, "Maple Sugaring: History of a Folk Technology," *Keystone Folklore Quarterly* 11 (1966):239-74.

A few of the publications providing background on the southern Appalachian region are Jack E. Weller, *Yesterday's People* (Lexington: University Press of Kentucky, 1965); Elmora Messer Matthews, *Neighbors and Kin: Life in a Tennessee Ridge Community* (Nashville: Vanderbilt University Press, 1965); John D. Photoiadis and Harry K. Schwarzweller, eds., *Change in Rural Appalachia: Implications for Action Programs* (Philadelphia: University of Pennsylvania Press, 1970); Bruce Ergood and Bruce E. Kuhre, eds., *Appalachia: Social Context Past and Present* (Dubuque, Iowa: Kendall/Hunt, 1978); Allen Batteau, ed., *Appalachia and America: Autonomy and Regional Dependence* (Lexington: University Press of Kentucky, 1983); Elinor Lander Horwitz, *Mountain Crafts, Mountain People* (New York: Lippincott, 1974); and David E. Whisnant, *All That is Native and Fine: The Politics of Culture in an American Region* (Chapel Hill: University of North Carolina Press, 1983).

Overviews of the study of folk art and material culture include John Michael Vlach, "American Folk Art: Questions and Quandaries," *Winterthur Portfolio* 15 (1980):345-55; Kenneth L. Ames, "Folk Art: The Challenge and the Promise," in *Perspectives on American Folk Art*, eds. Ian M.G. Quimby and Scott T. Swank (New York: Norton, 1980), 293-324; Simon J. Bronner, "Concepts in the Study of Material Aspects of American Folk Culture," *Folklore Forum* 12 (1979):133-72; Michael Owen Jones, "The Study of Folk Art Study: Reflections on Images," in *Folklore Today*, eds. Linda Dégh, Henry Glassie, and Felix J. Oinas (Bloomington, Ind.: Center for Language and Semiotic Studies, 1967), 291-394; Simon J. Bronner, ed., "Material Culture Studies: A Symposium," special double issue of *Material Culture* 17 (Summer-Fall 1985); Kenneth L. Ames, *Beyond Necessity: Art in the Folk Tradition* (New York: Norton, 1977); Simon J. Bronner and Stephen P. Poyser, eds., *Approaches to the Study of Material Aspects of American Folk Culture* (Bloomington, Ind.: Folklore Forum, 1979); Simon J. Bronner, "Material Culture and Region: Lessons from Folk Studies," *Kentucky Folklore Record* 32 (1986):1-16; Jules David Prown, "Mind in Matter: An Introduction to Material Culture Theory and Method," *Wintherthur Portfolio* 17 (1982):1-20; C. Kurt Dewhurst, "Epilogue: The Study of Material Folk Culture Study," in *Grand Ledge Folk Pottery: Traditions at Work* (Ann Arbor: UMI Research Press, 1986), 93-106; Michael Owen Jones and Verni Greenfield, "Art Criticism and Aesthetic Philosophy," in *American Folk Art: A Guide to Sources*, ed. Simon J. Bronner (New York and London: Garland, 1984), 31-50; and Simon J. Bronner, "Visible Proofs: Material Culture Study in American Folkloristics," and Kenneth L. Ames, "The Stuff of Everyday Life: American Decorative Arts and Household Furnishings," in *Material Culture: A Research Guide*, ed. Thomas J. Schlereth (Lawrence: University Press of Kansas, 1985), 127-53 and 79-112, respectively.

The eight-legged chair illustrated in figure 28 and mentioned in this chapter is smaller than perhaps it appears in the photo. The chair measures 37 inches high. The back posts are 19½ inches apart at the top. The seat, which is 18½ inches from the floor, is 17 inches deep; it is 9 inches wide at the front, 16½ inches wide toward the center, and 7½ inches wide at the back behind the back posts. The seven-legged chair is 4 inches shorter. The back posts are 20 inches apart. The seat, which is 17 inches from the floor, measures 18 inches deep; it is 12¾ inches wide in front, 20½ inches wide toward the center, and 6 inches wide at the back.

2 THE MASTERPIECE AND THE NEW DESIGN

On the subject of utility and ornament, see Michael Owen Jones, "The Useful and the Useless in Folk Art," *Journal of Popular Culture* 7 (1973):794-818. See also Burt Feintuch, "A Contextual and Cognitive Approach to Folk Art and Folk Craft," *New York Folklore* 2 (1976):69-78, who uses the concept of signs to argue that "a craft object exists on the level of the index, while art objects exist on the levels of icons and symbols."

One of the most extensive treatments by a folklorist of the process of imagining and creating objects is Verni Greenfield's chapter "Breaking the Gestalt: The Process of Conceptualizing," in her book *Making Do or Making Art: A Study of American Recycling* (Ann Arbor: UMI Research Press, 1986), 91-108. See also Simon J. Bronner, *Chain Carvers: Old Men Crafting Meaning* (Lexington: University Press of Kentucky, 1984), and Sylvia Ann Grider and Barbara Ann Allen, "Howard Taylor, Cane Maker and Handle Shaver," *Indiana Folklore* 7 (1974):5-25.

Some ethnographies with information throughout on creativity and aesthetics are Ruth Bunzel, *The Pueblo Potter: A Study of Creativity in Primitive Art* (1929 reprint; New York: Dover Publications, 1972); Lila M. O'Neale, *Yurok-Karok Basket Weavers*, Publications in American Anthropology and Ethnology 32 (Berkeley: University of California, 1932); John Adair, *The Navaho and Pueblo Silversmiths* (Norman: University of Oklahoma Press, 1944); Charles Briggs, *The Wood Carvers of Cordova, New Mexico: Social Dimensions of an Artistic Revival* (Knoxville: University of Tennessee Press, 1980); and Dorothy Jean Ray, *Artists of the Tundra and the Sea* (Seattle: University of Washington Press, 1961). See also Franz Boas, *Primitive Art* (1927 reprint; New York: Dover Publications, 1955).

Among the studies of individual composition of folksongs are Henry Glassie, "'Take That Night Train to Selma': An Excursion to the

Outskirts of Scholarship," *Journal of Popular Culture*, 2 (1968):1-62; Edward D. Ives, *Larry Gorman: The Man Who Made the Songs* (Bloomington: Indiana University Press, 1964); and Edward D. Ives, *Joe Scott: The Woodsman-Songmaker* (Urbana: University of Illinois Press, 1978).

In "Structure and Function, Folklore and the Artifact," *Semiotica* 7 (1973):313-51, Henry Glassie reports rules of composition he has abstracted from a study of folk architecture. Underlying these rules is a bilaterally symmetrical, tripartite concept apparent in 99.2 percent of 2,193 barns that he surveyed. See also his *Folk Housing in Middle Virginia: A Structural Analysis of Historic Artifacts* (Knoxville: University of Tennessee Press, 1975) for extensive illustrations and a discussion of his analysis of "rules."

Numerous films depict artists at work, revealing something about their methods and aesthetics. "The Art of Theora Hamblett" (22 min., color, 16 mm film, 1966; distributed by University of Mississippi) shows the painter at work and talking about both her memory paintings and visionary images. "Carved Visions, Painted Dreams: A Glimpse at Four California Artists" (30 min., color, ½" videotape, 1986; produced by Donna Reid and distributed by the Oakland Museum, Oakland, Calif., in cooperation with the UCLA Folklore and Mythology Center) presents vignettes of a black sculptor, a Maidu Indian painter, a chainsaw sculptor, and a Beverly Hills painter. "The Cowboy, the Craftsman, and the Ballerina" (52 min., color, ¾" videotape, 1981; produced and distributed by CBS Productions) concentrates on the artistry, aesthetics, and sense of tradition in three occupations; both masters and apprentices comment, providing an understanding of how and why tradition and the aesthetic impulse are vital in people's lives. "Clothesline" (30 min., black and white, 16 mm film, 1981; produced and distributed by Roberta Cantow) contains much excellent material on the aesthetics of domestic life—both the pleasures and positive associations, as well as the unpleasant and negative sides. "The Stone Carvers" (28 min., color, 16 mm film, 1984; directed by Marjorie Hunt and Paul Wagner, distributed by Direct Cinema Limited) captures the work and infectious spirit of a small group of Italian-American artisans who have spent their lives carving designs on the Washington Cathedral. "Silk Sarongs and City Streets" (28 min., color, ¾" video, 1987; directed by Eric Van Schrader and distributed by The International Institute) explores the ways Lowland Laotians, like many other refugees, use traditional music and dance to deal with the task of learning to live in an alien society. "Hearts and Hands" (58 min., color, 16 mm film; directed by Pat Ferrero and distributed by Ferrero Films) dramatically presents the role of women and textiles in the nineteenth century's great movement and events; in the process, it insightfully communicates how and why women made quilts.

3 MAN OF CONSTANT SORROW

Sara Selene Faulds and Amy Skillman provide an excellent overview of folkloristic research on individual artists and an extensive list of publications in their essay "Biographies" in *American Folk Art: Guide to Sources*, ed. Simon J. Bronner (New York: Garland, 1984), 99-116.

In "The Life Story," *Journal of American Folklore* 93 (1980):276-92, Jeff Todd Titon differentiates among biography, oral history, a life story, and a personal or life history. A few of the works with life history data on traditional artists and performers are the following:

Alvey, R. Gerald. *Dulcimer Maker: The Craft of Homer Ledford*. Lexington: University Press of Kentucky, 1984.
Beck, Jane C. "Newton Washburn: Traditional Basket Maker." In *Traditional Craftsmanship in America: A Diagnostic Report*, ed. Charles Camp, 67-71. Washington, D. C.: National Council for the Traditional Arts, 1983.
Bock, Joanne. *Pop Wiener, Naive Painter*. Amherst: University of Massachusetts Press, 1974.
Boyd, E. *Saints and Saintmakers of New Mexico*. Santa Fe: Laboratory of Anthropology, University of New Mexico, 1946.
Briggs, Charles. *The Wood Carvers of Cordova, New Mexico: Social Dimensions of an Artistic Revival*. Knoxville: University of Tennessee Press, 1980.
Bronner, Simon J. "An Experiential Portrait of a Wood Carver." *Indiana Folklore* 13 (1980):30-45.
──────. "Investigating Identity and Expression in Folk Art." *Winterthur Portfolio* 16 (1981):65-83.
──────. *Chain Carvers: Old Men Crafting Meaning*. Lexington: University Press of Kentucky, 1984.
Burrison, John A. *Brothers in Clay: The Story of Georgia Folk Pottery*. Athens: University of Georgia Press, 1983.
Cansler, Loman D. "Walter Dibben, an Ozark Bard." *Kentucky Folklore Record* 13 (1967):81-89.
──────. "He Hewed His Own Path: William Henry Scott, Ozark Songmaker." *Studies in the Literary Imagination* 3 (1970):37-63.
Carpenter, Inta Gale. *A Latvian Storyteller*. New York: Arno Press, 1980.

Dow, James R. "The Hand Carved Walking Canes of William Baurich-ter." *Keystone Folklore Quarterly* 15 (1970):138-47.

———. "He Says, 'I've Heard of you,' and I says, 'No Doubt': Status-Seeking through Storytelling." *New York Folklore Quarterly* 29 (1973):83-96.

Ferris, William R., Jr. " 'If You Ain't Got It in Your Head, You Can't Do It in Your Hand': James Thomas, Mississippi Delta Folk Sculptor." *Studies in the Literary Imagination* 3(1970):89-107.

———. *Local Color: A Sense of Place in Folk Art*. New York: McGraw-Hill, 1982.

Goldstein, Kenneth S. "William Robbie: Folk Artist of the Buchan District, Aberdeenshire." In *Folklore in Action*, ed. Horace P. Beck, 101-11. Philadelphia: University of Pennsylvania Press, 1962.

Grider, Sylvia Ann, and Barbara Ann Allen, "Howard Taylor, Cane Maker and Handle Shaver." *Indiana Folklore* 7 (1974):5-25.

Ives, Edward D. *Larry Gorman: The Man Who Made the Songs*. Bloom-ington: Indiana University Press, 1964.

———. *Joe Scott: The Woodsman-Songmaker*. Urbana: University of Illi-nois Press, 1978.

Joyce, Rosemary O. *A Woman's Place: The Life History of a Rural Ohio Grandmother*. Columbus: Ohio State University Press, 1983.

Lipman, Jean, and Tom Armstrong, eds. *American Folk Painters of Three Centuries*. New York: Hudson Hills Press in association with the Whitney Museum of American Art, 1980.

Marriott, Alice. *Maria, The Potter of San Ildefonso*. Norman: University of Oklahoma Press, 1948.

Marshall, Howard Wight. "Mr. Westfall's Baskets: Traditional Crafts-manship in Northcentral Missouri." *Mid-South Folklore* 11 (1974): 43-50.

Moore, Willard B. "An Indiana Subsistence Craftsman." In *Material Culture Studies in America*, ed. Thomas J. Schelereth, 259-68. Nash-ville: American Association for State and Local History, 1982.

Mordoh, Alice Morrison. "Two Woodcarvers: Jasper, Dubois County, Indiana." *Indiana Folklore* 13 (1980):17-29.

Oring, Elliott, ed. *Humor and the Individual*. Los Angeles: California Folklore Society, 1984.

Roberts, Warren E. "Ananias Hensel and His Furniture: Cabinetmak-ing in Southern Indiana." *Midwestern Journal of Language and Folklore* 9 (1983):69-122.

Vlach, John Michael. *Charleston Blacksmith: The Work of Philip Simmons*. Athens: University of Georgia Press, 1981.

Some works on the concepts of "personal documents" and "life history" are L. Gotschalk, C. Kluckhohn, and R. Angell, *The Use of Personal Documents in History, Anthropology and Sociology,* Social Science Research Council Bulletin 53 (New York, 1945); L.L. Langness, *The Life History in Anthropological Science* (New York: Holt, Rinehart & Winston, 1965); and L.L. Langness and Gelya Frank, *Lives: Anthropological Approach to Biography* (Novato, Calif.: Chandler and Sharp, 1981). For other works on ethnographic biography and life history, see Stanley Brandes, "Ethnography Autobiographies in American Anthropology," in *Crisis in Anthropology: Views from Spring Hill, 1980,* eds. E.A. Hoebel, Richard Currier, and Susan Kaiser (New York: Garland, 1982), 187-202; Gelya Frank, "Finding the Common Denominator: A Phenomenological Critique of Life History Method," *Ethos* 7 (1979):68-94; David G. Mandelbaum, "The Study of Life History: Gandhi," *Current Anthropology* 14 (1973):17-206; and Lawrence C. Watson and Maria-Barbara Watson-Franke, *Interpreting Life Histories: An Anthropological Inquiry* (New Brunswick, N.J.: Rutgers University Press, 1985).

When I began my research, only *The Use of Personal Documents* by Gotschalk et al., Langness's *The Life History,* and four works cited in the life history bibliography by Boyd, Goldstein, Ives, and Marriott were available. While there were other writings about biography in the fields of history and literature, along with many biographies of notable people and a few ethnographic biographies, the publications just mentioned interested and influenced me most. I knew I was not writing biographies of Chester Cornett and other chairmakers. I did seek biographical or life history information, however, to infer motivations, aspirations, values, and attitudes—knowledge of which would help in understanding why the craftsmen made certain forms with particular features. This information proved essential to analyzing how emotional states and processes sometimes were expressed through craft processes and products. It was also vital theoretically, leading to the realization that folk craftsmen are not simply passive recipients of a cultural heritage but may be active contributors to the traditions in which they participate.

For lists and descriptions of films, some of which concern individual artists, see William Ferris, "Films," in *American Folk Art: A Guide to Sources,* ed. Simon J. Bronner (New York and London: Garland, 1984), 255-68; and Carolyn Lipson, *American Folklore Films and Videotapes: An Index,* vol. 1 (Memphis: Center for Southern Folklore, 1976), and Ellen Slack, *American Folklore Films and Videotapes: An Index,* vol. 2 (New York:

Bowker, 1982). A ninety-minute film produced by Herbie Smith and Elizabeth Barret and distributed by Appalshop, Whitesburg, Kentucky, "Hand Carved" documents the construction of the last chair that Chester made.

Chester was unable to recall the words of "Man of Constant Sorrow" as sung by Robert Fields, a song that seems to have inspired his own composition, "My Old Kentucky Mountain Home." One rendition of "Constant Sorrow," however, that might approximate what Fields sang can be heard on Frank Proffitt's *Memorial Album* (Folk-Legacy FSA-36), side II, band 3; note "The place where I was borned and raised," a phrase and concept dominant in Chester's song.

Although I do not assume that Chester heard them, two nostalgic songs about the old home place that no longer exists are "Old Home Place" by Larry Campbell and the Country Playboys, *Bluegrass Mountain Home* (Rich-R-Tone Records), side II, band 6, and "Just a Corner Stone," *Roy Crockett and the Pleasant Valley Boys Present Gospel and Blue Grass Music* (D&R Recording Co.), side I, band 1.

"The Brier Losing Touch with His Traditions," a poem seemingly inspired by Chester and some of his experiences, concerns a chairmaker who manipulates the identity of traditional mountaineer; see Jim Wayne Miller, *The Mountains Have Come Closer* (Boone, NC.: Appalachian-Consortium Press, 1980), 44.

4   THE UNIQUE AND THE ANTIQUE

For remarks on the concept of style, see Ruth Bunzel, "Art," in *General Anthropology*, ed. Franz Boas (New York: D.C. Heath, 1938), 535-88; Meyer Schapiro, "Style," in *Anthropology Today*, ed. A.L. Kroeber (Chicago: University of Chicago Press, 1953), 287-312; and Adrian A. Gerbrands, "The Concept of Style in Non-Western Art," in *Tradition and Creativity in Tribal Art*, ed. Daniel Biebuyck (Berkeley and Los Angeles: University of California Press, 1969), 58-70.

Selected examples of stylistic analyses include Richard M. Dorson, "Oral Styles of American Folk Narrators," in *Folklore in Action*, ed. Horace P. Beck (Philadelphia: University of Pennsylvania Press, 1962), 77-100; Richard M. Dorson, "The Art of Negro Storytelling," in *Negro Folktales in Michigan* (Cambridge: Harvard University Press, 1956), 19-30; E. Boyd, *Saints and Saintmakers of New Mexico* (Santa Fe: Laboratory of Anthropology, University of New Mexico, 1946); Robert Thompson, "Abatan: A Master Potter of the Egbado Yoruba," in *Tradi-*

tion and Creativity in Tribal Art, ed. Daniel P. Biebuyck (Berkeley and Los Angeles, 1969), 120-82; and Adrian A. Gerbrands, *Wow-Ipits: Eight Woodcarvers of New Guinea* (The Hague, 1967).

A film of a nineteenth-century itinerant painter that emphasizes stylistic development and change is "New England Folk Painter—Erastus Salisbury Field" (33 min., color, 16 mm, 1967; distributed by Colonial Williamburg Foundation and also McGraw-Hill Films).

5   SECURITY, SECLUSION, AND SELF-ESTEEM

Economic matters are addressed in John Robert Vincent, "A Study of Two Ozark Woodworking Industries" (M.A. thesis, University of Missouri, 1962); L.J. Mayes, *The History of Chairmaking in High Wycombe* (London: Routledge & Kegan Paul, 1960); William Morgan Williams, *The Country Craftsman: A Study of Some Rural Crafts and the Rural Industries Organisation in England* (London: Routledge & Kegan Paul, 1958); Michael Owen Jones, "Folk Craft Production and the Folklorist's Obligation," *Journal of Popular Culture* 4 (1970):194-212; Michael Owen Jones, " 'If You Make a Simple Thing, You Gotta Sell It at a Simple Price': Folk Art Production as a Business," *Kentucky Folklore Record* 17 (1972):73-77, and 18 (1973):5-12, 31-40; Rosemary O. Joyce, " 'Fame Don't Make the Sun Any Cooler': Folk Artists and the Marketplace," in *Folk Art and Art Worlds*, eds. John Michael Vlach and Simon J. Bronner (Ann Arbor: UMI Research Press, 1986):225-41; and Rosemary O. Joyce, ed., "Marketing Folk Art," a double issue of *New York Folklore* 12 (1986).

For some terms and approaches to economic relations, see Eric R. Wolf, *Peasants* (Englewood Cliffs, 1966); George M. Foster, "The Dyadic Contract: A Model for the Social Structure of a Mexican Peasant Society," *American Anthropologist*, 63 (1961):1173-92; and E.E. LeClair, Jr., "Economic Theory and Economic Anthropology," *American Anthropologist* 64 (1962):1179-1203.

A few works on the grieving process are Katherine J. Bordicks, *Patterns of Shock* (New York: Macmillan, 1965); Herman Feifel, *The Meaning of Death* (New York: McGraw-Hill, 1959); Herman Feifel, ed., *New Meanings of Death* (New York: McGraw-Hill, 1977); Richard A. Kalish, *Death, Grief, and Caring Relations* (Monterey, Calif.: Brooks/Cole, 1981); Bernadine Kreis and Alice Pattie, *Up from Grief: Patterns of Recovery* (New York: Seabury, 1969); Colin Murray Parkes, *Bereavement: Studies of Grief in Adult Life* (New York: International Universities Press, 1974); and Robert Lester Fulton, *Death and Identity* (New York: Wiley,

1966). The behavior of some of the storytellers and singers mentioned by Henry Glassie (" 'Take That Night Train to Selma': An Excursion to the Outskirts of Scholarship," *Journal of Popular Culture*, 88 [1968], 1-62) could be interpreted from the point of view of grieving over a loss rather than a result of freedom from ordinary responsibilities or dissatisfaction with one's own culture, which are Glassie's main explanations.

The theme of creativity related to grief is also strongly implied in some of the biographical sketches in Pat Ferraro's excellent film, "Quilts in Women's Lives" (28 min., color, 16 mm or ¾" videotape; distributed by New Day Films, Franklin Lakes, N.J.). The most extensive treatment of folk art and the processes of coping and adjustment is Simon J. Bronner, *Chain Carvers: Old Men Crafting Meaning* (Lexington: University Press of Kentucky, 1985).

The quotes from C.G. Jung about "lonely island" and "seeing the Other" are from his *Psychological Types, or the Psychology of Individuation*, trans. H. Goodwin Baynes (New York: Pantheon Books), *Collected Works*, vol. 13, 480 and 500, respectively.

For information about the chair/coffin, see Mary S. Herrick, "A Chenango County Coffin," *New York Folklore Quarterly* 8 (1952):135-36.

The quote from the Kansas farmer (Albert Bodecker) is from Michael Owen Jones, "Traditions of a Kansas Farmer" (M.A. thesis, Indiana University, 1966), 345; his song and the circumstances surrounding its composition are discussed at some length by the farmer.

6 IT TAKES HALF A FOOL TO MAKE CHAIRS

For additional information about the chairs, tools, and techniques of construction of Chester and his kin, as well as other chairmakers mentioned in this chapter, see Michael Owen Jones, "Chairmaking in Appalachia: A Study in Style and Creative Imagination in American Folk Art" (Ph.D. dissertation, Indiana University, 1970), 685-855. See references to chapter 1 above for information about other chairs and chairmakers.

"Country Auction: The Paul V. Leitzel Estate Sale" (60 min., color, 16 mm film, 1985; produced by Aibel, Levin, Musello, and Ruby) demonstrates the importance of objects in people's lives as symbols and sources of associations. For more information about the community, see Christopher Musello, "Family Houses and Social Identity: Communicational Perspectives on the Homes of Ridge County" (Ph.D.

dissertation, University of Pennsylvania, 1986). Musello's study concerns "the structure of rules, roles, values, customs and beliefs which
organize how homes are used, how they are evaluated, and how they
come to assume meaning within this frame of reference."

7 THE BEAUTY PART AND THE LASTING PART

The information about traditional types of chairs is from Henry Glassie, *Material Folk Culture in the Eastern United States* (Philadelphia: University of Pennsylvania Press, 1968), 228-34. For other discussions of
tradition in craftwork, see Carlos C. Drake, "The Traditional Elements
in the Cooperage Industry," *Keystone Folklore Quarterly* 14 (1969):81-96,
and Lila M. O'Neale, *Yurok-Karok Basket Weavers*, Publications in American Anthropology and Ethnology 32, (Berkeley: University of California, 1932):161-65. *Potiki*, a novel by Patricia Grace (New York: Penguin,
1986), offers a compelling look at the role of tradition in people's lives;
see the review by Michael Owen Jones in the *The Book Review, Los
Angeles Times* (Sunday, 14 December 1986), 1, 2.

   For theoretical discussions of "tradition," including attempts to define or characterize the word or develop it into a technical term, see the
following: Dan Ben-Amos, "The Seven Strands of Tradition: Varieties
in Its Meaning in American Folklore Studies," *Journal of Folklore Research*
21 (1984):97-131; Kristin G. Congdon, "Finding the Tradition in Folk Art:
An Art Educator's Perspective," *Journal of Aesthetic Education* 20
(1986):92-106; Deirdre Evans-Pritchard, "The Portal Case: Authenticity,
Tourism, Traditions, and the Law," *Journal of American Folklore* 100
(1987):287-96; Richard Handler and Joycelyn Linnekin, "Tradition,
Genuine or Spurious," *Journal of American Folklore* 97 (1984):273-90; E.J.
Hobsbawm and Terrence Ranger, *The Invention of Tradition* (Cambridge
University Press, 1983); Lauri Honko et al., "Final Discussion: On the
Analytical Value of the Concept of Tradition," *Studia Fennica* 27
(1983);233-49; Susan L.F. Isaacs, "Retrospective Tradition: Potters and
Buyers in the Contemporary Redware Market Place," *New Jersey Folklife*
9 (1986):21-34; Colin Quigley, "Creative Processes in Musical Composi-
tion: French Newfoundland Fiddler Emile Benoit," Ph.D. dissertation
(UCLA, 1987); Max Radin, "Tradition," *Encyclopedia of the Social Sciences*
15 (New York: Macmillan, 1935); Sandra Stahl, "The Personal Narrative
as Folklore," *Journal of the Folklore Institute* 14 (1977):9-30; Carl Wilhelm
von Sydow, *Selected Papers on Folklore. Published on the Occasion of His 70th
Birthday* (Copenhagen: Rosenkilde and Bagger, 1948).

An important study often overlooked is Alfred L. Kroeber, "The Arapho," *Bulletin of the American Museum of Natural History* 18 (1902):36-150. Despite expectations to the contrary, Kroeber was unable to find any fixed system of symbolism in Arapaho art, discovering instead that individuals offered varied and variable interpretations (and sometimes no interpretations) of their own and others' designs.

For alternative ways of thinking about "art" and "folk," see chapter 4 ("Modern Arts and Arcane Concepts: Expanding Folk Art Study") in Michael Owen Jones, *Exploring Folk Art: Twenty Years of Thought on Craft, Work, and Aesthetics* (Ann Arbor: UMI Research Press, 1987).

The six factors in the Western elite concept of the aesthetic are discussed at length by Alan P. Merriam in chapter 13 of his *The Anthropology of Music* (Evanston: Northwestern University Press, 1964). See also chapter 9 ("Aesthetic Attitude, Judgment, and Response: Definitions and Distinctions") in Jones, *Exploring Folk Art*. In "The Meaning of Childhood Experiences: A Dialectical Hermeneutic" (Ph.D. dissertation, University of Pennsylvania, 1980), Cathy A. Brooks describes the "getting of taste."

For other writings on taste and aesthetics, see Russell Lynes, *The Tastemakers* (1954; reprint New York: Dover Publications, 1980), 339-41; Thomas C. Munro, *Toward Science in Aesthetics* (New York: Library Arts Press: Bobbs Merrill, 1956); Irvin L. Child, "Personal Preferences as an Expression of Aesthetic Sensitivity," *Journal of Personality* 30 (1962): 456-513; C.S. Ford, E. Terry Prothro, and Irvin L. Child, "Some Transcultural Comparisons of Esthetic Judgment," *Journal of Social Psychology* 68 (1966):27-33; M. Lawler, "Cultural Influences on Personal Preferences in Design," *Journal of Abnormal and Social Psychology* 61 (1955):690-92; Robert H. Lowie, "A Note on Aesthetics," *American Anthropologist* 23 (1921):170-74; W.A. McElroy, "Aesthetic Appreciation in Aborigines of Arnhem Land: A Comparative Experimental Study," *Oceania* 23 (1952):81-94; John Messenger, "Reflection on Aesthetic Talent," *Basic College Quarterly,* 4 (1958):20-24; Daniel J. Crowley, "An African Aesthetic," *Journal of Aesthetics and Art Criticism* 24 (1966), 519-24; Robert Farris Thompson, "Esthetics in Traditional Africa," *Art News,* 66 (1968):44-45, 63-66; Richard Bauman, "The LeHave Island General Store: Sociability and Verbal Art in a Nova Scotia Community," *Journal of American Folklore* 85 (1972):330-43; and Thomas A. Burns, "Aesthetic Judgement: The Interpretive Side of the Structure of Performance," *Keystone Folklore* 19 (1974):61-94.

Edward D. Ives distinguishes three levels of creativity in his article "A Man and His Song: Joe Scott and 'the Plan Golden Band,' " in

Folksongs and Their Makers, ed. Henry Glassie, Edward D. Ives, and John P. Szwed (Bowling Green, Ohio: Popular Culture Press, 1970), 71-146. On the concept of innovation, see H.G. Barnett, *Innovation: The Basis of Cultural Change* (New York, 1953), 208-12.

For information about industrial workers' creativity, see Bruce E. Nickerson, "Ron Thiesse: Industrial Folk Sculptor," *Western Folklore* 37 (1978):128-33; C. Kurt Dewhurst, *Grand Ledge Folk Pottery: Traditions at Work* (Ann Arbor: UMI Research Press, 1986); Yvonne R. Lockwood, "The Joy of Labor," *Western Folklore* 43 (1984):202-11; and Robert S. McCarl, "The Production Welder: Product, Process and the Industrial Craftsman," *New York Folklore Quarterly* 30 (1974):243-53.

For examples of studies of objects in the past using some of the methods of folklore studies, see Robert F. Trent, "Legacy of a Provincial Elite: New London Country Joined Chairs 1720-1790," *The Connecticut Historical Society Bulletin* 50 (1985):15-35; Kenneth L. Ames, "Meaning in Artifacts: Hall Furnishings in Victorian America," *Journal of Interdisciplinary History* 9 (1978):19-46; and Kenneth L. Ames, "Material Culture as Nonverbal Communication: A Historical Case Study," *Journal of American Culture* 3 (1980):619-41. See also Ellen and Bert Denker, *The Rocking Chair Book* (New York: Main Street Press/Mayflower Books, 1979), and Dell Upton, "Toward a Performance Theory of Vernacular Architecture in Tidewater Virginia," *Folklore Forum* 12 (1979):173-96.

Examples of attempts by collector-connoisseurs to characterize folk art and country furniture are "What is American Folk Art? A Symposium," *Antiques* 57(1950):355-62, and "Country Furniture: A Symposium," *Antiques* 93 (1968):342-71. See also Holger Cahill, *American Primitives: An Exhibit of the Paintings of Nineteenth-Century Folk Artists* (Newark, N.J.: Newark Museum, 1931); Holger Cahill, *American Folk Art: The Art of the Common Man in America, 1750-1900* (1932; reprint, New York: Arno Press for the Museum of Modern Art, 1969); Herbert W. Hemphill, Jr., and Julia Weissman, *Twentieth-Century American Folk Art and Artists* (New York: Dutton, 1974); Jean Lipman and Alice Winchester, *The Flowering of American Folk Art, 1776-1876* (New York: Viking Press for the Whitney Museum of American Art, 1974); and Robert Bishop, Judith Reiter Weissman, Michael McManus, and Henry Niemann, *Folk Art: Paintings, Sculpture and Country Objects* (New York: Knopf, 1983).

The development of interest in American folk art by collectors is traced in Beatrix T. Rumford, "Uncommon Art of the Common People: A Review of Trends in the Collecting and Exhibiting of American Folk Art," in *Perspectives on American Folk Art,* eds. Ian M.G. Quimby and

Scott T. Swank (New York: Norton, 1980), 13-53; and Simon J. Bronner, *Grasping Things: Folk Material Culture and Mass Society in America* (Lexington: University Press of Kentucky, 1986), 182-210. Criticisms of the collector-connoisseur approach are in Robert T. Teske, "What Is Folk Art? An Opinion on the Controversy," *El Palacio* 88 (1983):34-38; John Michael Vlach, " 'Properly Speaking': The Need for Plain Talk about Folk Art," in *Folk Art and Art Worlds*, ed. John Michael Vlach and Simon J. Bronner (Ann Arbor: UMI Research Press, 1986), 13-26; and the review of Jean Lipman, Elizabeth V. Warren, and Robert Bishop, eds., *Young America: A Folk-Art History* (New York: Museum of American Folk Art/Hudson Hills Press, 1986) by Charlene Cerny (Director of the Museum of International Folk Art, Santa Fe, N.M.) in *New York Times Book Review* (22 February 1987). Observing that definitions of art are highly political, Eugene W. Metcalf, Jr., examines "Black Art, Folk Art, and Social Control," *Winterthur Portfolio* 18 (1983):271-89.

For some of the varied forms studied by folklorists in recent years, see Jack Santino, "The Folk *Assemblage* of Autumn: Tradition and Creativity in Halloween Folk Art," in *Folk Art and Art Worlds*, ed. John Michael Vlach and Simon J. Bronner (Ann Arbor: UMI Research Press, 1986), 151-69; Katherine Rosser Martin, "Food Preparation and the Folk Aesthetic," *Kentucky Folklore Record* 25 (1979):1-5; Simon J. Bronner, "Links to Behavior: An Analysis of Chain Carving," *Kentucky Folklore Record* 29 (1983):72-82; Deidre Evans-Pritchard, "Vehicles for Expression: Two Decorated Cars in Los Angeles," *Folklore and Mythology Studies* 9 (1985):1-15; Leslie Prosterman, "The Aspect of the Fair: Aesthetics and Festival in Illinois County Fairs" (Ph.D. dissertation, University of Pennsylvania, 1982); Charles E. Martin, "Decorating the Appalachian House," in *Appalachia and America: Autonomy and Regional Dependence*, ed. Allen Batteau (Lexington: University Press of Kentucky, 1983), 14-27; E.N. Anderson, Jr., "On the Folk Art of Landscaping," *Western Folklore* 31 (1972):179-88; Elizabeth Mosby Adler, "Creative Eating: The Oreo Syndrome," in *Foodways and Eating Habits: Directions for Research*, ed. Michael Owen Jones, Bruce S. Giuliano, and Roberta Krell (Los Angeles: California Folklore Society, 1981), 4-10; Theodore Daniels, "The Grammar of Kindness: The Exchange of Homemade Gifts in Folklife" (Ph.D. dissertation, University of Pennsylvania, 1985); I. Sheldon Posen, "Storing Contexts: The Brooklyn *Giglio* as Folk Art," in *Folk Art and Art Worlds*, ed. John Michael Vlach and Simon J. Bronner (Ann Arbor: UMI Research Press, 1986), 171-91; Elaine Eff, "The Painted Screens of Baltimore, Maryland: Decorative, Folk Art, Past and Present (Ph.D. dissertation, University of Pennsylvania, 1984); and Michael Owen Jones, "L. A. Add-ons and Re-dos: Renovation in Folk Art and Architectural Design," in *Perspectives on American Folk Art*, ed. Ian M.G. Quimby and Scott T. Swank (New York: Norton, 1980), 325-63. See also the engaging film "Harmonize: Folklore in Five Families" (35 min., color, 16 mm, 1979; produced by Steve Zeitlin and distributed by the Center for Southern Folklore).

An example of the compromise that may be possible between the collector-connoisseur approach and the folklorist's is "From Memory to Canvas: The Work of a Visionary," in *Images of Strawberry Hill: Works by Marijana*, ed. Jennie A. Chinn (Topeka: Kansas State Historical Society, 1985), 33-51.

Research on folklore and folk art has direct applications to art education and art therapy. See Kristin G. Congdon, "A Theoretical Model for Teaching Folk Art in the Art Education Setting" (Ph.D. dissertation, University of Oregon, 1983); Jackie Christenson, "Ethnic Folklore and the School Art Curriculum," *New York Folklore* 2 (1976): 177-80; Mary Hufford, *A Tree Smells Like Peanut Butter: Folk Arts in a City School* (Trenton: New Jersey State Council on the Arts, 1979); Marsha MacDowell, "Folk Art Study in Higher Education in North America" (Ph.D. dissertation, Michigan State University, 1982); Marsha Mac-Dowell, ed., *Hmong Folk Arts: A Guide for Teachers* (East Lansing: The Museum, Michigan State University, 1983); Kristin C. Congdon and Doug Blandy, eds., *Art in a Democracy* (New York: Columbia Teacher's College Press, 1987); Simon J. Bronner, *Chain Carvers: Old Men Crafting Meaning* (Lexington: University Press of Kentucky, 1986), 150-56; and Barbara Weber, "Folk Art as Therapy with a Group of Old People," *American Journal of Art Therapy* 20 (1981):47-52.

For some applications of folklore studies to industry and organizations, see Michael Owen Jones, ed., "Special Section: Works of Art, Art as Work, and the Arts of Working—Implications for Improving Organizational Life," *Western Folklore* 43 (1984):172-221; Camilla Collins, "Twenty-four to the Dozen: Occupational Folklore in a Hosiery Mill" (Ph.D. dissertation, Indiana University, 1978); Robert S. McCarl, *The District of Columbia Fire Fighters' Project: A Case Study in Occupational Folklife* (Washington, D.C.: Smithsonian Institution Press, 1984); Michael Owen Jones, "On Folklorists Studying Organizations: A Reply to Robert S. McCarl," *American Folklore Society Newsletter* 14, no. 2 (April 1985):5-6, 8; Michael Owen Jones, "A Feeling for Form, as Illustrated by People at Work" and "Aesthetics at Work: Art and Ambience in an Organization," chapters 7 and 8, respectively, in *Exploring Folk Art*; and Michael Owen Jones, Michael Dane Moore, and Richard Christopher

Snyder, eds., *Inside Organizations: Understanding the Human Dimension* (Newberry Park, Calif.: Sage Publications, 1988).

Some conceptions of culture are set forth in Linda Smircich, "Concepts of Culture and Organizational Analysis," *Administrative Science Quarterly* 28 (1983):339-58. See also Elizabeth E. Hoyt, "Integration of Culture: A Review of Concepts," *Current Anthropology* 2 (1961):407-26; Simon J. Bronner, "Modern Anthropological Trends and Their Folkloristic Relationships," *Folk Life* 19 (1981):66-83; and George Mills, "Art and the Anthropological Lens," and John Ladd, "Conceptual Problems Relating to the Comparative Study of Art," in *The Traditional Artist in African Society*, ed. Warren L. d'Azevedo (Bloomington: Indiana University Press, 1973), 379-416 and 417-24, respectively.

Additional examples of an anthropological orientation to the study of art are Adrian A. Gerbrands, *Art as an Element of Culture, Especially in Negro-Africa* (Leiden: E.J. Brill, 1957); Roy Sieber, "The Visual Arts," in *The African World: A Survey of Research*, ed. Robert A. Lystad (New York: Praeger), 442-52; George Mills, "Art: An Introduction to Qualitative Anthropology," *Journal of Aesthetics and Art Criticism* 16 (1957):1-17; Alan P. Merriam, "The Arts and Anthropology," in *Horizons of Anthropology*, ed. Sol Tax (Chicago: Aldine, 1964), 224-36; Herta Haselberger, "Methods of Studying Ethnological Art," *Current Anthropology* 2 (1961):341-84; Charlotte M. Otten, ed., *Anthropology and Art: Reading in Cross-Cultural Aesthetics* (Garden City: Natural History Press, 1971); and Carol F. Jopling, ed., *Art and Aesthetics in Primitive Societies: A Critical Anthology* (New York: Dutton, 1971).

For sociological issues and concerns, see K. Peter Etzkorn, "On the Sphere of Social Validity in African Art: Sociological Reflections on Ethnographic Data," in *The Traditional Artist in African Society*, ed. Warren L. d'Azevedo (Bloomington: Indiana University Press, 1973), 343-78; James H. Barnett, "The Sociology of Art," in *Sociology Today*, ed. Roberk K. Merton, Leonard Broom, and Leonard S. Cottrell, Jr. (New York: Basic Books, 1959), 197-214; Alvin Boskoff, "From Social Thought to Sociological theory," in *Modern Sociological Thought*, ed. Howard Becker and Alvin Boskoff (New York: Dryden Press, 1957), 3-32; John H. Mueller, "The Folkway of Art: An Analysis of the Social Theories of Art," *American Journal of Sociology* 44 (1938):222-38; Rudolph E. Morris, "What Is Sociology of Art," *American Catholic Sociological Review* 19 (1958):310-21; and James H. Barnett, "Research Areas in the Sociology of Art," *Sociology and Social Research* 62 (1958):401-5.

Selected works on the psychology and psychiatry of the arts include Thomas Munro, "The Psychology of Art: Past, Present, Future," *Journal* of *Aesthetics and Art Criticism* 2 (1963):263-82; Lev Semenovich Vygotsky, *The Psychology of Art* (Cambridge: M.I.T. Press, 1971); and Norman Kiell, *Psychiatry and Psychology in the Visual Arts and Aesthetics: A Bibliography* (Madison and Milwaukee: University of Wisconsin Press, 1965). For suggestions on the use of Jungian psychology, see Carlos C. Drake, "Jungian Psychology and Its Uses for Folklore," *Journal of American Folklore* 82 (1969):122-31. For other psychoanalytical concepts, see Alan Dundes, "Projection in Folklore: A Plea for Psychoanalytic Semiotics," *Modern Language Notes* 91 (1976):1500-1533.

Thomas C. Munro provides an excellent history and criticism of art in his book *The Arts and Their Interrelations* (Cleveland: Press of Case Western Reserve University, 1967). For diverse materials and approaches, see volumes and issues of *The Journal of Aesthetics and Art Criticism*.

Some of the terms referring to what generally is called folklore are considered in Don Yoder, "The Folklife Studies Movement," *Pennsylvania Folklife* 13 (July 1963):43-56; Dan Ben-Amos, "Toward a Definition of Folklore in Context," *Journal of American Folklore*, 84 (1971):3-15; Bruce Jackson, "Folkloristics," *Journal of American Folklore* 98 (1985):95-101; William Thoms, "Folklore," in *The Study of Folklore*, ed. Alan Dundes (Englewood Cliffs, N.J.: Prentice-Hall, 1965), 4-6; and Simon J. Bronner, *American Folklore Studies: An Intellectual History* (Lawrence: University Press of Kansas, 1986).

For conceptions of "the folk," "a folk" and "ICENs," see Robert Redfield, "The Folk Society," *American Journal of Sociology* 52 (1947):292-311; Richard M. Dorson, *Bloodstoppers and Bearwalkers* (Cambridge: Harvard University Press, 1952), 9-11; Alan Dundes, "The American Concept of Folklore," *Journal of the Folklore Institute* 3 (1966):226-49; Beth Blumenreich and Bari Lynn Polansky, "Re-evaluating the Concept of Group: ICEN as an Alternative," in *Conceptual Problems in Contemporary Folklore Study*, ed. Gerald Cashion, Folklore Forum Bibliographic and Special Series, no. 12 (Bloomington, Ind, 1974), 12-17.

For relatively recent characterizations of the subject, see "Folklore" by Robert A. Georges in *Sound Archives: A Guide to Their Establishment and Development*, ed. David Lance (Milton Keynes, England: International Association of Sound Archives, 1983), 134-44; and Elliott Oring, "On the Concepts of Folklore," in *Folk Groups and Folklore Genres*, ed. Elliott Oring (Logan: Utah State University, 1986), 1-22.

For discussions of approaches or perspectives within folkloristics, see the references at the end of notes for chapter 1, particularly Bronner, "Concepts in the Study of Material Aspects of American Folk Culture"; Bronner, "Material Culture Study and Region: Lessons from Folk Studies"; Dewhurst, *Grand Ledge Folk Pottery*; and Jones and Greenfield, "Art Criticism and Aesthetic Philosophy."

Index

Figures in boldface refer to illustrations.